The ASIATIC MODE of PRODUCTION in China

CHINESE STUDIES ON CHINA

THE CHINESE COMMUNIST PARTY'S NOMENKLATURA SYSTEM
Edited by John P. Burns

THE ASIATIC MODE OF PRODUCTION IN CHINA
Edited by Timothy Brook

BASIC PRINCIPLES OF CIVIL LAW
Edited by William C. Jones

A delegation from Peter the Great of Russia arriving at the Great Wall of China in 1693, from Ysbrants Ides, *Three Years Travels from Moscow Over-Land to China* (London, 1706) courtesy of the Thomas Fisher Rare Book Library, University of Toronto.

The ASIATIC MODE of PRODUCTION in China

Edited By **Timothy Brook**

M. E. Sharpe, Inc.
Armonk, New York   London, England

Library of Congress Cataloging-in-Publication Data

The Asiatic mode of production in China / edited by Timothy Brook.
    p.   cm. — (Chinese studies on China)
    Articles translated from the Chinese.
    Bibliography: p.
    Includes index.
    Contents: Some questions concerning research on the Asiatic mode
of production / Wu Dakun — China's ancient society from the
perspective of the Asiatic mode of production / Ke Changji — The well-
field system in relation to the Asiatic mode of production / Zhao
Lisheng — The unproblematic Asiatic mode of production / the authors
of An Outline history of world antiquity — Some questions concerning
research on the theory of the Asiatic mode of production / Zhu Jiazhen
— Further comments on the "Asiatic mode of production" / Wang
Dunshu and Yu Ke — The "Asiatic mode of production" is not a
Marxist Scientific Concept / Qi Qingfu — The scientific validity of the
concept of the Asiatic mode of production / Song Min — The basic
meaning of the "Asiatic mode of production" and the origin of the term
/ Su Kaihua — The Asiatic mode of production and the theory of five
modes of production / Hu Zhongda — The theory of Marx's "Four
modes of production" / Ma Xin.
    ISBN 0-87332-542-7
    1. Asiatic mode of production—China. 2. Marxian economics.
3. Marxian historiography—China. I. Brook, Timothy, 1951–
II. Series.
HC427.A83   1989
338.6—dc19   89-4247
                                         CIP

Printed in the United States of America

For Joseph Needham,
who also thinks these questions matter

CONTENTS

ABBREVIATIONS

CCPE   Karl Marx, *A Contribution to the Critique of Political Economy* (Moscow: Progress Publishers, 1970)

LCW   V. I. Lenin, *Collected Works* (Moscow: Progress Publishers, 1960–1070)

MECW   Karl Marx and Friedrich Engels, *Collected Works* (New York: International Publishers, 1975–)

MEQJ   Karl Marx and Friedrich Engels, *Makesi Engesi quanji* (Complete works of Marx and Engels) (Beijing: Renmin Chubanshe, 1965–)

PCEF   Karl Marx, *Pre-Capitalist Economic Formations*, ed. Eric Hobsbawm (New York: International Publishers, 1965)

PCSF   Karl Marx and Friedrich Engels, *Pre-Capitalist Socio-Economic Formations* (Moscow: Progress Publishers, 1979)

CONTRIBUTORS

HU ZHONGDA is the chairman of the Department of History, University of Inner Mongolia, Huhehot.

KE CHANGJI is affiliated with Lanzhou University.

MA XIN is an associate professor in the Department of History, China People's University, Beijing.

QI QINGFU is an associate professor in the Ethnology Department of the Central Minorities Institute in Beijing.

SONG MIN is a member of the Jilin Provincial Academy of Social Sciences.

WANG DUNSHU is a professor of history at Nankai University, Tianjin.

WU DAKUN is a professor in the Department of International Economics, China People's University, Beijing.

YU KE is a professor of history at Nankai University, Tianjin.

ZHAO LISHENG is a member of the Department of History, Lanzhou University.

ZHU JIAZHEN is the head of the Research Section on the History of Economic Thought in the Institute of Economics, Chinese Academy of Social Sciences, Beijing.

The
ASIATIC MODE
of PRODUCTION
in China

TIMOTHY BROOK

1 | **Introduction**

The Asiatic mode of production (AMP) is a concept that Karl
Marx formulated late in the 1850s in the course of his research
into the history of private property and the emergence of capitalism. Marx never provided a definition of the concept, and most
of his dispersed comments on Asia deal with the social, political,
and juridical aspects of particular Asian states rather than the logic
of their historical development. The ambiguity of this sketchy concept, which a deepening awareness of Asia since Marx's time has
only intensified, spawned a controversy in the late 1920s and early
1930s among Marxist intellectuals in the Soviet Union, China, and
Japan. The controversy was revived early in the 1960s in the Soviet
Union and Europe, and since 1978 it has received considerable attention in China. Indeed, by forcing a full rethinking of the conventional Marxist model of history used in China, it has been the
most important debate within the realm of historical theory there
in the 1980s.

The Chinese voices in the debate on the AMP have largely
gone unheard in the West, although some of the writings of their
Soviet and European counterparts have been made available in
English.[1] Since China is one of the candidates for "Asiatic" society,
it behooves us to bring Chinese perspectives on the AMP into the
debate.[2] The present volume includes translations of eleven essays
published in Chinese about the AMP between 1980 and 1987, plus
a bibliography. This introduction is intended to provide a historical
framework for the debate, as well as a context for evaluating its
contribution to the revision of social theory currently underway in
China.

East and West

The division of the world into East and West has been a convention of European thought since the time of the Greeks. For Hippocrates and Aristotle, the world divided at the Dardanelles: civilization lay to the west, and barbarism, a world of despotic potentates and servile subjects languishing in tropical lassitude, lay to the east. This halving of the known world, while it reflected in some measure the mantle of ignorance and prejudice that lay over Greek society, was foremost a product of the tense international environment in the eastern Mediterranean during the formative epoch of Greek civilization. The Turkic peoples of Asia Minor were a palpable threat. Filtered through a complex consciousness of ethnic cultural superiority, this threat and the anxiety it provoked were sublimated by the Greeks into a model of polar political opposites of mythic force. It lent form and meaning to the intellectual discoveries of the seventeenth and eighteenth centuries, and it lingers as "Orientalism" in the popular mind down to the present. It also continues to haunt most attempts by Western theorists to conceptualize sociopolitical orders different from their own.

Once the sailors of fifteenth-century Europe cracked the secrets of ocean navigation and opened the world to exploration, Europeans came into contact with a far broader range of peoples than they had previously known, peoples whose very existence surprised them and whose customs and cultures baffled their notions of civilized order. Their success at colonization confirmed their conviction that the West was the East's superior. What they found there tended only to strengthen their conceptual partition of the world into East and West, reinforcing what the English romantic Thomas de Quincy in 1818 dramatized as "the barrier of utter abhorrence between myself and *them* . . . deeper than I can analyze."[3] In contrast, China's inability to block Western penetration caused the Chinese geometry of world division—a set of concentric circles, with Chinese civilization in the middle—to weaken toward the end of the nineteenth century in favor of an East-West dichotomy. That dichotomy placed China at a disadvantage, favoring the industrializing West and denigrating the agrarian East.

Back in Europe, successive generations of thinkers from the sixteenth century forward attempted to incorporate the new and expanding knowledge of hitherto unknown parts of the globe by building models of historical change on this dichotomy.[4] The earliest drew on Biblical myths about the Flood and the Dispersion after the fall of the Tower of Babel to explain who peopled what areas of the earth and with what consequences. The reinterpretation of such myths to these ends contributed in part to the decline of Christian historiography in the seventeenth century, as expanding knowledge could no longer tolerate the limits of strict adherence to Biblical myth. In its place grew new models that, like Christianity, conceived of history teleologically, though they usually replaced God and salvation with secular concepts of necessity and progress.

Standing in the wake of these views, Marx was powerfully influenced by the scheme of universal history laid out by G.W.F. Hegel in *The Philosophy of History* (1830-31). Hegel plotted progress—the progressive realization of a World Spirit and the development of freedom—along a linear sequence beginning with Asia, advancing through Greece and Rome, and reaching its apogee and end in Germany. Asia was a static place for Hegel, a place "without history" at the very beginning of the process of civilization, stranded without the possibility of being transcended by the next stage of civilization, Greece. Placing Asia at the beginning point of a Eurocentric theory of history, immune to the forces that had impelled European history forward, typifies, as Donald Lowe has observed, "the unresolved tension between European preoccupation and universal process."[5]

Karl Marx's conception of Asia drew directly from the intellectual traditions to which he as a nineteenth-century German was heir. Although fiercely critical of many aspects of Hegel's philosophy, Marx was deeply influenced by Hegel's world historical conceptions. Just as Hegel had divided the world into three separate macroregions of Asia, Greece and Rome, and Germany, so Marx in the *Grundrisse* regionalized world civilizations into Asia, the classical Mediterranean world, and Germanic Europe (though he occasionally distinguished the Slavic area as a fourth). Marx did this in relation to his materialist analysis of property, defining distinctive forms of property for each of these regions: the Asiatic form in Asia, the ancient in the classical world, the Germanic in

Northern Europe prior to the collapse of the Roman empire, and the feudal thereafter. Marx also conceived of some if not all of these forms of property as defining distinct modes of production, a concept that typologizes societies in terms of property relations and the technical environment in which production is carried out.

Hegel's arrangement of Asia, the classical world, and Germany in a linear chronological order was based on the development not of their economic structures but of their political institutions. In this respect, the content of the Hegelian sequence is completely different from Marx's economic analysis, as the fourth essay in this volume insists.[6] The parallelism between their logical structures is inescapable, however, and must be recognized if one is to understand Marx historically.

The importance of Marx's analysis of Asia is not that it derived from Hegel but that it functioned as an integral part of the process through which he constructed his theory of capitalism. To understand the genesis of the capitalist mode of production, Marx read widely on the various civilizations that existed before the eruption of capitalism. These included the social formations of Asia. The teleological imperative in nineteenth-century European thought impelled him toward the convention of portraying these *non*capitalist societies, which preceded capitalism chronologically, as logically *pre*capitalist, in the sense that they were seen to lead inexorably toward the emergence of capitalism. Marx felt that he could establish the full meaning of capitalism only by placing it in relation to its past.

In 1859 Marx summarized his conclusions on this sequence in the oft-quoted Preface to *A Contribution to the Critique of Political Economy*: "In broad outline, the Asiatic, ancient, feudal and modern bourgeois modes of production may be designated as epochs marking progress in the economic development of society."[7] The exegesis of this formula has been at the heart of the controversy over the AMP that began six decades ago. The conventional model of the chronological sequence of modes of production, established by Soviet scholars and blessed by Stalin in 1938,[8] allows for five modes through which all societies are deemed to have passed in some form or another. The first stage is the primitive communal mode, characterized by the absence of individual private property. It is followed by the ancient or slave mode, represented by the classical world of Greece and Rome. It is replaced by feudalism, in which serfdom is the most common economic relationship. Out of feudalism arises capitalism, and out of capitalism, socialism. All five modes of production have been the subjects of much dispute.[9] Most problematic from the present perspective, however, is the absence of an Asiatic mode from this model.

The Asiatic Mode of Production

The Asiatic mode stands out in several ways from the other modes Marx names in the Preface to the *Critique*. First, it is the only mode bearing a specifically geographic identity (though it could fairly be argued that "ancient," "feudal," and "bourgeois" are all terms highly specific to the history of European society). The second, fourth, and ninth essays in this volume tackle the question of why Marx chose a geographic term that embraces an extraordinarily diverse range of societies rather than a more general expression. By extension, "Asiatic" implies a dichotomy of East-West historical development that would seem to run counter to the universal intention of the formula.

Second, the Asiatic mode stands out because it occupies first place in the sequence in the Preface. This position suggests that it preceded the others at least historically, if not logically. The AMP therefore has to be seen not only on its own terms but in relation to modes of production that Marx observed elsewhere in the world. At one level, Marx has continued the eighteenth-century tradition of incorporating Asian societies in a teleological scheme that places them closer to the origin of human society than European societies were. Whether this relationship expresses a universal pattern of historical development that transcends the particular histories of Asia and Europe, Marx does not explicitly say.

Third, the term "Asiatic," unlike the others, is a highly colored word, freighted, at least in the twentieth century, with pejorative meanings rooted in the centuries of condescension of the West toward the East. It conveys all the negative images that the early-modern European mind associated with Asia, what de Quincy called the "awful images and associations" of "Asiatic things": "ancient, monumental, cruel, and elaborate."[10] These pejorative resonances have now been securely attached to the word "Asiatic" by virtue of the distinction made between it and the more neutral adjective "Asian." Even though this separation of nuances occurred after Marx's time, it influences how twentieth-century intellectuals respond to the idea of an Asiatic mode.[11]

The negative connotations of "Asiatic" are much weaker in Chinese. The noun from which the adjective "Asiatic" is derived, *Yaxiya*, first appears on the map of the world that the Jesuit missionary Matteo Ricci (1552–1610) drew for his Chinese acquaintances in 1584. A contemporary, Zhang Huang, obtained a copy of this map for his encyclopedia, *Tushu bian* (The illustrated compendium), where it has been preserved in the twenty-ninth chapter. The transliteration is thus of Jesuit origin. In the twentieth century, *Yaxiya* has become archaic: in Chinese usage today the word is reserved as a technical term for the AMP; in all other contexts the nineteenth-century expression *Yazhou* is used for Asia.

The ambiguities surrounding the AMP and its status within the modes of production named in the Preface to the *Critique* have driven several generations of Marxist historians to comb through the writings of Marx and Engels to better understand what the economic relationships specific to the AMP might be and what place, if any, the AMP had in the process of the development of society toward the capitalist domination of the world. This has proven difficult in part because, as one Western commentator has noted, "Marx's writings on Asia do not bulk large in the corpus of work he published in his lifetime."[12] Marx's richest writings on Asia have only come out piecemeal in this century.[13] Some of what Marx and Engels wrote about Asia, particularly in their letters, has yet to appear in English translation.

The greater problem facing those who wish to analyze Marx's concept of the AMP is that most of what he and Engels wrote deals with concrete social formations in Asia covering a wide range of place and time rather than a theoretical model designed to explicate the economic logic of a mode of production. Given their reliance on particularistic and cliché-ridden descriptions of various Asian societies, Lowe has argued that the AMP is "an unsystematized combination of a European process of history and the conventional idea of a static East" that does violence to historical materialism's "linear process of universal history."[14] Recognizing this threat, many Marxists have sought to dismiss the AMP by disputing the peculiarities of particular Asian societies rather than evaluate the internal coherence or validity of the concept. For the latter form of analysis, it is necessary to focus on Marx's discussion of property in the *Grundrisse*.

The Asiatic Form of Property

The *Grundrisse* is a set of voluminous notebooks Marx kept over the years 1857–58. A portion dealing with precapitalist societies, which contains his most theoretical discussion of Asian society, was published separately in English in 1965 under the title *Pre-Capitalist Economic Formations*. His concern in this text is not with modes of production, although the sequence of modes he offers in the Preface (written the following January) grew out of his thinking in the *Grundrisse*. Rather, he is interested in the different forms of property preceding capitalism, which he regards as the highest development of private property, and the relations of production such forms imply.

For Marx, capitalist private property is the apex of a sequence that began with the absence of private property (the communal property of primitive society) and will end with a dialectical return to the absence of private property through state ownership under socialism, and eventually the complete negation of property under communism. Marx's crusade in the 1850s was to demonstrate that private property was invented, not God-given. He needed to understand its emergence in order to trace property's subsequent development and thence proceed to a fully informed analysis of capitalist property relations, which he believed communism would eventually supersede.

His analysis in the *Grundrisse* is much more open-ended than his formula in the Preface. He identifies three main forms of property. (1) The "Asiatic" or "Oriental" form (one of "the fundamental forms") is founded on "tribal or common property." The community is the "hereditary possessor," but it is subordinated to the state, which is "the real owner, and the real precondition of common ownership."[15] (2) The "ancient classical" form ("the second form of property") is one in which, to use the example of Rome, "property formally belongs to the Roman citizen, [and] the private owner of land is only such by virtue of being a Roman."[16] (3) In the "Germanic" form, ownership is vested partly in the community itself and partly among the members of the community.[17]

All three are differentiated by the varying degrees of private ownership they embody, and they are sequenced in relation to the increasing inability of communal property to withstand the encroachment of private property. The Asiatic form is thus closest to property's primeval character as communal, belonging to the community in general but to no one individual exclusively. The difference between Asiatic property and the primitive-communal form of property that precedes it derives from the role of the state, which in the former has emerged to interpose itself by force between the community and its native right to property. The state claims to be the "highest owner," a claim it acts on by requiring the communities it dominates to submit a portion of their product as tribute for its own maintenance. State ownership is not yet private property, but it marks the first step in the alienation of property away from the producer. For Marx, who saw in capitalism the completion of this process of alienation, the alienation of property is what was most interesting about the form of property he thought he discerned in Asian societies.

Oriental Society

Most of the participants in the AMP debate draw upon the *Grundrisse*, yet they also continually circle back to the descriptive accounts of Oriental society that are scattered through Marx's and Engels' writings. The characteristics of Asian social formations in their work have been distilled by Wang Dunshu and Yu Ke in the sixth essay in this volume as follows.[18] (1) The main productive activity is agriculture, and the natural unity between agricultural and domestic handicraft labor has not been broken by commerce. (2) Agriculture depends on irrigation, which is facilitated by state-controlled hydraulic projects. (3) The basic social unit is the village community or commune, a simple organism that reproduces itself without exploitation. (4) Land is owned in common, though the state asserts ownership in such a way that there appears to be a legal absence of private property in land. (5) The representatives of the state exist as a class divorced from the rural dwellers, whom they rule despotically. (6) Tax is the principal form in which surplus is extracted, tax and rent forming a unity. (7) Social change is imperceptibly slow; society is stagnant.

With the exception of the sixth characteristic, the unity of rent and tax,[19] Chinese scholars have battled over all of these aspects, since each has specific implications for contending theories of the AMP. The most consistently denounced, partly because Wittfogel made it the foundation of his influential attack on Asian communism in *Oriental Despotism*,[20] is the notion of the hydraulic basis of Asian society (the second characteristic). Wittfogel's vision of Asian stagnation (the seventh) is also firmly rejected. This idea was deeply rooted in European thought when Marx described China in an article in the *New York Daily Tribune* as a "mummy preserved in a hermetically sealed coffin."[21] Europe was undergoing tumultuous change in the nineteenth century, and the convention of associating change with the West and stagnation with the East had considerable appeal. In 1858 Marx spoke of China "vegetating in the teeth of time,"[22] less out of ignorance, however, than for the rhetorical purpose of criticizing British imperialism, which was at mid-century giving time its teeth in China. If the issue is still grist for critical mills in China in the 1980s, it has more to do with polemics regarding the comparative weakness of Chinese economic development since 1949, particularly under Mao Zedong's leadership, than with misperceptions on the part of Marx.

There is similar political significance in Marx's and Engels' many references to the despotic nature of state power under the AMP (the fifth characteristic listed above). The English classical political economists who preceded Marx used "Oriental despotism" polemically. By showing the deleterious effect of state intervention in the Asian economy, they sought to validate their argument for free trade; and by demeaning the reputation of the Chinese government, they could justify imperialist intervention.[23] Marx and Engels had a different purpose in using the term. Conscious that all states assist the ruling classes in exploiting the people, they found in Asian states the most vivid examples of the oppressive relationship that must always arise between a state and its subject population.[24] They also turned the concept against imperialism by depicting Europeans in Asia as perpetrating a despotism equal to if not greater than that of the native rulers.[25] Some current proponents of the AMP in China, Wu Dakun, for example, have found in Marx's comments about despotism ammunition against totalitarian practices in China since 1949. Others, both pro- and anti-AMP, have sought to dissociate despotism from the AMP, regarding it as a political condition that can be found in any type of social formation.[26]

Taken together, the characteristics of Oriental society that Marx highlighted in his writings picture a world antithetical to Europe. But unlike his predecessors, Marx portrayed Asia in this fashion not to highlight what was good about Europe, but to point out what was wrong with Europe, to criticize the kind of exploitation that capitalism had built into European life and was carrying abroad to its colonies.[27] Oriental society thus served the rhetorical purpose of negating European capitalist society.

Rhetoric and Controversy

Rhetoric has had much to do with the fortunes of the AMP since Marx's time. Although Georgii Plekhanov was the first after Marx to apply the AMP, which he did to Russia, the history of the rhetorical uses of the AMP in the twentieth century properly begins with Lajos Magyar (1891–1940), a Hungarian who worked for the Communist International (Comintern) in China in the 1920s. On the basis of on-site research on China's rural economy which he undertook in the 1920s, Magyar wrote the first full sociological study of rural China.[28] In his book he argues that China before the coming of the West was dominated by the AMP, moderated by a certain level of commodity exchange. Imperialist encroachment disrupted the AMP in the nineteenth century by interfering with the tasks of the central government and breaking down the near self-sufficiency of the peasant communities. In its place it fostered capitalism. The old Asiatic ruling class— landlords, merchants, usurers, and officials—was weakened and then transformed into a new capitalist class. Magyar believed that it was against this class and its colonial masters that the Chinese revolution had to be waged.[29] The AMP thus provided him with a framework of analysis through which to address the destructive impact of imperialism. To characterize China as feudal, on the other hand, would direct the attention of the revolution to traditional class relations in the countryside, which Magyar maintained were already in decline. It would also view the nascent bourgeoisie as potential supporters of a revolution against feudal forces.

Not only was the bourgeoisie's revolutionary potential not realized, but the man deemed to represent this bourgeoisie, Jiang Jieshi (Chiang Kai-shek), turned on his Communist allies in 1927 and butchered the party into near extinction. Magyar's book was published the following year in Moscow, just when the Comintern was having painfully to rethink its analysis of the situation in China. Soviet opinion was initially divided, though the official view favored the feudal interpretation.[30] At a conference convened in Leningrad in 1931, which Magyar was not invited to attend, some Soviet scholars still defended the AMP as a legitimate attempt to incorporate Asian history into world history. The tide of opinion went against the AMP, however. Its implication that capitalism, not feudalism, was the real enemy of the Chinese revolution made it, in the words of one of its critics, "the wetnurse for the theoretical position of Trotskyism."[31] Although the advocates of the AMP appear not to have suffered direct sanctions for their views,[32] many, like Karl Wittfogel, found it difficult to publish their work subsequently. Later in the decade, some fell victim to Stalin's purges. Among them was Magyar, detained in 1934 and dead by 1940. The pro-Trotsky, anti-Stalinist aura that the AMP acquired at this time would feed its future rhetorical functions not only in the Soviet Union but in China as well.

Controversies over the AMP broke out in both China and Japan in response to the Soviet debate. Having just recently come to Marxism, Chinese and Japanese were naturally intrigued by Marx's views of Asia.[33] Not content with the decision at Leningrad, some hoped to find in the AMP a way to incorporate into what is essentially a European-based theory of social change the peculiarities of Asian society. Most, however, faulting the AMP for its reliance on East/West polarities, which they found uncomplimentary to themselves, preferred to remain within the more secure Marxist mainstream of historical development.

The AMP resurfaced as an issue among European and Soviet Marxists in the 1960s. The proximate cause of this renewal of interest was the publication in 1957 of Wittfogel's angry denunciation of Communist states in his *Oriental Despotism*. In that book a parody of the AMP provides the foundation for Wittfogel's critique of Stalin and Mao's "restoration" of Oriental despotism in twentieth-century Asia. Interest in the AMP was additionally prompted by the rising tide of militant anti-imperialist movements in the Third World and the realization that the only successful Marxist revolutions were those being waged outside of Europe, where capitalism was least fully developed. All this required that conventional categories of analysis be rethought. The most creative new interpretations of the AMP came from French Marxists, notably Maurice Godelier, who found the concept useful for the task of constructing "a multilineal scheme of the evolution of societies."[34] Toward the end of this round of discussion, in 1972, Umberto Melotti argued in his *Marx e il terzo mondo* (Marx and the Third World) that the AMP be rehabilitated as the "sixth mode of production." His book helped to spark the revival of debate on the AMP in China.

The Asiatic Mode of Production in China

With the exception of the years 1958–1959 (during the Great Leap Forward) and 1965–1977 (during and after the Cultural Revolution), the AMP has appeared every year in the scholarly press in China since 1951. Essays on the AMP were published through the 1950s and early 1960s at a rate of only about two a year,[35] indicating that the AMP was a relatively peripheral issue. Every author in this period denied or minimized its usefulness as a theoretical construct, preferring instead the five-stages model. The most popular interpretation among historians in the 1950s, including Wu Dakun, who was to become the strongest advocate of the AMP in the late 1970s, was that the AMP was a type of slavery. In the 1960s a minority view, represented by Tian Changwu, emerged that regarded the AMP as primitive society whose remnants had survived as a secondary formation within class society.[36] If there was a rhetorical function being served by the AMP in these early decades of the People's Republic, it was to deny Asian peculiarity and insist that China was moving forward toward its Communist goal just as Marxism predicted. Subsequently, during the Cultural Revolution decade, the AMP was dismissed as a Trotskyist heresy.[37]

By 1978, much had changed, including that conviction. Mao Zedong had died in September 1976, and his closest associates were soon removed from power. Deng Xiaoping had successfully returned to power and begun to steer China onto a very different course of economic development. Not coincidentally, calls for a reexamination of the framework by which Chinese history had been analyzed appeared in 1978 in leading publications.[38] And for the first time in thirteen years, two articles were published on the AMP. From the one signed article, which appeared in the conservative scholarly journal of Beijing University, it was not immediately clear what had changed. Ma Keyao, a senior historian at the university who specialized in the Zhou dynasty (first millennium B.C.), steadfastly opposed the notion that there was anything peculiar about China's historical development compared with the West. He argued that Marx and Engels had abandoned the concept of the AMP in the 1870s as their knowledge of Asian history and primitive society deepened.

The other article that year, carried in the journal of Jilin Normal University, was a report on a conference held under the joint sponsorship of Jilin Normal and Beijing universities. The report is mildly sympathetic to the possibility that further discussion on the AMP could produce new developments in historiography. Many scholars clearly thought so, for a flood of publications appeared in the following years. The better part of them come from North China, which is where interest in the topic has been strongest. This is partly because world history is more highly developed in North China than in Central and South China. Studies of early China are also more prominent in the North, fueled by the abundance of palaeolithic, neolithic, and bronze-age sites there. (Oddly, however, archaeologists, who should be uniquely qualified to contribute to discussions concerning the structure of early Chinese society, have declined to participate.[39]) Northern interest in the AMP may also be related to the comparative lack of class differentiation in the villages of North China, where undercommercialization has made the presence of the imperial state correspondingly greater than in villages in the South.[40]

The bibliography at the end of this volume provides a sense of how the debate over the AMP has developed in the past decade.[41] It lists ten articles published in 1979, eighteen in 1980, and thirty-five in 1981, not including reprints of earlier articles. In keeping with this increase in interest, a second conference on the AMP was held in Tianjin in April 1981. It was fully reported in academic journals and the popular press, and many of the papers delivered were subsequently published, several of them in the specialist journal *Zhongguo shi yanjiu* (Studies in Chinese history), the June issue of which was devoted exclusively to the topic. Debate continued at a moderate level (roughly fifteen articles a year) in 1982–83, declining to about half that level through 1986, followed by a small resurgence in 1987 (eleven). In addition, many articles dealing with other questions of Chinese history or historical theory have discussed the AMP.

The explosion of interest in the AMP that followed the first conference in 1978 was favored by the removal of some of the restrictions on intellectual inquiry that had been imposed during the Cultural Revolution decade. Far more important to the reemergence of the AMP, however, is its rhetorical function in relation to the post-Mao economic reforms, as John Rapp has observed.[42] The gradual abandonment of anticapitalist policies at the center and the reintroduction of the market in a wide range of commodities have encouraged Chinese social theorists to consider new ways of understanding economic growth, political development, ideology, and the role of the state. Just as economic planners are redefining socialism—what Deng Xiaoping has dubbed "socialism with Chinese characteristics"—so Marxist intellectuals are rethinking what Marxism means in other areas. The political theorist Su Shaozhi, who has been at the forefront of these revisions since 1978, has repeatedly called for applying the "basic methodology" of Marxism rather than holding dogmatically to the letter.[43] Su came under attack in 1987 for calling in his book *Democratization and Reform* for a fundamental reevaluation of Marxism and the abandonment of a slavish adherence to obsolete doctrines. Although the book was banned, the trend to develop "Marxism with Chinese characteristics" has continued unabated. The end of this liberalizing revision of Stalinist Marxism is still not in sight.

The reforms have prompted an equally powerful revision in historical theory. A sense of this change may be garnered from the writings of Tian Changwu at the Institute of History in the Chinese Academy of Social Sciences. In 1964, as already noted, Tian argued that the AMP was simply primitive society. The essay was also an appeal to other discussants to justify their interpretations on the basis of Marx and Engels' logical method, not a handful of literal quotations. Tian also urged that more extensive use be made of modern studies of primitive society. Two decades later, he continued these themes in an essay entitled "Establish a Marxist Historiography with Chinese Characteristics."[44] He makes largely the same point, but with a much stronger appeal that his colleagues work from the empirical evidence of Chinese history rather than rely excessively on findings based on the historical experience of Europe. The rules of historical development for China must be derived from Chinese historical conditions. Like Deng's call for the reform of socialism and Su's for Marxism, Tian literally pleads that historiography be free to adopt "Chinese characteristics." There can be no stronger call for making Marxist historical theory indigenous, and no clearer acknowledgment that the process is still not complete.

As Charles Burton has noted, though, of Deng Xiaoping's idea of "socialism with Chinese characteristics," this call for making the theory indigenous "is entirely *post hoc*, as it is derived exclusively from practical application." It provides no program for the reformulation of theory; at the same time, it throws open state ideology to "a crisis of legitimation."[45] Similarly, in historical circles, this aggressive, if directionless, new attitude has not resulted in a new program for historical research. It has, nonetheless, encouraged reconsideration of many of the established conventions of historical analysis since 1949, a process still very much underway.

The issue about which most pages have been printed in the 1980s has been the question of "the persistence of feudal society," beneath which lies the concern over why China has had such difficulties with modernization in this century, and why the "feudal" past has continued to dominate political and social processes even under socialism. The AMP is another way of getting at these questions of relative failure, but it is more challenging to the existing construction of Marxist theory in China. The "persistence of feudalism" issue can only address the question of how external social and political forces limited commerce's ability to destabilize the underdeveloped peasant economy and revolutionize the rural order (relying on the teleological theory of the "sprouts of capitalism," that feudalism has within it the ability to generate capitalism, even in China). The AMP recasts this question by suggesting that the rural order was not being victimized by external forces but was in some measure responsible, if only passively, for the inhibition of modernization in China. Rather than being hampered by the feudal state, this rural order naturally facilitated Asiatic state oppression. The critique of China's past (and present) that the AMP allows is thus far more sweeping, and its rhetorical force more potent, than the feudal persistence view.[46] Such prominent critics of the regime as Wang Xizhe and Lin Xiling, recognizing the political implications, have picked up the AMP interpretation.[47]

The AMP debate has not, however, been fueled entirely by political concerns. It has lasted as a current issue right up to the present because of the historiographical issues it raises. It is on these issues that the remainder of this introduction focuses in the course of introducing the eleven essays selected for translation. These essays have been chosen specifically in relation to the range of historiographical interpretations that the debate has spawned. The first three find the AMP applicable to China, although in different ways and to different degrees. The next four deny that the concept has any validity for historical analysis. The final four all support the AMP and use it to broach historiographically new ideas.

In Defense of the AMP

The writer for whom the rhetorical functions of the AMP are most explicit is Wu Dakun, its leading advocate. In the 1950s Wu spoke in favor of two different interpretations: first, that the AMP characterized the transition from primitive communalism to slavery, and then later, under criticism, that the AMP was simply an Oriental version of slavery.[48] In the opening essay in this volume, based on a talk he gave in 1979, Wu explains that it was reading Umberto Melotti's *Marx e il terzo mondo* (in its 1974 English translation) that led him to take a renewed interest in the AMP. That interest in turn encouraged him to abandon not only his earlier views of the AMP, but the entire five-stages theory, and to maintain instead that imperial China was a fully Asiatic state.

The AMP is for Wu, as for Wittfogel, an empiricist "ideological category."[49] He marshals it to criticize imperial China, the Soviet Union (which he calls "semi-Asiatic"), and the brutalities of the Cultural Revolution. The revival of the AMP issue, he says, has a revolutionary significance as a way of drawing attention to bureaucratism and providing a theoretical underpinning for the emergence of state-controlled capitalism in China. In a more detailed and carefully argued essay published in 1981, Wu Dakun continues his rhetorical argument by making the point that capitalism cannot spontaneously emerge from an Asiatic state, only from feudalism.[50] Lacking feudalism of the European type, China was subject to despotic political systems from imperial times down to the "Gang of Four" in the 1970s. The unambiguous implication is that the Communist state should withdraw from certain areas of economic and social activity where its influence previously has been "Asiatic" and has inhibited modernization.

The second essayist, Ke Changji, adopts a far more conservative position, reaffirming the Stalinist sequence and insisting that the AMP is simply primitive communalism by another name. Rather than using this equivalence to dismiss the AMP, however, Ke suggests that the concept be "extended" and made into "the economic category of rural communes."[51] In this extended sense, the AMP is for Ke a precise description of Asian society. He demonstrates the Asiatic character of China "from the last stage of primitive society to the beginning of capitalist society" by using examples of state land redistribution schemes from the last three millennia of Chinese history. In his final example, the land scheme of the Taiping rebel regime in the mid-nineteenth century, he takes what has conventionally been regarded as a revolutionary protocommunistic system and recasts it as an archaic and despotic throwback. The sensitive reader will quickly realize that Ke's essay is a polemic against the commune system, which had been set up by Mao Zedong in 1958 and was in the process of being dismantled when the essay appeared in 1981.

Senior intellectual historian Zhao Lisheng is the author of the third essay in his volume. Although here Zhao avoids rhetorical associations, in an earlier essay in 1981 he argues in favor of the AMP as a means by which "underdeveloped countries may explore why their progress has been slow and how obstacles to it might be removed, thus promoting their development." For China, he suggests that AMP-type state despotism—which he associates with the so-called Legalist tradition of political thought, deemed progressive in Cultural Revolution historiography—is the major obstacle to China's progress today.[52] In the essay translated here, Zhao applies the AMP to the well-field or nine-square land allotment system of the Western Zhou dynasty. According to this system, land was divided into nine plots (in the shape of the Chinese character for "well") and given to eight households to cultivate, each its own and all the ninth, the product of the latter going as a tithe to their lord.[53] The existence of the well-field system is widely disputed, but Zhao accepts it as a classic example of the kind of property arrangement that took shape in the AMP phase, a transition between primitive communalism and the emergence of the state.

For all three authors, the rhetorical significance of the AMP is unmistakable. Should one conclude, therefore, that the AMP has been revived solely, as has been suggested, for "Aesopian criticism"?[54] This characterization implies, on the one hand, that the rhetorical functions of historical studies must remain submerged beneath a false surface of pure academic inquiry, and, on the other, that the positions being taken and the points being made are choreographed principally in relation to the submerged rather than the stated issues. To some extent the AMP has been vulnerable to this kind of ideological use, particularly at the hands of authors like Wu Dakun and Ke Changji. John Rapp has described its rhetorical function as "a force for political reform and democratization."[55]

Yet I would argue that the political meaning of the AMP is only one aspect of the discussion in the 1980s. Equally at stake, besides the question of democratic reform, are legitimate questions of historiography and historical analysis. Even if most of the participants in the AMP debate are motivated to study the AMP out of personal concerns about the political and economic problems bequeathed by Maoist policies, those concerns do not negate the potential for pursuing a historical analysis of these problems. One should not forget that most of those who have written on the AMP are professional historians (in this collection, only political economist Wu Dakun and economist Zhu Jiazhen are not), and as historians they are seeking not just to polemicize but to identify the long-term social causes of China's twentieth-century political and economic woes. The political goal may be democratic reform, but the historiographic goal is to develop a theory of Chinese society that can place the present in a more meaningful relationship with the past, rather than simply jettison it altogether.

The rate of publication on the AMP declined in 1984, leading one American observer to suppose that it was no longer regarded as capable of providing answers to the pressing questions about China's failure to modernize.[56] The value of its rhetorical function may indeed have diminished, but the rate of publication since 1984 continues at a level much higher than it ever was in the 1950s, and it increased again in 1987. Rhetoric aside, the AMP still has the important historiographical function of challenging the dominant conventions framing the study of Chinese history in the People's Republic. History is being used, certainly, but it is also being served.

Advocacy of the AMP has remained a minority view among those who have taken part in the 1980s debate. This should caution against assuming that opposition to the AMP implies a rejection of the reforms. It may only signal a conservative unwillingness to proceed too quickly. In any case, I believe that the anti-AMP position is based on historiographical as well as political concerns. It is to this position that I now turn.

Denying the Uniqueness of the East: The AMP as Primitive Society

The next four essays in this volume interpret the AMP as Ke Changji did, as a restatement of the primitive mode of production. Unlike Ke, they deny the value of applying the concept to China.

This view was stated clearly in an essay published in 1979 by Lin Zhichun of Jilin University in collaboration with Liao Xuesheng at the Chinese Academy of Social Sciences. Both are leading authorities on the ancient world. Lin headed the group that produced the first volume of *Shijie shanggu shigang* (An outline history of world antiquity) in the same year, a well-received survey text that broke new ground in China by relying extensively on recent archaeological findings. This group entered the debate in 1980 with the fourth essay translated here under the intentionally provocative title "The Unproblematic AMP." (It was incorporated in revised form in 1981 as an appendix to the second volume of *An Outline History*.)

The authors argue that Marx and Engels formulated the concept of the AMP in the 1850s for primitive communal society, which was constituted by agricultural communities or communes existing in the absence of a state. Marx and Engels regarded the self-sufficient village commune of rural Asia as a remnant of this mode that continued to exist as a primitive form under colonial rule. After reading Lewis Morgan's *Ancient Society* (1877), however, they recognized that there existed an earlier, more primary social formation, the "primitive community," and that the agricultural community they had associated with the AMP was in fact a "secondary formation" that had appeared in the "transition from society based on common property to society based on private property."[57] The authors of *An Outline History* thus conclude that Marx and Engels' recasting of the agricultural community as an element in class society signifies that they no longer regarded the AMP as the primitive mode, and in fact no longer regarded it as having any theoretical applicability whatsoever. The "problem" of the AMP, according to the authors, arose because of attempts to conceptualize a mode of production unique to Asia that combined primitive communities with a state, which in Marxist terms are incompatible. They conclude that the five-stages model applies equally well to Asian societies as to European.[58]

Zhu Jiazhen offers in the fifth essay a more theoretical statement of the same view of the AMP as primitive society. Concerned about understanding the place of the village community in postcommunal society, he argues that slavery emerged alongside village communalism and did not simply absorb it. That absorption only happened under feudalism, though feudalism preserved certain of its primitive characteristics into the early modern period. By identifying the AMP with primitive communalism, Zhu divests it of any exclusive association with Asia.

The sixth essay is by Wang Dunshu and Yu Ke, specialists on the Mediterranean world and early modern Europe respectively. Rather than treating the AMP as equivalent to another, more familiar mode of production, they regard it as theoretically incoherent. Like the authors of *An Outline History*, Wang and Yu believe that Marx and Engels changed their minds later in life about primitive communalism. But they insist that the concept is far from "unproblematic." Where they differ is in asserting that Marx and Engels in the 1850s did in fact regard the AMP as a mode of production peculiar to Asia, though they subsequently abandoned the concept in favor of a universal model of development. The AMP thus describes not primitive society, but society in which remnants of primitive communalism continue to exist. Wang and Yu strongly oppose the solution proposed by the *Outline History* group of representing typically Asiatic societies as combinations of two different societies. Every society, no matter how mixed its components, is always a single totality.

Qi Qingfu, in the seventh essay, argues the abandonment view with the greatest force. In an earlier article published in 1980, Qi suggested that Marx's proposal for an AMP in the 1850s was experimental, and that Marx and Engels later repudiated the idea. Qi's 1985 essay, translated in this volume, seeks to show the incoherence of the AMP concept by comparing characteristics attributed to the AMP with aspects of the social world of the Dai nationality in Southwest China earlier this century. Qi regards the similarities as superficial, arguing that the feudal political structure of the Dais makes their society unlike the AMP. Indeed, he asserts that despotism is a feudal rather than an Asiatic form of political power. He concludes that the AMP is not a scientific concept.

The AMP as a Sixth Mode of Production

How are simple rural communities to be combined with a state structure in the absence of serfdom or landlordism? Rather than dismissing this conundrum as indicative of theoretical incoherence, a few scholars have tried to combine these halves of the AMP by locating it at a certain juncture in the history of human society: the point of transition between primitive communalism and ancient (i.e., slave) society.

Song Min published a total of nine essays on the AMP between 1979 and 1987, more than any other participant in the debate. He resolutely opposes the view that the AMP is simply a restatement of primitive society. The eighth essay in this volume, Song's most recent, is framed as a direct rebuttal of Qi Qingfu's accusation that the AMP is not scientific, though the main object of criticism appears to be the *Outline History* group. Song validates the AMP not just by distinguishing the "primitive" from the "village community," but by identifying a third, the "clan community." The clan community, bound by blood ties, signifies true primitive communalism. The primitive community, by contrast, is not constituted entirely on the basis of blood ties and hence is more advanced. This, he says, is the society to which Marx only late in life came to apply the AMP. The village or agricultural community, then, belongs to slave society. In other words, the AMP constitutes a sixth mode of production in the unilinear sequence of modes, between primitive communalism and slavery.[59]

Using roughly the same body of sources, Su Kaihua in an essay from the same year presents a similar historical sequence: from the clan community of the primitive period, to the tribal community of the Asiatic period, to the agricultural community of the ancient (slave) period. For Su the key historical characteristic of this intermediate tribal stage is its pastoralism. This was the nomadic age before society settled down to a sedentary agricultural way of life.[60] In this regard his explication is more satisfactory than Song's because it identifies a particular type of socioeconomic formation with the AMP. Indeed, this essay is one of the most original contributions of the 1980s. (It is also one of the most confusedly written and has been extensively edited in translation.)

Despite their originality in rethinking the phases of development of early society, both Su and Song nonetheless hold fast to the conservative notion of unilinear history. For both, the AMP represents not a stage unique to parts of Asia, but a universal historical stage found in the history of all cultures. The AMP is Asiatic not because it was exclusive to Asia, however. In another essay on the AMP published in 1986, Song says that Marx chose the name because the examples from which he derived his general principles of development for this stage came from Asia.[61] Su disagrees, arguing more creatively that Marx settled on the term because he regarded Asia as the historical origin of tribal society. In effect, Su is arguing that the history of human society be rewritten in Asian terms. His refusal, however, to cite any authority besides Morgan and Engels leaves his theory weakly defended.

Neither Song nor Su refers to the AMP as a "sixth mode of production," an expression mostly used by the AMP's detractors.[62] But this is what they are arguing for. If Song and Su have shunned the term, it is to avoid as much as possible the ideological rebuttals that it might elicit from more conservative Marxist historians.

Challenging Unilinear History

Using the AMP to propose a sixth mode is one challenge to the current orthodoxy in Marxist historiography; the other is to repudiate the idea that the history of all societies must follow the same path. Indeed, the AMP is specially suited to this challenge because it can claim the mantle of Marx's approval. The burden of proof is with the critics, who must argue that Marx either did not really mean what he said, or was mistaken and revised his views later on, or was simply wrong.

The challenge to unilinearism brings one back to the old East/West dualism that was implied by the AMP when Marx used it. The question today, now that so much more is known about Asian history, is slightly different: not how East and West differed, but whether it is more helpful in historical analysis to emphasize the universal or the particular, the structural commonalities among different societies or their structural peculiarities. Hu Zhongda and Ma Xin both opt for the latter.

Hu Zhongda's essay, which has been considerably shortened in the present translation (mostly by removing a discussion of feudalism at the end), sketches two multilinear models. The simpler model pictures the AMP as a single alternative to the ancient-feudal-capitalist sequence; the AMP and slavery thus represent two different routes out of primitive society. The other model, which Hu prefers, sees all three precapitalist modes—Asiatic, ancient, and feudal—as equally possible routes for leaving primitive communalism. None need lead to any other, which means that all belong to the same stage of development. Feudalism, which did not supersede slavery but grew from different conditions, is thus no more advanced as a social mode of production than slavery.[63] The only restriction in this model is that only feudalism leads to capitalism. Feudalism was a peculiarly Western European phenomenon that in turn made capitalism there a unique event in world history.

In the last essay in this volume Ma Xin offers another formula by associating the Asiatic, ancient, and feudal modes of production with the three main forms of property in *Pre-Capitalist Economic Formations*: tribal, classical, and Germanic. Like Su Kaihua, he views the AMP as tribalism, the universal first stage of development after primitive society. Unlike Su, however, he insists that there is no one route out of the AMP, and that slavery and feudalism can both emerge from it under certain circumstances.

These may seem like modest challenges to the Stalinist unilinear model, but within the historiographical climate in China they represent a major initiative. One response from the historical studies establishment has been to deflect the challenge by substituting "multiplicity" for "multilinearity." In 1985 Pang Zhuoheng and She Shusheng, two participants in the AMP discussions, published essays arguing that historical phenomena are necessarily multiple and variant, but that within this multiplicity and variation there is regularity and unity.[64] The unstated implication for AMP proponents like Hu Zhongda and Ma Xin is that they are losing sight of the larger pattern of world history that embraces all societies. Liao Xuesheng similarly argued recently for the great unity of historical development in all parts of the world, though it proceeds in different cultures at uneven rates. "Unevenness" (*bu pingheng*) is now the favored explanation among conservative historians for historical diversity. Liao points out, quite fairly, that the AMP controversy of the past decade was part of a larger dispute "over whether there are laws of development governing all societies, and if so, what these laws might be." He concludes that "the notion that we can indiscriminately divide up societies into 'Oriental' and 'Western' and should emphasize the differences in their courses of development is daily losing ground."[65]

Abandoning the Model

It is presumptuous of Liao to declare victory for his side, even though the intellectual mainstream in China generally prefers to emphasize structural commonalities over structural peculiarities. To judge from essays appearing recently in national publications, there are in fact indications that the mainstream may be shifting course in the late 1980s. Xiang Guanqi points out in his second contribution to the AMP debate in the December 1987 issue of *Lishi yanjiu* (Studies in history), the leading establishment history journal, that the Marxist five-stages theory is itself a product of history. He cautiously implies that the AMP may be its Achilles' heel. A more direct statement appeared in the national *Guangming Daily* on March 23, 1988: a pseudonymous article declares that the theory of a fixed sequence of social formations cannot be considered a law of historical development, since not all societies have passed through all the stages it dictates. Marx intended the model to apply only to Western Europe, the article insists, and the AMP debate arose precisely because historians have misapplied the theory elsewhere as though it had the authority of historical law.[66]

These indicators of a new direction suggest that Chinese historical theory is at a crossroads, and the AMP has largely been responsible for bringing it there. It is undeniable that Stalinist historiography is still largely intact in China, and that historical thinking continues to be dominated by categories rather than concepts, to be theological rather than critical in its reasoning. Yet the presence of the AMP in the new wave of debates on social formations in the last decade—as indeed at every other time it has surfaced among Marxists in this century— has reflected an awareness of the failure of prevailing theory to understand the influence of the past on present problems and future options. The latest round of debate has been weak on applying theory to reality and has not generated many new insights into Chinese history. The AMP controversy nonetheless has encouraged critical thinking about certain fundamental principles of social theory in China, propeling historians back to the once discredited idea that not all societies have experienced history through the same sequence of socioeconomic structures.

Those who shy away from multilinearism and hang onto the five-stages model do so out of a fear that China will sink back into peculiarity and be cast out of the charmed world-historical circle from which Hegel excluded it a century and a half ago. This is the anxiety that drove Chinese intellectuals to embrace Marxism in the 1920s, when China's place in the modern world was extremely insecure.[67] I rather doubt the value of keeping that anxiety alive in the 1980s. It is true that China's path forward under the new reforms is unclear, but social theorists in China should view this search for a new direction as an opportunity to provide a better understanding of the historical course that has led China to its present situation, rather than as an inducement to retreat to the well-worn theoretical postures of an earlier stage in the growth of Chinese Marxism.

The experience of Marxist historiography in Europe has shown that the creative revision of historical theory is not only possible but necessary if Marxism is to be transformed from a self-referential hermeneutics into a critical method for the study of society. Writing in that context, Perry Anderson has begged that the AMP "be given the decent burial that it deserves"[68] and a range of concepts of greater analytical power be developed for Asian societies. Chinese Marxist historians have not yet shown themselves ready to take up that challenge. Many want to hurry the AMP into a pauper's grave, but not always for the best of reasons. Social theory in China will only mature when the AMP has been transcended, but it must be done through a process of new theoretical construction, not simplistic rejection. For the foreseeable future, the presence of the AMP in Chinese historical debates should be taken as a healthy sign. As long as the AMP remains on the agenda, there is hope that Chinese scholars will not rest content with the Stalinist model of historical development but will move creatively in new directions to generate a more powerful analysis of Chinese society.

The preparation of this book has been in part a collaborative project involving the efforts of six graduate students at the University of Toronto: Alfred Chan, Ray Dragan, Paul Forage, Emily Hill, Li Anshan, and André Schmid. My own understanding of the AMP has been considerably strengthened in the course of working with them.

As editor I have exercised a very free hand, both in revising their translations and in substantially editing the original texts. Tangential points have been reduced to endnotes, and some unnecessary digressions removed entirely. These alterations have been done out of a conviction that a liberal rendering of the essays would better convey their logic and intentions than would a precise adherence to the conventions of Chinese academic prose. Of the nine authors who communicated with me concerning the translations of their essays, all approved of the changes that were made, and a few suggested further emendations. Their warm response to the project has been truly gratifying.

Finally, I would like to express my thanks to Joshua Fogel, John

Rapp, and Bin Wong, who read the introduction and offered helpful criticisms; to the Research Board of the University of Toronto, which provided me with a grant to aid in the preparation of the manuscript; to Douglas Merwin and Anita O'Brien of M. E. Sharpe, who injected enthusiasm into the project at every stage; and to Meg Taylor, who was unfailing in her editorial acumen and personal support through the year it took to get this project from conception to completion.

Notes

1. Anne Bailey and Josep Llobera, eds., *The Asiatic Mode of Production: Science and Politics* (London: Routledge and Kegan Paul, 1981). The only Asians included are a Vietnamese (Le Thanh Khoi) and two Turks (Huri Islamoglu and Caglar Keyder).

2. Chinese discussions of the AMP have been noted briefly in Benjamin Schwartz, "A Marxist Controversy in China," *Far Eastern Quarterly* 13 (February 1954): 143–54; Petr Skalník and Timoteus Pokora, "Beginning of the Discussion about the Asiatic Mode of Production in the USSR and the People's Republic of China," *Eirene* 5 (1966): 179–87; Arif Dirlik, *Revolution and History: The Origins of Marxist Historiography in China, 1919–1937* (Berkeley: University of California Press, 1978), pp. 191–207; and Joshua A. Fogel, "The Debates over the Asiatic Mode of Production in Soviet Russia, China, and Japan," *The American Historical Review* 93, 1 (February 1988): 56–79. The political context of the debates in the 1980s is analyzed in John Rapp, "Despotism and Leninist State Autonomy: The Chinese Asiatic Mode of Production Debates in Comparative Perspective," Ph. D. diss., University of Wisconsin, 1987. Some of Rapp's arguments have appeared in "The Fate of Marxist Democrats in Leninist Party States: China's Debate on the Asiatic Mode of Production," *Theory and Society* 16 (1988): 709–40.

3. Thomas de Quincy, *Confessions of an English Opium-Eater* (London: J. M. Dent, 1960), p. 241.

4. Pre-Marxian views of Asia are analyzed in Perry Anderson, *The Lineages of the Absolutist State* (London: New Left Books, 1974), pp. 462–72; Lawrence Krader, *The Asiatic Mode of Production* (Assen: Van Gorcum, 1975), ch. 1.

5. Donald Lowe, *The Function of "China" in Marx, Lenin, and Mao* (Berkeley: University of California Press, 1966), p. 6.

6. Marx accordingly singles out for criticism Hegel's theory that private property developed as an expression of the growth of the human will. See *Capital*, vol. 3 (New York: International Publishers, 1967), p. 615 n.26.

7. *CCPE*, p. 21.

8. Commission of the Central Committee of the Communist Party of the Soviet Union (Bolsheviks), ed., *History of the Communist Party of the Soviet Union (Bolsheviks): Short Course*, (Moscow: Foreign Languages Publishing House, 1951), pp. 194-99.

9. For recent disputes surrounding the idea of a slave mode of production, see Barry Hindess and Paul Hirst, *Pre-Capitalist Modes of Production* (London: Routledge and Kegan Paul, 1977), ch. 3; Chris Wickham, "The Other Transition: From the Ancient World to Feudalism," *Past and Present* 103 (May 1984): 6ff. There is a large literature in Chinese on the topic, arising out of the difficulty that Marxist historians have faced trying to discern a period in Chinese history when slavery could be regarded as the dominant economic relationship.

10. de Quincy, *Confessions*, p. 240.

11. The continuing power of the negative connotation of "Asiatic" is evident in the recent controversy surrounding Ernst Nolte's reference to the Holocaust as an "'Asiatic' deed." Nolte sought to mitigate the guilt of the German people by characterizing Hitler's atrocities as an understandable response to the barbarism of Stalin's purges in the USSR, not something that came from within the German people themselves. Nolte borrowed the term from the observation of Max Erwin von Scheubner-Richter in 1938 that the genocide of the Armenians by the Turks in 1915 was an "Asiatic" deed. See Richard Evans, "The New Nationalism and the Old History: Perspectives on the West German *Historikerstreit*," *Journal of Modern History* 59 (December 1987): 765. I am grateful to James Retallack for drawing my attention to this latest chapter in the life of a loaded word.

12. Norman Levine, "The Myth of Asiatic Restoration," *Journal of Asian Studies* 37, 1 (November 1977): 73.

13. *Pre-Capitalist Economic Formations* first appeared in a Soviet edition in 1938 and only became widely known after its publication in English in 1965 with an introduction by Eric Hobsbawm. Lawrence Krader published Marx's notes on Lewis Morgan, John Phear, Henry Maine, and John Lubbock in *The Ethnological Notebooks of Karl Marx* (Assen: Van Gorcum, 1972).

14. Lowe, *The Function of "China,"* p. 27.

15. *PCEF*, pp. 69–70.

16. Ibid., pp. 71, 74–75.

17. Ibid., p. 75. Marx also mentions a Slavonic form of property, which appears to be a modified version of the Asiatic.

18. Wang Dunshu and Yu Ke in fact distinguish only six characteristics, but for greater clarity I have subdivided their first into two. For a more thorough and critical account of the constituent elements of the AMP, see Krader, *The Asiatic Mode*, pp. 286–96.

19. The lack of critical analysis of the concept of the rent/tax couple is surprising, given the tendency among Western scholars to view this mode of appropriation as the weakest element of the AMP. See Hindess and Hirst, *Pre-Capitalist Modes of Production*, pp. 192–200; Chris Wickham, "The Uniqueness of the East," *Journal of Peasant Studies* 12, 2–3 (April 1985).

20. Karl Wittfogel, *Oriental Despotism: A Comparative Study of Total Power* (New Haven: Yale University Press, 1957).

21. Marx, "Revolution in China and in Europe" (1853), in Marx and Engels, *On Colonialism* (New York: International Publishers, 1972), p. 21.

22. Marx, *Marx on China, 1853–1860: Articles from the New York Daily Tribune*, ed. Dona Torr (London, 1951), p. 55. Sensitive commentators on Asia at

this time were able to see past the stability of China's social structure. Marx was familiar with the memoirs of Evariste-Régis Huc, a missionary in China in the 1840s, who observed that "the immutability of the Asiatics is one of those established ideas . . . which is founded on an utter ignorance of their history" (*A Journey Through the Chinese Empire*, vol. 2 [New York: Harper, 1855], p. 52).

23. Kong Lingping, " 'Dongfang zhuanzhizhuyi' gainian de yanbian" (The evolution of the concept of "Oriental despotism"), *Shixue yuekan* (History monthly) 2 (1983): 73.

24. E.g., Engels' characterization of Russia in a letter to Vera Zasulich, April 23, 1885, in Marx and Engels, *Selected Correspondence* (Moscow: Progress Publishers, 1965), p. 385.

25. E.g., Engels' description of Dutch rule in Java in a letter to Kautsky, February 16, 1884, in *On Colonialism*, p. 344.

26. One Chinese scholar, Chen Hongjin, not only denies that despotism is a characteristic of the AMP, but argues that the AMP has bequeathed to present-day China a communitarian democratic tradition (Chen Hongjin, 1981, pp. 9, 11).

27. Cf. Krader, *The Asiatic Mode*, p. 296.

28. Lajos Magyar, *Ekonomika sel'skogo khoziaistva v Kitae* (Moscow and Leningrad, 1928), translated into Chinese as *Zhongguo nongcun jingji yanjiu* (Research on China's rural economy) (Shanghai: Shenzhou Guoguang She, 1931).

29. Magyar lays out this view in his introductory chapter, "The AMP and Imperialism" (see especially pp. 26 and 37–40 in the Chinese edition). In his next book, *Ocherki po ekonomike Kitaia* (Moscow, 1930), translated as *Zhongguo jingji dagang* (An outline of the Chinese economy) (Shanghai: Xinshengming Shuju, 1933), Magyar eschews an explicitly Asiatic analysis, though his insistent critique of imperialism remains unshaken (Chinese ed., pp. 420–22). The only work by Magyar in English that I have seen is an abridgement of an essay first published in 1930, translated in Bailey and Llobera, *The Asiatic Mode*, pp. 76–94. Magyar's name is Russianized as Liudvig Mad'iar in most English-language works.

30. This inclination is indicated by the inclusion in the front of Magyar's book of a long preface by someone at the Research Institute on the China Question in Moscow disputing his interpretation. The same sort of disclaimer was used in the February 29, 1928, issue of *Bolshevik*, in which Wissarion Lominadze's AMP-based analysis of the Chinese revolution is preceded by an editorial identifying his view as a departure from Comintern policy, and followed by a fuller critique by Pavel Mif. See Kotake Kazuaki, "Rominaaze no Chugoku kakumeiron: 'Ajiateki seisan yoshiki ronso' to no kanren ni okeru shokai" (An introduction to Lominadze's view of the Chinese revolution as it relates to the "AMP controversy"), *Kindai Chugoku kenkyu kaiho* (Research reports on modern China) 8 (1986): 14.

31. Mikhail Godes, "The Reaffirmation of Unilinealism," in Bailey and Llobera, *The Asiatic Mode*, p. 104.

32. Stephen Dunn, *The Fall and Rise of the Asiatic Mode of Production* (London: Routledge and Kegan Paul, 1982), pp. 35–36.

33. Fogel, "The Debates over the Asiatic Mode," p. 74. The Japanese debate is surveyed in Germaine Hoston, *Marxism and the Crisis of Development in Prewar Japan* (Princeton: Princeton University Press, 1986), ch. 6.

34. Maurice Godelier, *Perspectives in Marxist Anthropology* (Cambridge: Cambridge University Press, 1977), p. 122.

35. Tian Renlong, 1981, pp. 158–59, provides a partial bibliography for the period 1951–1981. Chinese essays on the AMP are cited by only author and date in the notes; refer to the bibliography for full information.

36. Tian Changwu, "Makesi Engesi lun Yazhou gudai shehui wenti" (Marx and Engels on the question of ancient society in Asia), *Lishi congtan* (Essays on history) no. 1 (Beijing: Zhonghua Shuju, 1964), p. 41. Tian's position is summarized in Skalník and Pokora, "Beginning of the Discussion," pp. 185–86. Guo Moruo (1892–1978) in 1928 was the first Chinese scholar to interpret the AMP as primitive society. Tong Shuye (1908–1968) also wrote in this vein in 1951 and 1952. See Tian Renlong, 1981, pp. 147–53; Lin Ganquan et al., 1982, pp. 147–55.

37. Timothy Brook and René Wagner, "The Teaching of History to Foreign Students at Peking University," *China Quarterly* 71 (September 1977): 602.

38. E.g., *Shehui kexue zhanxian* (Social science frontline) 4 (1978); *Guangming ribao*, November 8, 1978.

39. Their absence from the debate has been noted by K. C. Chang, "Archaeology and Chinese History," *World Archaeology* 13, 2 (October 1981): 167.

40. Cf. Philip Huang, *The Peasant Economy and Social Change in North China* (Stanford: Stanford University Press, 1985), p. 29.

41. The bibliography covers the decade 1978–1988. It is reasonably complete for all but the last year, for which I could include only three titles before this book went to press. The most extensive Chinese bibliography on the AMP, though not complete, is the draft edition of *Makesizhuyi shehui xingtai wenti yanjiu lunwen mulu suoyin* (Bibliographic index to articles researching questions of Marxist social formations), compiled by Ben Muqin, Tao Shifu, and Xu Zhaoren and published by the History Department of China People's University in July 1988. I am grateful to Ma Xin for supplying me with a copy of this book.

42. Rapp, "The Fate of Marxist Democrats," pp. 714–21.

43. Su Shaozhi, "Developing Marxism under Contemporary Conditions," in Su Shaozhi et al., *Marxism in China* (Nottingham: Spokesman, 1983), p. 32.

44. Tian Changwu, "Jianshe you Zhongguo tese de Makesizhuyi lishixue," *Lishi yanjiu* (Studies in history) 1 (1984).

45. Charles Burton, "China's Post-Mao Transition: The Role of the Party and Ideology in the 'New Period,' " *Pacific Affairs* 60, 3 (Fall 1987): 437.

46. Peter Perdue has noted that the feudal-persistence and AMP proponents share a common view of the past as "a unified, unchanging presence," which amounts to a repudiation of China's past more thorough than at any time since the iconoclastic May Fourth Movement in 1919. "The Western concept that asserted the inevitable superiority of the West and the backwardness of the East is now fervently adopted by young Chinese themselves to overcome their own backwardness" (*Exhausting the Earth: State and Peasant in Hunan, 1500–1850* [Cambridge: Council on East Asian Studies, Harvard University, 1987], pp. 6–7). Their historiographical implications are, however, quite different.

47. Rapp, "The Fate of Marxist Democrats," pp. 720–21.

48. Lin Ganquan et al., 1982, p. 150. Wu participated in discussions but did not

publish anything on the AMP in the 1950s.

49. Hindess and Hirst, *Pre-Capitalist Modes of Production*, pp. 180–83. Wu has sharply criticized Wittfogel's analysis in Wu Dakun, 1982.

50. Wu Dakun, 1981, repr. 1983, pp. 55–56. This essay is summarized in Rapp, "The Fate of Marxist Democrats," pp. 725–27.

51. The phrase *nongcun gongshe* has been variously translated in these essays as "agricultural community," "village community," and "rural commune," depending on the context or the phrasing of existing English translations of passages from Marx and Engels cited by the authors. Sometimes another term, *gongtongti* (*kyodotai* in Japanese), is used for "community;" it appears to have come to China from Japanese scholarship on the AMP in the 1930s.

52. Zhao Lisheng, 1981, p. 26.

53. The earliest attempt to analyze the well-field system in relation to the AMP is M. Kokin and G. Papaian, *"Tszin-Tian,"* agrarnyi stroi drevnogo Kitaia (*Jintian*, the agrarian order of ancient China) (Leningrad, 1930), for which Magyar wrote a lengthy introduction (see note 29). A Chinese translation was published in Shanghai in 1933.

54. Fogel, "The Debates over the Asiatic Mode," p. 79.

55. Rapp, "The Fate of Marxist Democrats," p. 733.

56. Gilbert Rozman, *The Chinese Debates about Soviet Socialism, 1978–85* (Princeton: Princeton University Press, 1987), p. 8.

57. Marx to Zasulich, March 8, 1881, third draft, in *PCEF*, p. 145.

58. See Zuo Wenhua, 1980, for a critique of this essay. The same group published again on the AMP in 1982 to answer charges that their analysis failed to take account of the state in Marx's Asiatic formulations. Naming Wittfogel, but perhaps implying Wu Dakun, they assert that arguing for an AMP state is slandering Chinese socialism as "bureaucratic collectivism."

59. Zhang Yaqin and Bai Jiufu, 1981, p. 34, criticized Song for his transitional stage and argued that it should be seen as an "economic formation" within which communal property was being eroded, rather than a "socioeconomic formation."

60. This tribal stage, which Marx discusses briefly in *Pre-Capitalist Economic Formations*, p. 68, is usually regarded as a transitional phase rather than a distinct stage in its own right (as Wang Dunshu and Yu Ke argue). For a review of recent attempts to distinguish stages in the development of primitive society, see Qiu Pu and Li Qinghe, "Guanyu yuanshi shehui de fenqi wenti" (The question of periodizing primitive society), *Sixiang zhanxian* (Ideological frontline) 4 and 5 (1984).

61. Song Min, " 'Makesi yu dongfangxue ji qita' yiwen shangque," p. 139.

62. E.g., Li Yongcai and Wei Maoheng, 1986.

63. Conceiving of slavery and feudalism as alternative routes rather than a single sequence out of primitive society is now receiving wide support. See, e.g., Xue Huizong, "Yuanshi shehui hou bu yiding shi nuli shehui" (What follows primitive society is not necessarily slave society), *Jiang-Han luntan* (Jiang-Han forum) 2 (1982).

64. Pang Zhuoheng, "Lishi de tongyixing, duoyangxing yu lishi de bijiao yanjiu" (Unity and multiplicity in history and comparative historical research), *Tianjin shehui kexue* (Social sciences in Tianjin) 1 (1985); She Shusheng, "Lishi fazhan de

changguixing he bianyixing de tongyi" (Unity of regularity and variation in historical development), *Shehui kexue pinglun* (Critical essays in social sciences) 1 (1985).

65. Liao Xuesheng, "Guanyu nuli zhanyouzhi shehui de yixie sikao" (Some thoughts on slave-owning society), *Shixue lilun* (History and theory) 1 (1988): 56. Curiously, Hu Zhongda in the same issue of *Shixue lilun* takes much the same position, saying that variations in historical development should be understood in terms of uneven rates of development, not differences of social types ("Lun shijie lishi fazhan de bu pingheng xing" [On unequal development in world history]).

66. Qi Liang, "Shehui xingtai lilun yu lishi guilü bianyi" (Distinguishing between the theory of social formations and historical laws), *Guangming ribao*, March 23, 1988, p. 3. The five fixed social formations model was further challenged in articles by Li Yongchang, Liu Youcheng, and Yuan Lin in *Shixue lilun* 3 (1988): 147–82.

67. E.g., Guo Moruo, *Zhongguo gudai shehui yanjiu* (Studies in ancient Chinese society) (repr., Beijing: Renmin Chubanshe, 1977), preface, p. vii.

68. Anderson, *Lineages of the Absolutist State*, p. 548.

WU DAKUN

2 | # Some Questions Concerning Research on the Asiatic Mode of Production

As the capitalist economies of the West have stagnated in the 1970s, Western scholars have been making great progress in research on Marxist thought. Meanwhile, Marxism has become unfashionable among younger Chinese, who would rather talk about Western bourgeois things, but in the West the situation is just the reverse. The developed capitalist countries as well as underdeveloped countries in the Third World are now facing serious economic problems that cannot be solved using bourgeois economics. Some scholars and leftists in Western countries have turned their attention to Marx and are beginning to study him again, and their achievements in this area have been impressive. In Italy, for example, Umberto Melotti published a book in 1972 entitled *Marx e il terzo mondo*, a specialized study of Marx's Asiatic mode of production. I have gained much from an English translation of this book published in 1974 (*Marx and the Third World*). The book rekindled my interest in the concept of the AMP, which had influenced my thinking in the past, and it has convinced me of the great need for further research in this area.[1] I wish to take this opportunity to ask for guidance on certain problems that came to

From *Xueshu yanjiu* (Academic research) 1 (1980): 11–18, based on a talk given to the Economics Association of Guangdong on September 29, 1979, entitled "On the Relation Between the Asiatic Mode of Production and Imperialism." Translated by Emily Hill.

mind while I was reading the book. These questions are certain to be controversial, but I put them forward in the spirit of promoting true "contention among a hundred schools of thought."

Five or Six Modes of Social Production?

Most of the works on Marxist historical science published in China or the Soviet Union speak of five modes of production in the history of society, though a few distinguish six. The five modes are primitive communism, slavery, feudalism, capitalism, and socialism. In his classic Preface to *A Contribution to the Critique of Political Economy*, however, Marx actually stated that "the Asiatic, ancient, feudal and modern bourgeois modes of production may be designated as epochs marking progress in the economic development of society."[2] This shows that Marx conceived of an Asiatic mode of production preceding the slave stage of development, which brings to a total of six the number of modes of production.

There was great controversy over the AMP in the Soviet Union during the 1920s and 1930s. The debate was originally theoretical and academic, but it became linked with political issues as some of the advocates of the AMP, later labeled Trotskyists, were judged to have committed serious political errors. As a result, scholars in other countries interested in the AMP became reluctant to continue discussing it for fear of being considered Trotskyist. Trotskyist crimes are one thing, but the AMP was actually one of Marx's theories. Discussion of the AMP need not stop just because the Trotskyists talked about it, any more than all mention of Mao Zedong Thought must cease because Lin Biao and the "Gang of Four" talked about it. Furthermore, the situation is different now that we have Marx's *Pre-Capitalist Economic Formations* and *The Ethnological Notebooks*, which were unknown when the AMP was being discussed in the Soviet Union in the 1920s and 1930s.[3]

Melotti has clearly spent much time and effort researching the AMP to write his book, and his well-documented argument is most persuasive. On the basis of Marx's original view, he holds that there are six rather than five modes of social production in history, and that we must accept the AMP as a distinct mode of production. People have been afraid to treat Marx's AMP as a separate mode of production because it is not mentioned in the second section of the fourth chapter of the *Short History of the Communist Party of the Soviet Union (Bolsheviks)*, compiled under Stalin's direction in 1938.[4] It lists only five modes of production, so Soviet academic discussion was limited to five modes. But Marx unambiguously mentioned the AMP. Soviet scholars therefore devised two explanations to resolve this contradiction. One approach was to identify the AMP with the primitive communal system. This explanation is not very persuasive, because in Marx's description of society under the AMP the state had already formed. If the state existed, society must have been divided into exploiting and exploited classes. Land was owned by the Asiatic state, which was the highest landlord and extracted taxes and rents from all the producers ("rents" and "taxes" were for a period of time conflated in the Asiatic state). The Asiatic state relied on the peasantry to support a large bureaucracy, and its bureaucracy was in fact an exploitative class just like the landlord and bourgeois classes of feudal and capitalist states. It makes no sense to equate the AMP with primitive communalism when there was already a state and a class of exploiters supported by rents and taxes.

The second approach was developed by later Soviet scholars, who worked hard to explain the AMP in the wake of Stalin's declaration. Vasilii Struve (1889–1965), followed by many other so-called Oriental historians, identified the AMP as underdeveloped slavery in order to reconcile Marx's view with Stalin's prescription of five historical stages. Struve racked his brain to come up with the explanation that two types of slave society could be distinguished within the slave mode of production. Ancient Greek and Roman society was a developed form of slavery, whereas Asiatic society was an underdeveloped form. While I myself once accepted the theory of five modes of production and found Struve's explanation theoretically satisfactory, I now feel after reading Melotti's book that it is necessary to reconsider this question.

It may be acceptable in a certain sense to identify the AMP with an underdeveloped slave system, for slavery existed in AMP states, but slaves did not become the main producers for the state. Furthermore, to call the system "underdeveloped" leads one to expect that it should later become a developed slave system, following the law of material progress from underdeveloped to developed forms. History has shown, however, that slavery remained underdeveloped in states based on the AMP. No Asiatic state ever developed into a slave society in which slaves were the main producers as they were in Greece and Rome. This is one drawback to the interpretation of the AMP as an underdeveloped form of slavery.

From the present perspective, the main weakness of the explanation that there were actually two types of slave system is that, in *Pre-Capitalist Economic Formations*, Marx treats the Asiatic (or Oriental) mode as a mode of production comparable to the classical (ancient, or slave) and Germanic modes. Furthermore, the status of the main producers was not the same in these different modes of production. In the Asiatic state, the main producers were always peasants, whereas in classical Greece and Rome the main producers were slaves and, in the Germanic mode, serfs.

Whether there have been five or six modes of production in history has become an important theoretical question very much worth reconsideration. If it were proved on the basis of both theory and historical evidence that there were indeed six rather than five, then great changes would follow in many fields of knowledge, including world history, Chinese history, historical materialism, and political economy in the broad sense. We must not hesitate to face the implications, however troublesome; scholarship will not flourish if we avoid complex issues and differences of opinion.

Is Social Development Unilinear or Multilinear?

According to Stalin's unilinear view of history, slavery succeeds primitive communalism, feudalism follows the disintegration of slavery, feudalism is in turn followed by capitalism, and socialism follows the collapse of capitalism. Is this model in accordance with Marx's original intention? And does it fit the facts of world historical development? We now know from the correspondence between Marx and his acquaintances that he based his analysis of the historical development of society mainly on the history of Western Europe. He did not recommend that his conclusions be applied to the history of all continents. In fact, he even cautioned his friends against muddling up his formulas. Melotti entitled his book *Marx and the Third World* because in Third World countries, actual historical development has not resembled Stalin's unilinear pattern. Given the low level of social productivity when primitive communalism collapsed, different geographical conditions throughout the world led to the emergence of dissimilar developmental paths: the Asiatic, the ancient Greek and Roman, and the Germanic. Among the nations of the world, democratic revolutions occurred only in Western Europe, allowing the feudal states there to develop into capitalist states. In other countries the capitalist system has developed only under external influences.

Why capitalism emerged only in Western Europe is a question very much worth further study. According to Melotti, the answer is that historical development is multilinear rather than unilinear. Two points must be clarified here. The first is that the term "Asiatic" used by Marx was not a geographic term. Marx first used it to refer to Egypt, which is outside of Asia. Japan, though an Asian country, had, according to a note in *Capital*, the same type of feudalism as the West, and hence it cannot be referred to as "Asiatic" in Marx's sense. The second point is that both unilinear and multilinear historical development are in accordance with Marx's basic principle of historical materialism; that is, both are "single origin" theories of history. To discuss more than one "line" of development is not the same thing as discussing more than one "origin" of history. A theory of multiple lines is a strict application of Marxist principles of historical materialism, for it reflects the concrete conditions of world historical development more accurately than Stalin's unilinear scheme, and it seems more helpful in clarifying both historical issues and the problems of the present.

Understanding the Nature of Soviet Society Today

Melotti's *Marx and the Third World* discusses the world today as well as history. Although his ideas are not necessarily always correct, they are at least useful for us to think about. According to Melotti's research, tsarist Russia may be categorized as a semi-Asiatic society, while imperial China was typically Asiatic. Scholars all over the world have been arguing about the nature of Soviet society since the Soviet military occupation of Czechoslovakia in 1968. The unrestrained violence of that event showed the true face of the Soviet Union's socialist imperialism. How can Soviet imperialism be explained theoretically? One current explanation is that capitalism has been restored in the Soviet Union. This explanation is not very convincing because the means of production are not privately owned, nor is there a private bourgeoisie. Another explanation is that the Soviet Union is a state monopoly capitalist society. This explanation is not convincing either, because the United States is also a state monopoly capitalist society but is obviously very different from Soviet society. A third explanation, held by certain radical thinkers in the West, says that the Soviet Union has created new exploiting and exploited classes, thereby becoming a new type of exploitative state. There is as yet no name for this historically unprecedented exploitative society.

Melotti has suggested a fourth explanation, but this is one that is insulting to China, for he places China in the same category as the Soviet Union. In his view, Russia and China are both bureaucratic collectivist societies. Setting aside for the moment the question of China, I can accept Melotti's view of the continuity between the Russia of today and the Russia of the past even without having studied that country myself. Because prerevolutionary Russia was a semi-Asiatic society, bureaucratic traditions were very strong. Lenin himself discovered after the October Revolution that bureaucratism was deeply entrenched in the Soviet system, and he believed that the socialist revolution could not be completed nor socialism established until bureaucratism had been eradicated. Lenin's goal was not achieved even after his death, for Stalin was not able to eradicate bureaucratism either. At the Nineteenth Party Congress, held in 1956 after Stalin's death, Georgii Malenkov, in summarizing shortcomings in the party's work, devoted one-third of his report to the problem of Soviet bureaucratism. By the time of Stalin's succession by Khrushchev, the Soviet rulers had already stopped working on the bureaucracy problem and had degenerated into a bureaucratic monopoly capitalist class.

There is no need for a bureaucratic monopolistic bourgeoisie to divide the means of production among themselves. Through redistribution made possible by its control of the incomes of its citizens, the state has the power to use almost all of the surplus value created by laborers to support its swollen military and bureaucratic structures. These structures, divorced from popular supervision and control, will inevitably become oppressive domestically and chauvinistic in foreign relations and will evolve into organs carrying out the military and economic expansion of an unalloyed socialist-imperialist state. Just as the Asiatic despotic state described by Marx was formed through state ownership of land as princes became the highest landlords and exploited the peasants by compelling them to provide corvée labor, so the despotism in the Soviet Union today is a result of state ownership of the means of production. Soviet rulers have become the highest capitalists of their country, able to exploit all laborers by compelling their labor. In my opinion, the degeneration of Soviet society can be fully explained in this way. But I believe that Melotti is wrong to place Chinese and Soviet societies in the same category. He formed this mistaken view mainly because he came to China during the period of the Cultural Revolution. Prior to 1972, when Melotti's book was first published, Lin Biao and the "Gang of Four" were still in power, and Melotti's personal impressions of Chinese conditions were therefore mistaken. He was naturally even less aware of how the situation in China would change to become what it is today.

Periodization of Premodern Chinese History

Nonetheless, I do agree with Melotti that historical China can be understood as a typical Asiatic state. There has long been disagreement among Chinese historians over how Chinese history should be periodized. The reason for this is that Stalin's scheme of five modes of production had shackled our thinking, including my own. We forced Chinese history into Stalin's pattern, and all manner of controversies developed because it did not fit. If we now take into account the one other mode of production Marx mentioned, the AMP, we will perceive that the Asiatic state he referred to became established in China during the Xia, Shang, and Zhou dynasties (second and first millennia B.C.) in the wake of the dissolution of primitive communalism.[5] Through the changes of the Spring and Autumn and Warring States periods (722–221 B.C.), this immature Asiatic state became centralized and despotic, evolving into the true Asiatic state of the Qin, Han, and later dynasties.

The political and economic characteristics of Chinese bureaucratic society sketched by Mao Zedong in "The Chinese Revolution and the Chinese Communist Party" are actually the features of the typical Asiatic state.[6] In my view, Mao would have realized that he was describing an Asiatic state with characteristics very different from European feudalism if he had been able to read Marx's *Pre-Capitalist Economic Formations*. In China, the state has always been the highest landlord. The emperor and all of his bureaucratic agents relied on the benefits of peasant "rents" and "taxes." The land could be freely bought and sold, however, and peasants were the main producers. Though the peasants suffered great oppression and exploitation, they were certainly not completely bound as serfs to the land. In a year of famine they could flee. In medieval Europe, land could not be bought and sold, and serfs were bound to the land. Because land was not a commodity, money earned in trade and industry after capitalism began to develop could only be invested to expand trade and industry. This caused the formation and strengthening of the bourgeoisie, which eventually led to the overthrow of feudalism in Western Europe.

The situation was different in China, where political control was in the hands of the bureaucratic representatives of the landlord class. There were some sprouts of capitalism in China, too, but Chinese merchants and industrialists were able to invest their accumulated capital in land, and consequently commercial capital, usury, and landlordism fused together to form a triad system of rule. The formation of an independent bourgeoisie was not possible, nor was the formation of a true proletariat. Suffering extreme oppression, the peasants rose in rebellion, but all they could change was the reigning dynasty. It was not possible for them to establish capitalism, the new type of society that formed in Western Europe. In pursuit of profit, the Western European bourgeoisie advocated bourgeois "democracy" and encouraged the development of science and technology. The despotic rulers of China, in contrast, did not need to promote the expansion of industry and commerce or the development of science and technology, because as representatives of the landlords they relied primarily on exploitation of peasant labor. And they were naturally even more opposed to "democracy." So even though science and technology were advanced in ancient China compared to other parts of the world, when they were unrelated to the development of agriculture they were suppressed after the formation of the centralized despotic state during the imperial period. (Ancient advances in fields astronomy and calendrical measurement, mathematics, and hydraulic engineering were all related to the development of agriculture.[7]) With the establishment of the imperial examination system during the Tang dynasty (A.D. 618–906), the intelligence and talents of Chinese intellectuals were completely diverted from science and technology and shackled into the "eight-legged essay" system down to the end of the imperial period in 1911. As a result, even though the level of science and technology was high, China did not succeed in inventing the steam engine or developing toward capitalism. This was not an accidental outcome but was determined by the nature of China's Asiatic society.

The Political Significance of Studying the AMP

In my view, studying the Marxist theory of the AMP not only will contribute to our understanding of Chinese history but is especially important for a better understanding of the importance and theoretical basis of the policies now being promoted by the Chinese Communist Party. This is because the main political characteristic of the AMP is bureaucratic rule. As we all know, the greatest recent contribution of the party has been to steer China onto the path of building a fully modernized socialist state after completely smashing the tyranny of the "Gang of Four." As historical materialists, we cannot consider accidental the degeneration of Russia into a social-imperialist state, or the appearance in China of Lin Biao and the Gang of Four. In my view, Marx's description of the AMP can be related to the development of these evils in socialist nations. It is now popular to refer to the despotic ruling methods of Lin Biao and the Gang of Four as "feudal fascism." This is certainly permissible as an everyday expression, but scientifically speaking it is not appropriate. Fascism is the autocracy of the monopolistic capitalist class and does not appear in feudal society. The activities of Lin Biao and the Gang of Four in fact revived the Oriental despotism of ancient Asiatic states. The cruelty of this Oriental despotism was even worse than that of modern fascism. We need only remember that when Dimitrov, secretary-general of the Third Communist International, was arrested by the German fascists, he was still able to exercise his right to legal defense. He voiced his Marxist-Leninist beliefs and his opposition to fascism in court and was finally released.[8] Far worse was the imprisonment of Zhang Zhixin under Lin Biao and the Gang of Four.[9] As products of China's long-established Asiatic society, they knew that Zhang would scream slogans at the point of death, so they made sure to cut her throat before torturing her further. Has such cruelty occurred in any other country in the modern period?

With united purpose, the Chinese people are now working to achieve the four modernizations under the leadership of the party, and unprecedentedly favorable conditions have developed across the country. Certain obstacles to progress remain, however. Bureaucratism is one of these obstacles. Keeping in mind the example of the Soviet Union, we must treat bureaucratism as a very serious problem and absolutely ensure that it does not develop further in the Soviet manner. Like Lenin in 1919, we must resolve to eradicate bureaucratism completely because it obstructs socialist revolution and socialist construction. The method of eradication will be the rule of socialist democracy and the enforcement of socialist law. We must also greatly increase the scientific and cultural knowledge of the Chinese people and strengthen scholarly, cultural, and scientific communication with other nations. The despotism of Lin Biao and the Gang of Four perpetuated the ignorance and superstition of the Chinese people, and it is essential that we reverse this tendency.

To speed China's four modernizations, the party has adopted the method of joint-venture cooperation with foreign multinational companies. There is some concern that this form of cooperation might be inappropriate for socialist modernization. We are all aware that multinationals have economically and politically impaired the sovereignty of Third World nations. The Chinese state, however, is a dictatorship of the proletariat and will be able to maintain autonomy, without fear of multinationals. My view of the joint-venture enterprises is that they fall into the Leninist category of "state capitalism," which is not the same thing as the state capitalism in capitalist countries. In a report delivered at the Eleventh Congress of the Russian Communist Party (March 27, 1922), in which he criticized those who confused "state capitalism" in the Soviet Union with "state capitalism" in capitalist countries, Lenin said: "When we say 'state' we mean ourselves, the proletariat, the vanguard of the working class. State capitalism is capitalism which we shall be able to restrain, and the limits of which we shall be able to fix."[10] This statement, together with Lenin's series of essays entitled "The Tax in Kind," provide the theoretical basis of the Chinese Communist Party's present policy of cooperation with foreign countries. Lenin's writings show us that we no longer need to fear capitalism, but that bureaucratism remains a serious threat. On the problem of bureaucratism, Lenin wrote, "Capitalism is a bane compared with socialism. Capitalism is a boon compared with medievalism, small production, and the evils of bureaucracy which spring from the dispersal of the small producers."[11] Lenin emphasized the disastrous nature of bureaucratism and recognized that its economic basis was the "atomized and scattered state of the small producer with his poverty, illiteracy, lack of culture, the absence of roads and *exchange* between agriculture and industry, the absence of connection and interaction between them."[12]

China's present situation is slightly more favorable than was Russia's at that time. Russia's backwardness then was a result of civil war, while China's present situation is the result of the Gang of Four having had free rein for a decade. In any case, it will be impossible to achieve socialist revolution and socialist construction in a formerly Asiatic state as long as we are plagued with bureaucratic rule divorced from the people. Opposition to bureaucratism is an essential task for the revolutionary vanguard of the Chinese proletariat in the course of socialist revolution and socialist construction. Because the Chinese people under the leadership of the party are wholeheartedly supporting the policies of promoting socialist democratic rule and strengthening socialist law, I believe that we will triumph in this endeavor.

Notes

1. The Chinese translation of Melotti, *Makesi he disan shijie*, trans. Gao Sian et al. (Beijing: Shangwu Yinshuguan, 1980), was produced under my supervision.

2. *CCPE*, p. 21. Editor's note: The first Chinese translation of Marx's *A Contribution to the Critique of Political Economy* was done by Guo Moruo (1892–1978) and published in Shanghai in 1931 (*Die Werke von Karl Marx und Friedrich Engels in China: Katalog und Auswahlbibliographie* [Trier: Schriften aus dem Karl-Marx-Haus, 1984], p. 126).

3. The Chinese edition of Marx's *Pre-Capitalist Economic Formations*, translated by Ri Zhi, was published in 1963. Lawrence Krader, who edited and pub-

lished *The Ethnological Notebooks of Karl Marx* in 1974, has argued in his book *The Asiatic Mode of Production* (Assen: Van Gorcum, 1975) that, given the large volume of writings on the AMP by Marx during his later years, Marx and Engels cannot be said to have discarded the theory of the AMP.

4. Editor's note: Commission of the Central Committee of the Communist Party of the Soviet Union (Bolsheviks), ed., *History of the Communist Party of the Soviet Union (Bolsheviks): Short Course* (Moscow: Foreign Languages Publishing House, 1951), pp. 194–99. The authority of this textbook in China, where it was once unquestioned, has been under challenge in the 1980s.

5. Cf. my *Zhongguo de nulizhi jingji he fengjianzhi jingji lungang* (Outline theory of the Chinese slave economy and feudal economy) (Beijing: Sanlian Shudian, 1963), in which I discuss the Xia, Shang, and Zhou dynasties as Bronze Age slaveholding states, distinguishing them from the Iron Age slave-holding states of Greece and Rome. Actually all slave-holding states established during the Bronze Age were Asiatic states in the Marxist sense.

6. *Selected Works of Mao Tse-tung*, vol. 2 (Peking: Foreign Languages Press, 1965), pp. 305–308.

7. Editor's note: China's considerable advances during the imperial era in the realms of protochemistry, medical biology, metallurgy, and magnetism, to mention only a few, would suggest that the author's assertion here is more polemical than factual.

8. Editor's note: Georgii Dimitrov (1882–1949) was one of a group of Communists accused by Hitler's Social Democratic Party in the Leipzig Trial of 1933 of setting fire to the Reichstag. He headed the Bulgarian Communist Party after the war.

9. Translator's note: Zhang Zhixin (1930–1975) was a high-ranking member of the Communist Party Committee of Liaoning province who was sentenced to death in 1975 for opposition to Cultural Revolution policies. She was posthumously declared a revolutionary martyr in 1979.

10. Lenin, "Political Report of the Central Committee," *LCW*, 33:278.

11. Lenin, "The Tax in Kind," *LCW*, 32:350.

12. Ibid., p. 351.

KE CHANGJI

3 | # Ancient Chinese Society and the Asiatic Mode of Production

The Asiatic mode of production (AMP) is the crystallization of Marx's Asiatic theory and the epitome of his successful search for the route traveled by early civilization. After several decades of controversy, however, there is still no consensus as to the meaning of the term, yet its clarification could lead to the solution of many specific problems regarding Asia and China through the ancient and medieval periods.

The Genesis of Marx's Asiatic Theory

Marx's Asiatic theory arose in connection with the growth of social science and the academic investigation of primitive societies. Reminiscing about this process, Engels wrote in 1881:

> In 1847, the pre-history of society, the social organization existing previous to recorded history, was all but unknown. Since then, Haxthausen discovered common ownership of land in Russia, Maurer proved it to be the social foundation from which all Teutonic races started in history, and by and by, village communities were found to be, or to have been, the primitive form of society everywhere from India to Ireland. The inner organization of this primitive Communistic society was laid bare, in its typical form, by Morgan's crowning discovery of the true nature of the gens and its relation to the tribe.[1]

From Lanzhou daxue xuebao (Lanzhou University journal) 3 (1983): 16-25. Translated by Alfred Chan.

Why was 1847 the watershed for research on the prehistory of society? In that year Haxthausen, an adviser to the Prussian government, in his book *The Russian Empire: Its People, Institutions, and Resources,* was the first to reveal the widespread existence of communal ownership among Russian peasants. The appearance of Maurer's *A General Discussion of the Mark System, Village System, City System, and Political Power* in 1854 further confirmed Haxthausen's inference about the character of ownership in human prehistory, proving that public ownership of land was the earliest form of ownership. Morgan's *Ancient Society,* published in 1877, revealed the kind of social organization that fit with this type of ownership.

Marx and Engels pursued their research on primitive society independently of these three writers. In *The German Ideology,* written between 1845 and 1846, they had already pointed out that "the first form of ownership is tribal ownership."[2] This is their first conceptualization of the system of ownership in primitive society. In 1850, they discovered vestiges of the Indian village community (or rural communes) still in general existence and came to the following conclusion:

> A careful study of Asiatic, particularly Indian, forms of communal property would indicate that the disintegration of different forms of primitive communal ownership gives rise to diverse forms of property. For instance, various prototypes of Roman and Germanic private property can be traced back to certain forms of Indian communal property.[3]

Clearly, Marx's method—using the existing vestiges of the rural communes to construct a prototype of primitive society—is identical to that of Haxthausen and Maurer. The only difference is that the Asian, especially the Indian, rural communes appear to be older than the Russian and German. Therefore, this type of Asian rural commune became excellent raw material for Marx to probe into primitive society and its forms of ownership; from then on, Marx used "Asiatic" as a technical term extensively, eventually formulating his Asiatic theory. The fruits of his research appear in *Pre-Capitalist Economic Formations,* a section of the *Grundrisse* manuscript written between 1857 and 1858, and *A Contribution to the Critique of Political Economy,* published in 1859, followed by amplifications in *Capital.* In these works, Marx and Engels re-examined their earlier ideas of primitive society, and by using the material on Asian, and particularly Indian, rural communes, they furthered their investigation into the internal structure of tribal ownership. From then on the geographic term "Asiatic" acquired a specific meaning, though Marx continued to use the term in different senses depending on the context. For example, "Asiatic history" can refer to both the ancient and medieval history of Asia,[4] whereas Engels in *The Condition of the Working Class in England* uses "ancient Asia" (i.e., Asiatic antiquity) to refer to the slave societies of Asia. "Asiatic" is a polysemy, and this is the key. If this is not grasped, then we cannot understand Marx's writings, nor can we comprehend Marx's Asiatic theory.

How to Interpret the Asiatic Mode of Production

Marx wrote, in the Preface to *A Contribution to the Critique of Political Economy:* "In broad outline, the Asiatic, ancient, feudal and modern bourgeois modes of production may be designated as epochs marking progress in the economic development of society."[5] This "Asiatic mode of production" is controversial, and there are presently many different interpretations of the concept within China. I believe that Guo Moruo is correct in interpreting the AMP as primitive communal society.[6] The notion of "epochs marking progress in the economic development of society" implies the replacement of obsolete and lower modes of production by new and higher ones; in this case, of primitive ("Asiatic") society by slave ("ancient") society. What Marx is expounding here is the universal law of development of human society. If the AMP were interpreted in any other way, then the fundamental Marxist principle of social development would not be tenable, clearly contradicting Marx's original intention.

Therefore, the AMP as mentioned in the Preface, like the ancient, feudal, and capitalist modes of production, is a general term meant to indicate primitive society. These various modes of production rise and fall in turn as four independent socioeconomic formations in a complete sequence of development. Only when interpreted this way can we make correct sense of this sentence.

It is important to point out that we are referring here to the AMP in its extended, not its original, meaning. Its original meaning is the mode of production of the Asian rural commune. Marx was very clear on this:

> The obstacles presented by the internal solidarity and organiza-
> tion of pre-capitalistic, national modes of production to the cor-
> rosive influence of commerce are strikingly illustrated in the in-
> tercourse of the English with India and China. The broad basis of
> the mode of production here is formed by the unity of small-scale
> agriculture and home industry, to which in India we should add
> the form of village communities built upon the common owner-
> ship of land, which, incidentally, was the original form in China as
> well. In India the English lost no time in exercising their direct
> political and economic power, as rulers and landlords, to disrupt
> these small economic communities. English commerce exerted a
> revolutionary influence on these communities and tore them
> apart only insofar as the low prices of its goods served to destroy
> the spinning and weaving industries, which were an ancient in-
> tegrating element of this unity of industrial and agricultural pro-
> duction.[7]

In common usage, "mode of production" refers to a socio-economic formation comprising a specific relationship between the forces and relations of production that exists at a certain historical stage. Yet in the writings of Marx and Engels this is not always the case. Sometimes it refers only to the relations of production, as in "the contradiction between the forces of production and the mode of production." At other times it refers to certain productive sectors or economic categories, as in "historically determined mode of production, viz., the production of commodities."[8] In Marx's analysis of the disruption of Indian society by the British, "mode of production" is used in this original sense to represent the form that production took in the Indian rural commune. Thus, the AMP refers in the Preface to the primitive mode of production, but in Marx's descriptions of India it signifies the form of production typical of the Asian rural commune (a unity of small-scale agriculture and domestic handicrafts).

Why, then, is the mode of production of the Asian rural commune used to represent primitive society in the Preface? In his letter to Engels of March 14, 1868, Marx wrote that the form of collective property of the Asian rural commune also existed widely in Europe and was the source of all property systems there. Isn't it apparent that Marx was using the example of collective property in the Asian rural commune to depict the earliest form of ownership in primitive society in general? The text of this letter reads:

> At the Museum have among other things worked through old Maurer's . . . writings. . . . He demonstrates very fully that private property in land is of later origin, etc. . . . Interesting just at this moment, that the Russian practice of redistributing the land at fixed intervals (in Germany initially every year) survived in Germany here and there until the eighteenth and even the nineteenth century. Though Maurer knew nothing of the view I have put forward, namely, that the Asiatic or Indian forms of property constitute the initial ones everywhere in Europe, he provides further proof of it.[9]

Originally, the "Asiatic or Indian forms of property" was a geographic reference to collective ownership in the Asian rural commune, of which the Indian commune is most typical. In this letter, however, it is used as a universal concept of primitive communal ownership. This is because the vestiges of primitive communal ownership were more plentiful, authentic, and representative in the Asian rural commune than in other parts of the world. Hence Marx and Engels speak elsewhere of Asian and Indian communities in terms of "primitive communism" and "the original communism."[10] As Marx describes it, "the constitution of these communities varies in different parts of India. In those of the simplest form, the land is tilled in common, and the produce divided among the members."[11]

The Asiatic or Indian formation, the oldest specimen of the primitive system of common ownership that had yet been discovered, was quite similar to the clan communes outside Asia. For these reasons, the AMP was used in the Preface to represent the mode of production of the primitive commune and of primitive society in general.

Ancient Chinese Society and the Asiatic Mode of Production

The AMP is the essence of Marx's Asiatic theory. As the economic category of rural communes (rather than as the primitive mode of production), it had a long existence extending from the last stage of primitive society to the beginning of capitalist society. Its substantive character means that Marx's discussions of the AMP are connected to a whole series of complicated issues regarding ancient and medieval Asian history. There are at least three important aspects, each of which will be addressed in turn.

Monarchical State Ownership of Land

Landownership solely by the emperor is a manifestation of the monarchical system of state ownership of land. Marx believed "that in India, as in most Asiatic countries, the ultimate property in the soil vests the Government."[12] This type of land relation, where "the State [is] the real landlord,"[13] he called "the Asiatic system." A comparable situation can be found in China. During the Western Zhou, all land was proclaimed to be under the ownership of the Son of Heaven: "Under the wide heaven, All is the king's land."[14] The buying and selling of land belonging to the king was forbidden, hence the saying, "Fields and residences in the hamlets [when once assigned] could not be sold."[15] In the Spring and Autumn (770–476 B.C.) and Warring States (475–221 B.C.) periods, land gradually came to be traded like a commodity, and the monarchical system of state ownership collapsed.

State ownership made a brief comeback during the failed restoration movement of Wang Mang (33 B.C.–A.D. 23), which "change[d] the title of all land under heaven into royal land."[16] From the Northern Wei (386–534) to the Tang (618–907) dynasty, the system of state ownership of land was widely restored in the form of the equal-field system, although its original form, the royal fields of the Western Zhou, was not duplicated. Initially, equal-field land was allowed to be bought and sold within certain limits. According to the land regulations of the Northern Wei, "those with surplus land can sell, although they should not sell more than their allotted share; those with inadequate land can buy, but not in excess of what they need."[17] During the Tang, the restrictions were relaxed even more, and the limit on the quantity bought and sold was abolished: "Commoners who move from one village to another or are too poor to bury [their parents] can sell their inherited land. Those who move from a locale with little land to a locale with much land are allowed to sell their allotted land."[18] Such changes in the economic system are inevitable, because "as long as land is private property, any constraints imposed upon its mobilization are harmful and reactionary."[19] To consolidate its rule and not to repeat the mistakes of Wang Mang, the feudal government had to make some concessions in the face of economic laws.

Generally, in all these dynasties, it did not take long for the equal-field system to be disrupted. Succeeding dynasties nonetheless took great pains to resurrect it in the same localities. The impulse for doing so was that in the situation where all laborers were equally poor or half-starved, state ownership of land under the guise of the equal-field system could bring immense wealth and prosperity to the centralized feudal state, providing the power structure with a stable economic foundation. What feudal historians of the past praised in the equal-field system was nothing more than this enhancement of the center.

With the abolition of the equal-field system in the mid-Tang, monarchical state ownership of land was gone forever. This was inevitable given the development of the commodity economy and private ownership. Although the emperor no longer enjoyed absolute control over the land, he could exercise his despotic power by claiming to be highest owner of all land in the realm, both nominally and politically. Acting according to the principle of "we own all states,"[20] he could suppress the private ownership of land at will. For instance, early in the Hongwu era (1368–1398), "there was a certain Hua Xingzu whose family was extremely wealthy." Even though Hua had not committed any crime, "a decree was issued to have his family property confiscated."[21] A similar example occurred in 1379, when "all the properties of the big clans located in the lower reaches of the Yangzi River were confiscated one by one."[22]

The emperor could also rely on the state machinery to do the opposite. By handing out private landholdings on a grand scale, he could establish the image that he was "the first to dispense favors"[23] and the highest authority over land in the country. We offer three examples: After suppressing the Hmong rebellion in the border regions of Hunan/Hubei, Sichuan, and Guizhou in 1600, the Ming government immediately ordered that "the people of these three provinces [be] allowed to receive land that either was without owners or had been confiscated by the officials." In the first year of the Qing dynasty (1644), an imperial edict ordered that "all uncultivated land in the provinces, counties, and prefectures should be distributed among the refugees and soldiers to be held in perpetuity . . . and seals and licenses should be issued."[24] Finally, Yuhuan Island, abandoned because of the anti-Qing rebellion along the Zhejiang coast at the beginning of the dynasty, was being resettled in 1726, and the same policy of "issuing seals and licenses and distributing land according to the number of individuals"[25] was proposed. Such instances demonstrate that the emperor regarded the realm as within his power of ownership.[26]

To summarize, monarchical state ownership of land was in its heyday in the Western Zhou period, restored during the Northern Wei and Tang, but from the Song to the Qing declined and existed in name only. (Heyday, restoration, and decline also describes the route taken by the rural commune, its close associate.) In an agricultural society in which landed property was "the dominant relation of production in society,"[27] the centralized claim to the ownership of land subject to the whims of the supreme ruler could determine the future of the national economy and the people's livelihood. This was the basis for the emperor's political power, yet it was a great misfortune for the people. Clearly, this is one of the factors responsible for the slow and tortuous development of Chinese history.

The Persistence of the Rural Commune

Engels has put it bluntly: "Where the ancient communes have continued to exist, they have for thousands of years formed the basis of the cruelest form of state, Oriental Despotism, from India to Russia."[28] In addition, Indian scholars have verified that "the village republics which were established in India in early times are in one sense extant to this day."[29] One of the major characteristics of the Asian rural commune is the special form of common ownership preserved within it:

> As is the case in most Asiatic fundamental forms it is quite compatible with the fact that the *all-embracing unity* which stands

above all these small common bodies may appear as the higher or *sole proprietor*, the real communities only as *hereditary* possessors. ... The individual is then in fact propertyless, or property ... appears to be mediated by means of a grant (*Ablassen*) from the total unity to the individual through the intermediary of the particular community. The despot here appears as the father of all the numerous lesser communities, thus realizing the common unity of all.[30]

In this Asiatic formation, the despot, representing the state entity, was the true landowner of the small collectives. The communes merely occupied the land; individual commune members had in fact no right to private landownership. In other words, the commune member had only the right to farm the land as delegated to him by the state.

The oldest Asiatic formation in China is the well-field commune within the royal-field system of the Western Zhou.[31] Mencius describes the well-field system as follows:

If those who own land within each *jing* befriend one another both at home and abroad, help each other to keep watch, and succor each other in illness, they will live in love and harmony. A *jing* is a piece of land measuring one *li* square, and each *jing* consists of 900 *mu*. Of these, the central plot of 100 *mu* belongs to the state, while the other eight plots of 100 *mu* each are held by eight families who share the duty of caring for the plot owned by the state. Only when they have done this duty dare they turn to their own affairs.[32]

They are called well-fields because the small collective drank water from the same well (*jing*). The well formed the center of the grass-roots production and social unit.[33] Naturally, the relationship between labor and livelihood was intimate. The lines "those who own land within each *jing* befriend one another both at home and abroad, help each other to keep watch" were merely window-dressing included by Mencius to promote his political views. The relationship of each of the eight households to its one hundred *mu* was usufruct rather than ownership. This right was obtained at the price of rendering to the state corvée and land rent on the collectively farmed common field.

The ancient philosopher Lao Zi has vividly described life under the well-field commune:

> The state may be small; its people may be few.
> Let the people have tenfold and one-hundredfold of utensils,
> But never make use of them.
>
> Let the people weigh death heavily
> And have no desires to move far away.
> Though there be boats and carriages,
> No one will ride in them.
> Though there be armor and weapons,
> No one will exhibit them.
>
> Let the people return to tying knots and using them.
> Relish their food,
> Appreciate their clothes,
> Secure in their homes,
> Happy with their customs.
>
> The neighboring states will be so close
> that they can see each other,
> and hear the sounds of roosters and dogs.
> But the people will grow old and die,
> Without having visited each other.[34]

The word "states" refers to other communes in the area. On the surface the portrait is charming, but in reality the living standard was extremely low, daily necessities lacking, and transportation inadequate. Yet the people were happy in their poverty and content with their ragged clothes and inferior food. They lived alone and independently, feeling no need to socialize their labor or to communicate with civilization outside. Instead, they kept records by tying knots and spent their entire lives growing old and dying in the same place. This kind of independent and benighted small collective enabled the state to exploit the people at will.

There is no doubt that well-field communes existed in history, and this fact can be corroborated by the "vestiges of tribal organization and the primitive commune"[35] still preserved by the Qiawa tribe in southwest China. "The Qiawa people do not have their own land; land is farmed by all. They do not have private property;

they have only their tribe and their ethnic group."[36] The Asiatic formation of the ancient well-field communes is of precisely the same mold.

Another type of rural commune was known as the *shushe*. According to the record of Guan Zhong (d. 645 B.C.), "when King Wu attacked Zhou, the troops who went along obtained *shushe*"[37] as spoils. Guan Zhong himself "was given three hundred *shushe*" by Duke Huan for his meritorious service as prime minister of Qi.[38] First of all, what is a *she*? "*She* is the earth god. Since the earth is too extensive for the god to be worshipped at only one location, the land is divided into *she* to offer sacrifices."[39] Hence *she* is the earth god of a certain area, and by extension the altar to the god. But what about *shu*, which literally means "writing"? According to the historian Sima Qian (ca. 145–ca. 90 B.C.) "In ancient times, twenty-five households formed a *li*; each *li* set up its own *she* [altar]. Hence the term *shushe*: the names of the members of the *she* were written [*shu*] in the public registers."[40] Since a *she* was said to be "six *li* square,"[41] a *shushe* was a village of approximately this area with twenty-five households. The households of this rural commune worshipped a common earth god, and the names of every member were recorded in the commune register. *Shushe* were important not only in agriculture but also in the military activities of the state. For example, because the state of Qi was afraid that the Jin might attack, it begged the state of Chu for help. "The viscount of Chu . . . sent Wei Qijiang to Qi on a friendly visit, and to be informed as to the time of meeting [with the Marquis of Qi]. The marquis *shesou junshi* that the visitor might see them."[42] *Shesou junshi* means to order the *shushe* to conduct military exercises in preparation for combat. Therefore, under the monarchical system of state ownership of land, *shushe*, which were contemporary with the well-field communes, belonged also to the Asiatic formation. They were one more form of the ancient rural commune characteristic of the Orient, originating in the area governed by the Shang dynasty.

The well-field commune and monarchical state ownership of land disappeared at the same time, and this change was reflected in law, politics, and social life. The Qin dynasty "used the methods of Lord Yang of Shang (d. 338 B.C.), and the institutions of the Rulers of Old were changed. [Hence] was abolished [the system of] *jingtian* [well-fields], and the people were allowed to sell and to buy [land]. The rich [bought up so much land] that their fields were connected along both north-south and east-west roads, while the poor had not even [enough] land into which to stick an awl."[43]

The disappearance of the well-field system was not complete, for we find property being held in common later in Chinese history. In the Han dynasty, for instance, although the mountains, forests, rivers, and lakes were owned by the state, they remained open to common use by farmers, woodcutters, herdsmen, and hunters and could not be reduced to the category of private property. The government even came into conflict with imperial relatives and large landowning officials over this public land.

With the revival of monarchical state landownership during the Northern Wei, Zhou, Qi, Sui, and Tang dynasties, the ancient rural commune was resurrected in the form of the equal-field commune composed of 100 to 125 households. In the Northern Wei, the law required that "there should be a *lin* [group] leader for every five households, a *li* [neighborhood] leader for every five *lin*, and a *dang* [ward] leader for every five *li*. The *dang* leader should be chosen from among the strong and circumspect villagers."[44] The equal-field commune of the Tang dynasty appears to be larger than that of the Northern Wei, as the Tang government stipulated: "A hundred households form a *li* [ward], five *li* form a *xiang* [canton]."[45] Despite the provision for a cantonal level, in reality the activities of the communes were carried out at the ward level, as we read: "Each ward should have one supervisor to control the households, promote agriculture and sericulture, investigate crimes, and levy taxes and corvée."[46] The organizational structure of the communes was thus identical to the base level of the administrative structure.

For this reason, determining the membership of the communes was very complicated, for apart from the equal-field peasants, there were people of other social strata, such as owner-cultivators and landlords. It should be noted that the most important power—distributing and adjusting land allotments—was in the hands of the local officials and was not included among the various functions of the communes. The stipulation that "the county magistrate is in charge of the retrieval and reallocation of land"[47] shows that under the equal-field system, the communes had no power regarding landownership; they just implemented decisions from above. "The various ward supervisors should distribute land according to the statutes and tax agriculture and sericulture."[48] Their duty was merely to enforce the legal statutes and to provide the state with reliable economic and manpower support.

Although the property relations of the equal-field communes belonged to the Asiatic formation, they were subject to change. Under the Northern Wei, for example, "all males age fifteen and above should receive forty *mu* of open fields" and "the fields should be returned in the case of old age or death."[49] The recipient of land was merely a temporary occupier with the right to land use. On the other hand, the system also had a non-Asiatic element, for each adult male received twenty *mu* of mulberry fields from the government, specified by law as being "hereditary property not to be returned at death."[50] Therefore the peasants of the equal-field communes were those who had lost their land under the Asiatic formation, but simultaneously they were also the private owners of small tracts of land. Basically, the members of the equal-field communes labored under this double burden of property relations.

After the mid-Tang, the rural communes characteristic of the Asiatic formation generally disappeared from Chinese history. Private landownership and the tenancy system prospered and gained the upper hand at the expense of state landownership. However, the emperors constantly dreamt that this small production collective, which depended upon imperial favors, could return to the historical stage, even partially and temporarily. During the Yong-zheng (1723–1735) era there was an attempt to restore the well-field system by running experiments in four counties in Zhili:

> First well-fields were created on twenty-four thousand *mu* of official land in Xincheng and Guan counties. One hundred selected Banner households were allotted one hundred *mu* each, and another hundred *mu* were to be farmed collectively. Afterward, this pattern was repeated at Bazhou and Yongqing, but with poor results. At the beginning of the Qianlong era (1736–1795), they were changed into regular villages.[51]

The experiment failed almost immediately because this system of production had become obsolete. Yet it had acquired a certain sacred quality in the consciousness of the people, leading to its reappearance in the "Land System of the Heavenly Dynasty" of the Taipings:

> For every twenty-five families there must be established one public granary . . . the work of the potter, the blacksmith, the carpenter, the mason, and other artisans must all be performed by the corporal and privates. . . . At the time of harvest, every sergeant shall direct the corporals to see to it that of the twenty-five families under his charge each individual has a sufficient supply of food, and aside from the new grain each may receive, the remainder must be deposited in the public granary. . . . The division of land must be according to the number of individuals, whether male or female.[52]

Thus twenty-five households formed a base-level unit of administration and production, combining agriculture and handicraft industry. Commodity exchange was eliminated and property was placed under public ownership, but land was distributed to the households for individual farming. The picture that emerges is an idealized version of the ancient rural commune. Under the Taiping revolutionaries, the management of these communes was indeed different from what it would have been under the feudal rulers. However, the goal of enabling everyone to have sufficient food and clothing could never have been accomplished using such a utopian form. At the stage when the productive forces were not able to generate a new social formation, the economic basis of feudalism could not undergo a fundamental change, but the Asiatic commune persisted.

The Status of the "General Slave"

Regardless of the type of Asiatic rural commune, the laborers were degraded to the level of what Marx has called "general slavery."[53] A well-field commune member was looked down upon as a debased "savage" who could never "go beyond the confines of his village."[54] His entire life was restricted to his commune. It was the same with the equal-field peasants of the Northern Wei, who were "forbidden to change their residences without reason." The distribution of thirty *mu* of land to "slaves and dependent freemen for every adult male or ox" shows that the laborers were ranked equally with slaves and cattle in the distribution of land. During the earlier Wei dynasty (A.D. 220–266), pioneer communes modeled on well-fields were created by force in many parts of the country.[55] (There were two forms: sixty people formed a military colony, and fifty people formed a civilian colony.) On the surface, the members—soldiers and pioneers—appeared to be free men, but the reality was entirely different. A Western Jin imperial edict ordered: "The official slaves of Yexi are to man the new city to replace the field soldiers who are planting rice. Fifty slaves should form one colony, and each colony should establish one sergeant, completely in accordance with the law governing military colonization."[56] The members of this kind of colony, which was like the rural commune during China's slave period, were slaves in reality if not in name. This status is a peculiarity of ancient and medieval Asia.

The AMP in a general way reflects the specific characteristics of Asian society and throws light on some unsolved problems concerning ancient and medieval Asia. Both in theoretical terms and in its concrete context, however, the AMP fettered the people, pulled society backward, and refused to let history advance. The system of monarchical state landownership in China and its residual influence in various forms of communal ownership fully demonstrate this characteristic of the AMP. This is one of the major reasons why Chinese feudal society stagnated and was unable to develop into capitalist society. To wipe out the remnants of the AMP in a theoretical sense must be the historical mission of Marxist historians today.

Notes

1. K. Marx and F. Engels, *Manifesto of the Communist Party* (Beijing: Foreign Languages Press, 1965), p. 32.

2. K. Marx and F. Engels, *The German Ideology* (New York: International Publishers, 1970), p. 43.

3. *CCPE,* p. 33.

4. See my "Lun 'Yaxiyade' " (On the term "Asiatic"), *Wenzhou shifan xueyuan xuebao* (Wenzhou Teachers' College journal) 1 (1963).

5. *CCPE,* p. 21. On the earlier debate on the AMP, see Lü Zhenyu, *Zhongguo shehui shi zhuwenti* (Questions regarding the history of Chinese society) (repr. Shanghai: Renmin Chubanshe, 1979), pp. 32-37.

6. Guo Moruo, *Zhongguo gudai shehui yanjiu* (Studies of China's ancient society) (Shanghai: Qunyi Chubanshe, 1947), p. 197.

7. Marx, *Capital,* vol. 3 (Moscow: Progress Publishers, 1971), pp. 333–34.

8. Ibid., 1:80.

9. Marx to Engels, March 14, 1868, in *PCEF,* p. 139.

10. Engels to Kautsky, February 16, 1884; K. Marx, *Theories of Surplus Value,* vol. 3 (Moscow: Progress Publishers, 1971), p. 422.

11. Marx, *Capital,* 1:337.

12. K. Marx, "Lord Canning's Proclamation and Land Tenure in India," in K. Marx and F. Engels, *On Colonialism* (New York: International Publishers, 1972), p. 190.

13. Marx, "India," in *On Colonialism,* p. 79.

14. *The She King,* trans. James Legge (repr. Hong Kong: Hong Kong University Press, 1960), p. 360.

15. *Li Chi,* vol. 1, trans. James Legge (repr. New Hyde Park, New York: University Books, 1967), pp. 227–28.

16. *Han shu* (Standard history of the Han Dynasty), ch. 99, "Wang Mang zhuan zhong," (Hong Kong: Zhonghua Shuju, 1970), p. 4111.

17. *Wei shu* (Standard history of the Wei dynasty) (Beijing: Zhonghua Shuju, 1974), p. 2854.

18. *Xin Tang shu* (New standard history of the Tang dynasty), ch. 51 (Shanghai: Zhonghua Shuju, 1975), p. 1342.

19. *LCW,* 20:301.

20. *Song dazhaoling ji* (Collection of Song imperial edicts) (Beijing: Zhonghua Shuju, 1962), ch. 187, p. 684.

21. *Renhe xianzhi* (Gazetteer of Renhe county) (1549; 1893 repr.), 13.31b–32a.

22. Xu Yuanpu, *Wusheng qiebi* (Humble jottings on Suzhou gazetteers) (repr. Changsha: Shangwu Yinshuguan, 1939), p. 7.

23. *Liangshan xianzhi* (Gazetteer of Liangshan county) (1894; 1935 repr.), 1.85.

24. *Huangchao wenxian tongkao* (Critical history of documents of the present dynasty), ch. 1, "Tianfu kao."

25. *Yuhuan zhi* (Gazetteer of Yuhuan subprefecture) (1732), 1.13b.

26. Editor's note: The author's argument about the late imperial state's power to intervene despotically in landholding is not fully substantiated by his sources in this paragraph. In each case, the state was seeking to get uncultivated land under the plough to stimulate tax revenue and reduce the unstabilizing effect of vagrancy. In Yuhuan, the territory being resettled had been previously vacated by government order for military reasons. The use of language reminiscent of early imperial land reallocation schemes should not obscure the substantial differences between those and the late imperial resettlement projects.

27. Marx, *Theories of Surplus Value,* pt. 3, p. 399.

28. F. Engels, *Anti-Dühring* (Moscow: Foreign Languages Publishing House, 1962), p. 250.

29. Humayun Kabir, *The Indian Heritage* (Bombay: Asia Publishing House, 1955), p. 46.

30. *PCEF,* p. 69.

31. It has been argued that the well-field system was also implemented in the Xia and Shang dynasties. Su Shi (1036–1101) of the Song dynasty made this claim

(*Song wenjian,* ch. 104, "Quan qinmu"), which accords with historical development.

32. *Mencius,* trans. D. C. Lau (Harmondsworth: Penguin, 1970), pp. 99–100 (III.A.3).

33. It was impossible for the well-field communes to have had only nine hundred *mu* of land. Since the level of agricultural technology in the Western Zhou was not high, in practice land was rotated in three-year cycles. The communes would therefore have to have had additional land in fallow.

34. Lao Tzu, *Tao te ching,* trans. Paul Lin (Ann Arbor: Center for Chinese Studies, University of Michigan, 1977), p. 141.

35. *Renmin ribao* (People's daily), December 14, 1963.

36. Guo Guopu, *Zai Angmeina de buluo li* (Among the Angmeinas) (1959), p. 229.

37. *Guanzi,* trans. W. Allyn Rickett (Princeton: Princeton University Press, 1985), p. 147.

38. *Xunzi jianzhu* (Concise annotation of the *Xunzi*) (Shanghai: Renmin Chubanshe, 1974), ch. 7, p. 55.

39. Ying Shao, *Fengsu tongyi* (A compendium on popular lore), "She shen" (The earth god).

40. Sima Qian, *Shiji* (Records of the historian) (Beijing: Zhonghua Shuju, 1959), ch. 47, p. 1932.

41. *Guanzi,* p. 121.

42. James Legge, trans., *The Ch'un Ts'ew and the Tso Chuen* (repr. Hong Kong: Hong Kong University Press, 1960), p. 508.

43. *Han shu,* ch. 24, "Shihuozhi," p. 1137, translated in Nancy Lee Swann, *Food and Money in Ancient China* (Princeton: Princeton University Press, 1950), pp. 180–81.

44. Du You, *Tongdian* (Encyclopedic history of institutions) (801) (repr. Zhejiang Shuju, 1896), ch. 3, "Xiangdang" (Rural collectivities), pp. 9–10.

45. *Tang liudian,* ch. 3, "Shangshu hubu."

46. Du You, *Tongdian,* ch. 3,"Xiangdang," p. 12.

47. *Xin Tang shu,* p. 1319.

48. *Tang lü shuyi* (The Tang code with commentary) (737), ch. 13 (Shanghai: Shangwu Yinshuguan, 1936), p. 7.

49. *Wei shu,* p. 2853.

50. Ibid.

51. Wang Qingyun, *Xichao jizheng* (The record of governance of the Kangxi era), vol. 4 (1898), p. 20.

52. Franz Michael, *The Taiping Rebellion, History and Documents,* vol. 2 (Seattle: University of Washington Press, 1971), pp. 313–15. Editor's note: The earliest association of the Taiping regulations with "the original primitive forms of 'Asiatic' society" was made by the pro-AMP scholar S. A. Dalin in 1928; see Marian Sawer, *Marxism and the Question of the Asiatic Mode of Production* (The Hague: Martinus Nijhoff, 1977), pp. 90–91.

53. *PCEF,* p. 95.

54. *Mencius,* p. 99.

55. According to *Sanguo zhi* (Records of the Three Kingdoms), ch. 15 (Beijing: Zhonghua Shuju, 1971), pp. 467–68, Sima Lang recommended to Cao Cao: "It is better to revive the well-fields. In the past, the people had hereditary ownership of land, and it was difficult to expropriate it. This has been the case up to now. Since the time of chaos there have been no owners and all land has become public land, so it is opportune to revive them." Although Sima Lang's advice was not taken, the system of military colonies was really a version of this suggestion, though the term "well-field" was not used.

56. *Jin shu* (Standard history of the Jin dynasty) (Beijing: Zhonghua Shuju, 1974), p. 787.

ZHAO LISHENG

4 | The Well-Field System in Relation to the Asiatic Mode of Production

The "well-field" or nine-square system is a major system in Chinese history, and indeed a major type of landownership in world history. According to this system, a square of land was subdivided into nine smaller squares, creating a pattern like the Chinese character *jing* (well). In this essay I shall examine it in relation to Marx's theory of the Asiatic mode of production (AMP).

From the outset of planned agriculture, ancient man faced the problem of dividing up the land. The Duke Liu ode in the Greater Odes section of the *Shijing* (Book of songs) states that the duke

> noted the shadows and the height of the hills,
> Which parts were in the shade, which in the sun,
> Viewed the streams and the springs.
> To his army in three divisions
> He allotted the low lands and the high,
> Tithed the fields that there might be due provision.[1]

The Greater Minister of Instruction section of the *Zhouli* (Rites of Zhou) states further: "He measures further the depth of the soil by means of a gauging tablet; he seeks the center of the ground at the height of the midday sun,"[2] and then "discerns [the names and products of] its mountains, groves, rivers, marshes, craggy terrain, embankments, flats, and plateaus."[3]

From *Shehui kexue zhanxian* (Social science frontline) 3 (1982): 109–15. Translated by Ray Dragan.

Land survey was the first step. The second step was to divide the land into squares and then to build boundaries. In the Duke Wen of Teng chapter of the *Mencius* it is stated, "When boundaries are not properly drawn, the division of land according to the well-field system and the yield of grain used for paying officials cannot be equitable."[4] This was a later statement made out of concern for inequality among the nobility. Long before, the people were principally concerned with whether all members of the commune had equal plots. Only this ancient egalitarianism could lead to the division of land into regular-sized plots, ensuring that the people possessed set land allotments around which boundaries were built. In this way the land took on a checkerboard pattern.

These conditions already existed in the latter period of primitive society. With the emergence of class society came an aristocracy and a "king"; however, for various reasons (i.e., the forces of production were too low, the sense of private property had not been adequately entrenched, and despotism had not yet developed), they could not possibly smash up these even plots in one sweeping land reform. And so they preserved them, using the old frame of square plots to exploit the products of surplus labor. These circumstances are what we refer to as the well-field system in Chinese history.

This kind of land system was a frequent subject of discussion in later periods. I think that the objective existence of well-fields and the well-field system in ancient history is irrefutable. Furthermore, it is absolutely clear that the system was not devised by the "sagely lords and upright ministers," who for some unknown reason racked their brains to produce the system (whereas, for instance, the later equal-field system did show traces of being devised by the mental efforts of "sagely lords and upright ministers").[5] It was the result of the natural evolution of the economy of late primitive society and early class society, not of the subjective will of certain individuals. Though we cannot deny that the Xia, Shang, and Zhou dynasty rulers regulated the well-field system, its basic content took form naturally. Of course, the system varied in different dynastic eras, different fiefs, and different regions: for instance, the area of the field varied from fifty *mu* to seventy *mu* to as much as one hundred *mu*.[6] Different types of fields had different names:

public fields (*gongtian*), private fields (*sitian*), fallow fields (*laitian*), or bestowed fields (*guitian*). Among laborers there were "householders" (*jia*), "cultivators" (*fu*), and "unmarried cultivators" (*yufu*). The possible layouts included "the public field in the middle of the private fields," "the public field outside the private fields," "fields following ditches and watercourses,"[7] and land arranged vertically and horizontally into large stretches of "eastern acres" and "southern acres."

It is because of this variation that I argue that the "well-field system" should not be defined too narrowly but should rather be seen as a concept of considerable breadth. Thus, it signifies a land system that began with the first division of land into regular plots of fixed area along with the building of flood-proof boundaries and lasted until these boundaries were completely overrun and the regular field plots thrown into disorder.

Let us now consider the issue of Marx's theory of the AMP and its relation to the well-field system in ancient China. Karl Marx's penetrating analysis of capitalist society from the 1850s to the 1880s led him to discover a peculiar type of structure (which was first and foremost an economic structure). Since he saw this structure as a mode of production and derived his initial data for it from India, Marx named it the "Asiatic mode of production." Actually, this production system existed in precapitalist class society as a remnant, transformed and parasitic. It existed in this form during China's well-field era, though when compared with the more typical ancient "Asiatic" kingdoms in the Orient, the AMP structure in well-field China was incomplete. Still, in comparison with its remnant existence in other periods of China's history, it was relatively substantial. The AMP must therefore be analyzed in conjunction with the well-field system.

Prior to the 1930s, Soviet scholars divided the characteristics of the "Asiatic" mode into four categories: (1) state ownership of land, (2) irrigation, (3) agricultural communes, and (4) despotism. Some scholars added a fifth element, the unity of rent and tax. For the present we should not reject any of these characteristics out of hand, nor should we dogmatically include all of them and squeeze them into one theory. These characteristics could not possibly have been of equal importance. Soviet scholars seem to have treated the agricultural commune as the primary defining characteristic. According to Marx, the agricultural commune was a later form of the primitive commune and as a result already possessed a dual nature, embracing both public and private ownership. How, then, did the concrete conditions in ancient China manifest this kind of dual nature? Land was the main component of property holdings. At the agricultural commune stage, it was no longer under primitive public ownership or full collective ownership, since by this time there was already an exploiting class. However, the parasitic capabilities of the exploiting class of this era (the "king" and the various grades of nobility) still had limits. In ancient China, the purer kind of private ownership subject to the will of the individual owner of private property did not as yet exist. In addition, the owner of private property still had no political representative in the form of the (despotic) state. Full public ownership had already disappeared, and a relatively complete system of private ownership and state ownership had not yet come into being. Various rights (the rights of use, benefit, and inheritance) were still not concentrated in the hands of the state but dispersed throughout society. The agricultural laborer had the right to use and derive benefit from his share of land, but on the large field beyond his plot he was duty-bound to supply frcc surplus labor, and the benefits went to the nobility. The highest noble, the "king," was in name the overlord of all land in the kingdom, as reflected in the line of poetry: "Everywhere under Heaven is no land that is not the king's."[8] Aside from the agricultural laborers and the king and nobility, there was the old community (*gongtongti*) of long standing, the village commune. It was not an institution of merely nominal existence. The village commune controlled the distribution and rotation of land as well as certain public functions. These public functions were gradually being transformed into the basic structure of a bureaucratic system. And as this transformation was completed, a despotic state with a centralized bureaucracy took form.

This description of land rights shows that they were not concentrated in one set of hands but scattered among three. It demonstrates the dual nature of public and private ownership within the "Asiatic" mode. Clearly, we still are unable to speak of "state ownership of land," since the obligation of agricultural laborers to provide free surplus labor in the large fields indicates that the king and nobility only possessed the right to extract benefit from limited parts of the territory.

As for the characteristic of irrigation, I consider that it is related to specific geographical environments. These specific geographical conditions are found "extending from the Sahara, through Arabia, Persia, India, and Tartary, to the most elevated Asiatic highlands."[9] In this area, the peculiarities of the climatic and soil conditions created among the people a fear of drought and a reliance on irrigation. Therefore, the huge number of irrigation workers in these "Asiatic" states had a very important position. China, however, was different. The main area occupied by the people of the Xia, Shang, and Zhou dynasties did not extend beyond what is today northern and western Henan, southern Shanxi, southern Hebei, and the "land within the passes"[10] all the way to western Shandong. The people in this area relied on natural rainfall, and their fear was of floods caused by excessive rainfall, not drought. Ancient China had irrigation ditches, but they served primarily to drain flood waters. Of course, there is never a sharp separation between drainage and irrigation. In the process of flood drainage, excess water may be stored in reservoirs. However, the kind of connection that arose between the construction of hydraulic works and the slack periods in agricultural production in Arabia and the Indian subcontinent was lacking in China's well-field era.

In an overall perspective, the history of China's well-field period clearly bears the "Asiatic" brand, even though not all of the "Asiatic" characteristics were fully developed. Yet no matter how imperfectly developed the characteristics were at the time, Marx's theory of the "Asiatic" mode is most definitely a key for our analysis of the inner workings of the well-field system.

In the foregoing remarks I have offered some general comments about the well-field system and have introduced a few quasi-theoretical issues. Below, I will examine historical references to the well-field system, including the village commune and the distribution and rotation of land; the distribution of ditches, fields, and paths; the boundaries between "public fields" and "private fields" and their disappearance; the quality and quantity of exploitation (tribute payments, mutual aid, the share system, and taxation based on acreage); and the status of laborers in the well-field system.

Let us begin with the commune. Can its existence in ancient times actually be ascertained? Generally speaking, the Chinese ideograph *she* has an original sense as well as a secondary sense. Its original sense refers to the facilities for worshipping ancestors and agricultural gods. The Greater Minister of Instruction section of the *Rites of Zhou* states: "He sets up the altar mounds for the gods of the soil and grain and erects field tablets made of wood from the locale [to represent the spirits]. Subsequently he names the soil altar and locale [according to the name of the wood used]."[11] The "field tablet" (*tianzhu*) was in fact the ancestral spirit of the land, which was none other than the god of the field. The Special Sacrificial Animals of the Suburban Sacrifices section in the *Liji* (Book of Rites) states that during the great *bala* winter sacrifices, the Son of Heaven sacrificed to the embankments (*fang*), sacrificed to the ditches, invoked the cat spirit, invoked the tiger spirit, and sacrificed to the inter-well-field watchhouses.[12] The general purpose for these rites was described as follows:

> May the ground no sliding show,
> Water in its channels flow,
> Insects to keep quiet know;
> Only in the fens weeds grow![13]

These concerns were all very primitive and very practical. From a certain angle, they reflected the earliest activities and functions of the altar to the god of the soil (*she*). The altar to the soil was the focus of a collective organization. Its staff included, for instance, men responsible for cutting ice, the ice men (*lingren*); and people who controlled the distribution and rotation of land, called grand officers of the outer districts (*suiren*).[14] *Xia xiaozheng* is allegedly an account of the Xia dynasty that Confucius obtained while investigating social conditions in the states of Qi and Song.[15] In it, there is only a small number of titles for these kinds of workers, but in the later *Rites of Zhou*, when the communal staff slowly began evolving into a basic bureaucratic structure, there was a great increase in the different designations and numbers.

The commune gradually expanded and its functions increased.

Most important were the supervision of household registration, landholdings, military affairs, corvée labor, public security, and so on. The *Rites of Zhou* is an ancient classic that has been considered apocryphal and, for a long time, not at all reliable. However, this book contains a considerable amount of valuable information that was preserved despite the many periods of instability during the Han dynasty. First, we shall discuss household registration. In the "Annals of Zhou" of the *Guoyu* (Conversations of the states), these words of Zhong Shanpu are recorded: "The ancients did not count the people but they knew how many there were."[16] This statement reveals that the commune controlled household registration. In the Minister of Land section of the *Rites of Zhou*, descriptions of several official positions include the phrase "investigates laborers and households." The grand officer of the outer districts not only "investigates his subjects" but also "gives them their land,"[17] referring to the distribution and rotation of land.

Under the Minister of Instruction chapter in the Minister of Land section of the *Rites of Zhou*, there are three instances mentioning the distribution of land. Of the two main references, one has to do with the Greater Minister of Instruction and the other, the Grand Officer of the Outer Districts. The references are slightly different but essentially the same in implication. In general, the Greater Minister of Instruction was in control of estates (*shi*), or households, within the capital. "He gave families that cultivated their land annually plots of one hundred *mu*, families that cultivated their land once every two years two hundred *mu*, and families that cultivated their land once every three years three hundred *mu*."[18] The grand officer of the outer districts supervised the cultivators (*fu*) who constituted the main labor force, and the unmarried cultivators (*yufu*) in rural areas.

> In areas where the land was of superior quality, a cultivator received a dwelling, one hundred *mu* of arable land, and fifty *mu* of land lying fallow; an unmarried cultivator received the same amount of land lying fallow. In areas where the land was of average quality, a cultivator received a dwelling, one hundred *mu* of arable land, and one hundred of land lying fallow; an unmarried cultivator received the same amount of land lying fallow. In areas where the land was of inferior quality, a cultivator received a

dwelling, one hundred *mu* of cultivated land, and two hundred of land lying fallow; an unmarried cultivator received the same amount of land lying fallow.[19]

These differences in allotments reflect the contrast between the core of the capital and the periphery of the countryside. Since there was more uncultivated land in the periphery, allotments were slightly larger.

There are slight discrepancies in records concerning the number of families forming a small collective on these distributed lands. In the Duke Wen of Teng chapter of the *Mencius* it is stated: "A *jing* is a piece of land measuring one *li* square, and each *jing* consists of 900 *mu*. Of these, the central plot of 100 *mu* belongs to the state, while the other eight plots of 100 *mu* each are held by eight families who share the duty of caring for the plot owned by the state."[20] This was one model. The Lesser Minister of Instruction section in the *Rites of Zhou* states: "He arranges their fields and divides them into nine squares. Nine cultivators (*fu*) comprise one well-field and four well-fields form a district (*yi*)."[21] This was another model. Aside from these examples, it is entirely possible that there were other models, such as the "eastern fields" and "southern fields," which were lined up in a pattern of strips of land. Public fields were either contained within the private fields forming the nine-square land system or were separated spatially from their private counterparts, sometimes far removed from each other, as reflected in the Futian ode in the Lesser Odes section of the *Book of Songs:*

> The clouds o'erspread the sky in masses dense,
> And gentle rain down to the earth dispense.
> First may the public fields the blessings get,
> And then with it our private fields we wet![22]

Given China's immense geographical area, no single standard could be strictly enforced.

Alongside the fields were ditches and pathways of varying size, the three coming to be thought of as forming a set of standard features. In ancient times, the ditches were called "drainage ditches" (*gouxu*). The *Mencius* does not mention these drainage ditches when speaking of the well-field era. The *Analects* of Confucius speaks of the mythical emperor Yu who was noted for the fact that "all his energy went into draining and ditching."[23] As we can see, the use of ditches to displace water was practiced in very early times. The "Record of Public Works" (*Kaogong ji*) in the *Rites of Zhou* records drainage ditches built by "construction workers" (*jiangren*). Plows were usually paired in those days. A single plowshare was five inches in width, and a double plowshare could dig a trench one foot deep and wide. Such a trench was dug between fields and called a small drain (*quan*). At the top of the fields, the width and breadth of the trenches were doubled to two feet by two feet and called a drain (*sui*). Between well-fields, the trenches were four feet wide by four feet deep and were called ditches (*gou*). An area of ten square *li* was called a *cheng*, and the trenches between *cheng* were eight feet wide by eight feet deep and called moats (*xu*). The larger area of one hundred square *li* was called a *tong*. The trenches between *tong*, sixteen feet wide by sixteen feet deep, were called channels (*guai*) and were connected to natural rivers.

Whether the arrangement of the ancient drainage system was as clear-cut as this theoretical plan suggests is a problem we will not consider here. In general, however, it is unlikely that the account was fabricated without any basis in reality. The main function of these drainage ditches was the displacement of water. The "Record of Public Works" in the *Rites of Zhou* also states: "All ditches must follow the flow of existing water courses, and embankments (*fang*) must follow the terrain. Good ditches are cleaned out with the water that runs through them. Good embankments are reinforced by the deposits from the water that washes them."[24] From this passage, we discover that (1) the ancient drainage ditches followed the natural topography, which accorded with reason but was by no means a utopia, and (2) with the ditches there were also embankments, which were dikes used to block the flow of water.

The *fang* embankments worshipped in the *bala* winter sacrifices are the same embankments spoken of here. Moreover, the *yong* ditches worshipped in winter were actually the drainage ditches of the well-field system. Both the embankments and the ditches were designed to control floods, though they were never completely effective. Often when there was excessive rainfall, the water would collect and form pools, and these would serve as primitive reservoirs. However, these pools were not essential to agricultural production in ancient times. In the Li Lou chapter of the *Mencius*, it is stated: "If a thing has no source, it is like the rain water that collects after a downpour in the seventh and eighth months. It may fill all the gutters, but we can stand and wait for it to dry up."[25] Thus we can see that reservoirs were still not essential in those times.

Let us turn to an examination of the "public fields" and "private fields." The terminological distinction between these two types of land existed very early in China. In the *Xia xiaozheng* there are the statements: "Farmers hastily plowed their fields," and "First they would serve on the public fields." According to Dai De of the Western Han, "In ancient times there were public fields. The ancient people first served on the public fields and then worked on their own fields,"[26] meaning the "private fields." Dai De's account tallies with the passage in the *Mencius* that reads: "Only when they have done this duty [i.e., cared for the state-owned plots] dare they turn to their own affairs."[27] Thus the distinction in name between "public fields" and "private fields" existed at a very early time.

What, then, was the criterion for differentiating between public fields and private fields? I contend that at the close of the era of classless society, it was the distinction between necessary labor and reserve labor; after the emergence of classes, kings, and nobility, it was the distinction between necessary labor and surplus labor.[28] Generally speaking, the agricultural laborers during the well-field era were slaves or commune staff, but this need not be decided here. They did, however, have families who needed to be fed; that is, they had to sustain their own "self-reproduction." No documents or archaeological discoveries have been found suggesting the existence of communal dining halls. The laborers lived as separate families in their homes where "there are sowbugs in this room; there were spiders' webs on the door."[29] Going to work "with my wife and children, bringing hampers to the southern acre,"[30] each family would squat together at the side of the field and eat. These were the private fields on which necessary labor had to be expended. If both the public and private fields belonged to the nobility, there would be no opportunity for necessary labor to realize its own value, and the laborers would be unable to maintain their own reproduction. Such a situation would make no sense.

The private field was an allotment of land. To maintain reliable rights to use and benefit from this plot of land (i.e., the "constant means of support" referred to in the *Mencius*: "Those with constant means of support will have constant hearts"[31]), the laborer in a classless society had to go to the public field to expend his reserve labor. The product of this kind of reserve labor was offered as public tribute. The tribute (*gong*) system that later emerged in the time of the mythical emperor Yu evolved more or less from this reserve labor on public fields. Was this tribute system expressed through material goods or by labor? Did it resemble Long Zi's words in the *Mencius*, "the payment due is calculated on the average yield over a number of years,"[32] or some other method? Owing to the great antiquity of the tribute system, no one is able to answer these questions.

The standard taxation method, which was extremely common during the well-field era, was called "mutual aid" (*zhu*) or "tributary cultivation" (*jie*). It is not simply a matter of hearsay that people performed this tribute. The *Mencius* states: "There is 'public land' only when *zhu* is practiced. From this we see that even the Zhou practiced *zhu*."[33] Textual commentators of the eastern Han dynasty provide very accurate explanations. Zhao Qi (d. A.D. 201) said: "Tributary cultivation (*jie*) is the same as the character meaning 'to borrow' (*jie*), which is found in the expression 'borrowing the people's strength to cultivate public fields.' "[34] Similarly, Zheng Xuan (A.D. 127–200) stated: "Tributary cultivation (*jie*) refers to the character 'to borrow,' as in 'to borrow the people's strength to cultivate the public fields.' . . . That which the people cultivated themselves was not taxed."[35] The ratio of labor on private fields to that on public fields was approximately ten to one. Therefore, "the ancient people had one-tenth of their produce levied by mutual cultivation [of the public fields rather than] paying taxes [out of the produce from their private fields]." This became an absolute standard in the consciousness of the ancient

Chinese. This kind of "ten-to-one" labor system was a manifestation of one of the "Asiatic" characteristics: the unity of rent and tax. Zheng Xuan's statement that the people's private produce was not taxed corresponds with the words of Karl Marx that "there could never again be a tax that is different from this land rent format." Therefore, when the state of Lu "began levying part of the produce from all acres" and taxing according to acreage, the Gongyang and Guliang commentaries to the *Spring and Autumn Annals* both protested that it was "improper." Furthermore, they stated that the "ten-to-one labor system" was "the justest and most correct for all under the sky," and "if more than this tenth be taken, we have great Jies and little Jies. If less we have great Mos and little Mos."[36] People had not yet realized that an increase in the products of surplus labor was an objective necessity.

Comparing the conditions described in the *Rites of Zhou* with what has been outlined above, we find a great deal of variation. As I see it, there are primarily two changes: (1) an increase in the number of commune staff, leading to the formation of base-level bureaucratic agencies, which represent the sprouts of despotism; and (2) the separation of the unity of rent and tax—an "Asiatic" characteristic—and, responding to the need for taxation, a division by the base-level agencies of the laborers' land into state dwellings (*guozhai*), gardens (*yuanpu*), inner suburbs, outer suburbs, satellite walled cities (*shao*), imperial domains (*dian*), counties (*xian*), cities (*du*), and so on. They also divided the public fields into residential land (*zhaitian*), officers' land (*shitian*), merchants' land (*gutian*), administrative land (*guantian*), pasture (*niutian*), grazing land (*mutian*), imperial domain fields (*gongyi zhi tian*), private domain fields (*jiayi zhi tian*), small city fields (*xiaodu zhi tian*), large city fields (*dadu zhi tian*), and so on.[37]

On the basis of this kind of rezoning, taxes were set at five levels of 5 to 25 percent. All of these had become pure tax, a direct economic manifestation of the existence of a state mechanism. Was the surplus labor that the laborers expended for the nobles then canceled? Historical records lack explicit evidence to that effect. However, there was probably no exemption, for the *Rites of Zhou* refers to "doing corvée labor on the land." In these various ways, the burden borne by the well-field peasant far exceeded the "ten-to-one" ratio, eventually surpassing even a "ten-to-five" ratio. The comprehensive term for this is the share system (*che*). Jin Jingfang has proposed that the Chinese ideograph representing the share system was originally that for "wheel ruts," which represents a kind of compound taxation system.[38]

There are many troublesome issues arising from the five-stages theory of modes of production, the status of the laborers being one. Naturally, it cannot be denied that the five-stage theory has had its positive functions, for it was the first comprehensive expression of the regularity of development of human society. If we adopt, however, the larger principle of establishing a universal standard and then making all local variations conform to it when they in fact do not, we will end up neglecting actual circumstances and acting in a Procrustean manner, "cutting the foot to fit the shoe." Actually, in the period before capitalism had emerged and after primitive society had disintegrated, the differences between slave society and feudal society and between the status of slaves and that of serfs were not all that sharp.

The status of agricultural laborers in the well-field era accordingly was multiple. For instance, the main work force was what textual sources called the "common people" (*shuren*). What status did these common people have? On pages 237 and 243 of the first volume of China's national university textbook, *Zhongguo shigao* (Draft history of China), it is stated unequivocally that the common people were slaves involved in agricultural production,[39] but do the facts actually support this? I will offer five pieces of evidence to the contrary:

1. The Great Plan section in the *Book of History* states that every time there was a major event, the state would "consult with its nobles and officers" and would also "consult with the masses of people." "If . . . the nobles and officers, and the common people all consent to a course, this is what is called a great concord."[40] Does the status of the common people in this case resemble that of slaves?

2. The Juan'a ode in the Greater Odes section of the *Book of Songs* was a eulogy used by the rulers of the Zhou dynasty for sacrifices to their first ancestor. In it there are cadenzas of two stanzas, one of which states: "Loving you, the son of Heaven," and

the other states: "and loving the multitudes of the people."[41] Could there have ever been a slave owner who would offer his respect to mere slaves during ancestral sacrifices?

3. The fourth part of the "Annals of Jin" in the *Annals of the States* records that "the common people live off their own efforts," which means that they relied on their independent labor to grow their own food. In this way they differed from the merchants and artisans who "lived off officials" and the great officers of state who "lived off land grants."

4. The account of the thirty-second year of Duke Shao in the *Zuo zhuan* records the words of Shu Xiang of the state of Jin that "the surnames of the sovereigns of the three [previous dynasties] are now borne by men among the [common] people."[42] This means that members of the nobility had been reduced to the status of common people. It is unthinkable, however, that nobles could suddenly become slaves.

5. The second year of Duke Ai in the *Zuo zhuan* records Zhao Jianzi of the state of Jin as encouraging military service and promoting the warrior spirit by saying, "A common man [i.e., a farmer], a mechanic, or a merchant [who follows his superior into battle and distinguishes himself in battle against Zheng, shall receive] the privilege of becoming an officer."[43] The last part of this passage clearly implies that slaves who make a military contribution may be released as free men. The first part, however, says that those who follow their superiors into battle can become officials, which was something the average slave could not expect to achieve. Given these five examples, the view that the "common people" were slaves involved in agricultural production is untenable.

The common people may not have been slaves, but they bore the main burden of agricultural production. At that time, village communes were widespread, so the common people were members of the village communes. Of this I am certain. We must ask, however, whether the members of the village communes were freemen, and the answer is, not necessarily. We must assume that there could be many intermediate statuses between nonfree people (slaves) and freemen. At that time, the members of the village communes were no longer members of the primitive communes. Just as the village commune possessed the dual nature of public and private ownership, the members of the village communes had the dual status of being partly free and partly exploited. On the one hand, they had families, land ("private fields" or "constant means of support"), and a small-household economic base. They were not prisoners, and they did not belong to the category of industrial and commercial slaves who relied on the officials for their livelihood.

The restrictions on their freedom were still very great. For instance, regarding migration, the *Mencius* states: "Neither in burying the dead, nor in changing his abode, does a man go beyond the confines of his village."[44] Under the professional title of community leader (*bizhang*) in the Minister of Earth section of the *Rites of Zhou*, it is stated: "If families migrate within the capital or the suburbs, then he [the community leader] will accompany them and present them to their new leader; if families migrate to other areas, then he will make them a waymark and permit them to go on their way. If an individual changes his place of residence without the necessary permit or waymark, then he is imprisoned."[45] That is to say, those who had no migration permit were arrested. This practice was very restrictive.

Furthermore, an individual's duties vis-à-vis the community were very heavy. The Lesser Minister of Instruction heading in the Minister of Land section of the *Rites of Zhou* states that there were at least three duties to be observed by all members: (1) "joining the armed forces," which involved both military service and battle action; (2) "performing corvée labor," which involved group labor in the public fields; and (3) "serving as runners" (i.e., police duty), which involved apprehending criminals. These duties follow the principle that "the family does not provide more than one individual," though extra labor called "surplus" (*xian*) could be called up. When performing corvée labor and police duty, people were required to "do so to the utmost." When going to war, people were summoned with a large flag of a bear (symbol of martial valor), and those who disobeyed orders were executed. In other words, the primitive authority of the community was great enough to have people executed. Hence, commune members were not free with respect to these duties. Third, the common people provided free surplus labor for the nobility, compounded with extreme extortion, as in the verses:

> And take those foxes and wild-cats
> To make furs for our Lord. . . .
> The one-year-old [boar] we keep;
> The three-year-old we offer to our Lord.[46]

There was only a fine line separating this from the economic and extraeconomic coercion of feudalism.

Aside from the typical commune member, there were probably other members of lower status. For instance, in the first section of the "Annals of Jin" in the *Conversations of the States*, Shi Su and the other great officers of Jin, discussing the problem of Li Ji,[47] said, "Just like servile peasants (*linong*), even though they obtain fertile land and diligently cultivate it, they will not be able to hold feasts for others."[48] The servile peasant spoken of here and the serfs of medieval Europe belong to two completely different eras, yet this quotation reveals that even though the well-field peasants were able to obtain allotments of good land and to rotate them, most of the product of their surplus labor was expropriated by force, leaving them little they themselves could enjoy. Why were they willing to accept this kind of treatment? The reason was that they were in a relationship that involved a certain degree of bondage. To cite another example, when Wang Anshi (1021–1086) read the passage "[the inspector] discerns the number of working men and women, people, and fields being cultivated or lying fallow,"[49] he assigned the inspector to one rank and the "people" to another, interpreting the "people" as "slaves of the people."[50] In other words, people of this rank were commune members of servile status. In summary, the status of commune members was not uniformly fixed, and it was even less one of absolute "independence" or "freedom." The dispersed character of ownership and the lack of collective ownership at the time produced this multiplicity of statuses.

At that time there were still no clear class distinctions, and those differences that did exist were only of rank. Of course, this kind of distinction by rank harbored class content. The record of the seventh year of Duke Zhao in the *Zuo zhuan* states: "The day has its ten divisions of time, and of men there are ten classes. . . . Hence, the king makes the duke [the prince of a state] his servant; the duke, the great officer; the great officer, the [simple] officer; the officer, the lictor; the lictor, the crowd of underlings; the underling, the menials; the menial, the laborer; the laborer, the servant; the servant, the helper. There are also grooms for the horses, and shepherds for the cattle."[51] This passage provides many insights into the contemporary social structure: (1) This kind of distinction by rank was very crude and not at all refined or strict; (2) ranking the ruling exploiters together with those who were ruled and exploited throws the modern conception of class into confusion; (3) this is largely a description of China's nobility and their hordes of retainers; and (4) the "common people" alone were not included in the list. The reason for this last point is very simple. The common people were seen as "country bumpkins" who should not be listed because they belonged to the village communes. Some people rely only on the inscription on the Great Bowl Caldron[52] to say that the "common people" were actually slaves whose status was even lower than that of attendants (*yu*), yet why then were the "common people" not listed at the end of the ten ranks, or between the "officer" and the "lictor"?

In conclusion, exactly what was the landownership system of the well-field era? Perhaps the process of elimination will provide an answer to this question. First, the well-field system was no longer a primitive form of ownership but a well-developed public or communal landownership system. Second, it was not completely a state ownership system since the centralized despotic state and its authority to intervene in property had not yet matured. Third, and even more obviously, there is little indication (beyond a very few examples that should not be dismissed out of hand) that during the well-field era, land belonged to private owners and could be disposed of according to individual choice, even bought and sold. Therefore, in the final analysis, the well-field system could only have been the amalgamation of imperfect communal property and imperfect royal and noble property. In short, it was a relatively standard ancient landownership system of the "Asiatic" type.

Notes

1. Arthur Waley, trans., *The Book of Songs* (London: George Allen & Unwin, 1954), pp. 245–46.

2. Based roughly on the French translation by Feu Edouard Biot, *Le Tcheou-Li ou Rites des Tcheou*, vol. 1 (Paris: Imprimerie Nationale, 1851), p. 200.

3. Ibid., pp. 192–93.

4. D. C. Lau, trans., *Mencius* (Harmondsworth: Penguin, 1970), p. 99 (III.A.3).

5. Editor's note: The equal-field system was developed in the fifth century A.D. as a method by which the state redistributed land to tillers and brought independent landowners under firmer control.

6. Editor's note: One *mu* is roughly equivalent to one-sixth of an acre or one-fifteenth of a hectare.

7. See Cheng Yaotian (1725–1814), *Guoxu jiangli xiaoji* (A brief account of ditches and boundaries) (1860).

8. Waley, *The Book of Songs*, p. 320.

9. Marx, "The British Rule in India," in *On Colonialism*, p. 37.

10. Editor's note: The "land within the passes" refers to the homeland of the Zhou dynasty in southern Shanxi province south of the Great Wall.

11. See Biot, *Le Tcheou-Li*, 1:193.

12. Translator's note: The cat spirit and tiger spirit were invoked as a religious means of decimating the field mouse and wild boar populations.

13. James Legge, trans., *Li Chi: Book of Rites*, vol. 1 (repr., New Hyde Park, N.Y.: University Books, 1967), p. 432.

14. Translator's note: The outer districts (*sui*) were established beyond the suburbs of city-states, each district comprising 12,500 households.

15. The *Xia xiaozheng* is a chapter in the *Da Dai li*; however, it is sometimes treated as a work in its own right (see note 26).

16. *Guoyu* (Shanghai: Guji Chubanshe, 1978), p. 24.

17. See Biot, *Le Tcheou-Li*, 1:336–46.

18. Ibid., pp. 206–207.

19. Ibid., pp. 340–41.

20. *Mencius*, p. 100 (III.A.3).

21. Translator's note: See Biot, *Le Tcheou-Li*, 1:226. Zhao erroneously attributes this passage to the *Book of Rites*.

22. James Legge, trans., *The Book of Poetry* (New York: Paragon Book Reprint Corp., 1967), p. 292.

23. Arthur Waley, trans., *The Analects of Confucius* (London: George Allen & Unwin, 1938), p. 137.

24. See Biot, *Le Tcheou-Li*, 2:569–70.

25. *Mencius*, p. 131 (IV.B.18).

26. Dai De, *Xia xiaozheng* (Taibei: Taiwan Shangwu Yinshuguan, 1965), p. 9.

27. *Mencius*, p. 100 (III.A.3).

28. Editor's note: According to Marx, necessary labor is the "portion of the

labor process [during which the laborer] produces only the value of his labor-power, that is, the value of his means of subsistence." Surplus labor is the labor expended above and beyond what is necessary to reproduce the laborer. "The essential difference between the various economic forms of society . . . lies only in the mode in which this surplus labor is in each case extracted from the actual producer, the laborer" (*Capital*, vol. 1 [New York: International Publishers, 1967], pp. 216–17).

29. Waley, *The Book of Songs*, p. 116.

30. Ibid., p. 164.

31. *Mencius*, p. 97 (III.A.3).

32. Ibid., p. 98.

33. Ibid.

34. Zhao Qi, *Mengzi Zhao zhu shisijuan* (Zhao commentary to the *Mencius* in fourteen chapters) (Taibei: National Palace Museum, 1970), 5:5b.

35. Zheng Xuan, *Liji (Zhengshizhu)* (Zheng commentary to the *Book of Rites*) (Shanghai: Zhonghua Shuju, 1924), 4:10a.

36. Translator's note: James Legge, trans., *The Ch'un Ts'ew with the Tso Chuen*, in *The Chinese Classics*, vol. 5 (Hong Kong: Hong Kong University Press, 1960), pp. 68–69, citing the Gongyang commentary to the eighth line of the fifteenth year of Duke Xuan in the *Spring and Autumn Annals*. In this passage, overtaxation is associated with the infamous last king of the Xia dynasty, Jie, and undertaxation with a barbarian tribe, the Mos, in the north.

37. See Biot, *Le Tcheou-Li*, 1:276–77. A satellite walled city refers to a city situated at least three hundred *li* away from the royal city.

38. See Jin Jingfang, *Lun jingtian zhidu* (On the well-field system) (Jinan: Qi-Lu Shushe, 1982), p. 33.

39. Guo Moruo, ed., *Zhongguo shigao* (Draft history of China) vol. 1 (Beijing: Renmin Chubanshe, 1976).

40. Adapted from James Legge, trans., *The Shoo King*, in *The Chinese Classics*, 3:337.

41. Translator's note: James Legge, trans., *The Book of Poetry*, in *The Chinese Classics*, 4:493–94. These represent the last lines of the seventh stanza and eighth stanza respectively. Zhao wishes to show that in this ode, the common people were the object of respect.

42. Legge, *The Ch'un Ts'ew with the Tso Chuen*, p. 741.

43. Adapted from ibid., p. 799.

44. *Mencius*, p. 99 (III.A.3).

45. See Biot, *Le Tcheou-Li*, 1:260–61.

46. Waley, *The Book of Songs*, p. 165.

47. Translator's note: Li Ji was a woman taken captive when Duke Xian of Jin attacked the Lirong people (located east of Xi'an). The ministers viewed her being made duchess with much apprehension.

48. *Guoyu*, p. 258.

49. See Biot, *Le Tcheou-Li*, 1:284.

50. Translator's note: Wang Anshi, *Zhouguan xinyi* (Yueyatang Congshu, 1853), 6:21b. Zhao's misquotation has been corrected.

51. Legge, *The Ch'un Ts'ew with the Tso Chuen*, p. 616.

52. Translator's note: The Great Bowl Caldron is one of the largest bronze caldrons (*ding*) of the early Western Zhou period, with an inscription of 291 characters. It was unearthed in 1821.

The Unproblematic Asiatic Mode of Production

The AMP Is the Mode of Production of the Ancient Period

In the Preface to *A Contribution to the Critique of Political Economy*, written in January 1859, Marx placed the "Asiatic mode of production" (AMP) unambiguously at the head of a progressive series of epochs.[1] Marx himself assigned it this position, ahead of the ancient mode of production in the scheme of historical development. Any attempt to place it in parallel with the ancient mode—to divide the slave societies of the ancient civilized world into an "ancient Orient" and a "classical world"—not only directly contradicts Marx's universalist principle but amounts to a complete rejection of it.

The AMP refers to the naturally occurring or self-generated communal property of the primitive period. This public ownership is the most primitive form of property, the original form of all later types, as Marx observes in a footnote in the *Critique*:

> A careful study of Asiatic, particularly Indian, forms of communal property would indicate that the disintegration of different forms

From *Lishi yanjiu* (Studies in history) 2 (1980): 3-24. Translated by Timothy Brook. The two-volume *Shijie shanggu shigang* (Outline history of world antiquity) was published by Renmin Chubanshe (1979, 1981) and compiled under the editorship of Lin Zhichun.

of primitive communal ownership gives rise to diverse forms of property. For instance, various prototypes of Roman and Germanic private property can be traced back to certain forms of Indian communal property.[2]

Marx wrote the Preface shortly after composing this note, so it is clear that his reference to the AMP in the Preface is equivalent to the communal ownership of the primitive period cited in this note. Any attempt to drag the AMP from the primitive epoch into the period of class society and civilization directly contradicts what Marx says in the *Critique*. Fifteen years later, Marx incorporated this footnote unchanged into the second edition of the first volume of *Capital*,[3] showing that his view of the AMP as primitive communal ownership had not changed in the 1870s.

In 1887, four years after Marx's death, Engels prepared for publication the English edition of the first volume of *Capital*. In a passage concerning the Asiatic and ancient modes of production he parenthetically inserted the word "primitive" and the phrase "in a primitive tribal community." The resulting text reads as follows:

> In the ancient Asiatic and other ancient modes of production, we find that the conversion of products into commodities, and therefore the conversion of men into producers of commodities, holds a subordinate place, which, however, increases in importance as the [primitive] communities approach nearer and nearer to their dissolution. . . . Those ancient social organisms of production are . . . founded either on the immature development of men individually, who have not yet severed the umbilical cord that unite them with their fellow men [in a primitive tribal community], or upon direct relations of subjection.[4]

In this passage, the "ancient Asiatic" mode is associated with the period of the primitive tribal community, whereas the "ancient" mode is linked to the slave period of class subjection. It is obvious that the one follows the other. They cannot coexist during the same historical epoch. In equating the AMP and primitive society, Engels was not altering Marx's original meaning but making it more explicit. The equation remained intact and was not abandoned in the 1880s, as some argue.

The AMP Is the Universal Primitive
Socioeconomic Formation

Marx speaks of the "Asiatic" mode in the Preface. In the introduction to the *Grundrisse*, he refers to "oriental economics."[5] Neither "Asiatic" nor "Oriental" is a geographical term. Rather, they are generalized, abstract concepts indicating the earliest stage in the history of property or socioeconomic formations of all civilized peoples: "the primitive form of society everywhere from India to Ireland," as Engels noted in the 1888 English edition of the *Manifesto of the Communist Party*.[6] Marx occasionally simply spoke of primitive communal ownership as "the Asiatic or Indian form of property," as he does in his letter to Engels of March 14, 1868, pointing out that these forms "constitute the initial ones everywhere in Europe."[7] According to Marx, one can speak of the Asiatic form of property in relation to Europe as readily as to Asia. "Asiatic" or "Oriental" forms of property are simply alternative expressions for communal ownership. It would thus be incorrect to limit "Asiatic" and "Oriental" references in the *Grundrisse* and elsewhere to Asia, thereby separating the "ancient Orient" from the "classical world" and placing the Asiatic and ancient modes of production on parallel tracks.

Marx Did Not Inherit the AMP from Hegel

Marx's "AMP" and "Oriental society" were not derived from the concepts of "Asia" and "the Orient" in Hegel's *The Philosophy of History*. Marx did not inherit these concepts from Hegel.

In the history of modern thought, Hegel was the first philosopher to identify Asia as the point of origin of world history. He divided history into four worlds: Oriental, Greek, Roman, and German. The unfolding of history sequentially through these four stages was for Hegel at the same time the process of "the progress of the consciousness of freedom": from the freedom of the one (Oriental despotism) to the freedom of some (the Greek and Roman republics) to freedom generally (German constitutional monarchy).[8] Marx and Engels did not adopt this view of history. They never regarded "Oriental despotism" as the starting point of history, but rather saw it as something to be found at certain points in both Eastern and Western history. There was Roman despotism just as there was Oriental despotism.[9]

In the 1840s, Marx and Engels in *The German Ideology* stated that "the first form of ownership is tribal ownership."[10] During this period there was neither private property nor the state, the forces of production were weakly developed, and people occupied themselves with fishing, hunting, and agriculture. The only slaves were domestic, and the tribal leaders were patriarchal chiefs, not Hegelian Oriental despots. What Marx and Engels were explicating in this text was the developmental process from tribal ownership, to ancient communal and state ownership, to feudal ownership, and finally to modern private property. This is a process totally incompatible with Hegel's system of four worlds.

In their writings of the late 1840s, Marx and Engels restricted their comments to the stages of development of civilized or class society and did not deal with the primitive period. They were systematizing world history only from ancient to modern times. References to such prehistoric matters as "tribal ownership" simply do not appear.[11] They make an appearance once Marx and Engels begin to formulate comprehensive descriptions of history that include the primitive epoch. It is in the 1850s, as a result of further research, that Marx and Engels start referring to Oriental communal property, frequently substituting "Asiatic" (in the Preface to the *Critique*) or "Oriental" (in the Introduction to the *Grundrisse*) for the expression "tribal ownership," which they used earlier in *The German Ideology*. For this reason, we believe that Marx's concept of Asiatic or Oriental property did not come from Hegel's "Oriental despotism" but developed out of their earlier idea of "tribal ownership." By the winter of 1857-58, Marx was referring to "tribal ownership" under the new rubric of the Asiatic or Oriental form of ownership.[12]

Why "Asiatic"?

If the AMP represents tribal ownership and communal ownership in the primitive period and is common to the history of all civilized peoples, why did Marx and Engels use a geographical term for its name? Neither glosses his reason for using "Asiatic," but we can find clues in their writings.

The choice of the term is probably linked to their opposition to Mikhail Bakunin (1814–1876) and other pan-Slavics who sought to equate the common property of the Russian peasants with communism. When Marx and Engels began their research on common property in the early 1850s, right from the beginning they paid attention to peasant ownership in Russia in order to counter "the old pan-Slavic DODGE of transmogrifying the old Slav system of communal property into communism and depicting the Russian peasants as born communists."[13] Common property among the Russian peasants had first been pointed out by the Prussian Government Councillor Haxthausen in 1845.[14] Bakunin and his followers misunderstood the significance of these primitive communal remnants and capitalized on their discovery for political purposes. Given that private property had dominated people's consciousness for many thousand years by this time, it is hardly surprising that Haxthausen's discovery would lead some to argue that the communism of the peasant commune not only was more advanced than capitalism but was the modern communism for which the proletariat was struggling. Bakunin thought that communist society could be achieved in one step without going through the necessary historical stages.

Marx and Engels expended much energy opposing this kind of antihistorical theorizing, and from roughly 1853 onward they studied the question of common property with this concern in mind. They started by investigating specific communities, particularly the Scottish clan and the Indian commune.[15] The materials on which they based their studies of Asia were mostly recent reports, which certainly limited them in terms of proof.[16] Aside from Russia and India, there was also a certain amount of material on communal ownership available from Ireland and Germany, and by the end of the 1850s Marx and Engels had mastered most of it.

By the time that Marx wrote the *Critique*, he was thus ready to deal with the question of common property. Among the issues he had to tackle was what name to use. Bakunin had insisted that the only peasant communal ownership was among the Slavs. Marx criticized this "absurdly biased view" in a footnote to the *Critique*, and in a letter to Engels in 1868, written when he was reading Maurer's writings on common property among the Germans, he indirectly criticizes Bakunin when he observes that "the Russians now lose even the last traces of a claim to originality, even in this line."[17] Two years later in a letter to Ludwig Kugelmann, Marx emphatically pointed to India as the origin of communal ownership, saying that it could also be detected in the early history of European civilization.[18] Five years later, in 1875, Engels took this a step further to say that "communal ownership of the land is an institution which is to be found among all Indo-Germanic peoples on a low level of development, from India to Ireland."[19] In 1888 he concluded that village communities had been "the primitive form of society everywhere from India to Ireland."[20] The idea that common property was unique to the Russian peasantry was thus consistently repudiated.

This series of quotes shows that Marx dubbed communal ownership "Asiatic" or "Oriental" not simply because he found that Asia at the time provided representative examples, but because he was criticizing Bakunin's notion of natural communism in Russia. This does not mean that Marx and Engels were denying the validity of using the more common expression "primitive common property" for the same thing. Rather, they used both expressions at the same time. "Asiatic" and "Oriental" did not replace "primitive" but simply showed that the primitive form of ownership and mode of production were to be found not just in Russia but also in the East.

What Problem Did the AMP Solve?

By proposing the AMP as the first socioeconomic formation, what problem did Marx hope to solve? Put simply, it was the problem of primitive property.

The long history of private ownership meant that nineteenth-century Europeans viewed it as God-given. It is for this reason that common property among the Russian peasants was regarded as so unusual. But as Marx and Engels determined in the 1850s, "history rather shows common property (e.g. in India, among the Slavs, the early Celts, etc.) to be the original form."[21] On this basis, Marx formulated the "AMP" in the Preface to the *Critique*. Communal property in the primitive epoch thus serves as the starting point for the dialectic formula for property: from public to private to public, that is, modern communism.[22]

The AMP and Oriental Despotism

Being a concept based on communal ownership, the AMP cannot be applied to class society, lacking both private property and the state. By its very nature, the Asiatic or Oriental commune has nothing to do with despotism, nor can it produce despotism. However, we do find cases in which communes existed under the rule of a despot. The remnants of Indian and Russian communes, for instance, existed within the framework of the despotic state, the former under Mogul or British imperialism, the latter under the rule of the tsar. Javanese communes under Dutch imperialism were in the same situation. Under such conditions, the AMP does bear some relationship to the despotic state.

In *Pre-Capitalist Economic Formations* (1858), Marx points out that communal property in land "can realize itself in a variety of ways."[23] The Indian commune is a commune under a despotic monarchy; the Slavonic commune is sometimes placed within the framework of the state and sometimes not; the ancient Celtic commune is uniformly outside the state. It is easy to misread these references and fail to recognize that the communes under despotic monarchies are only a limited part of the communes to which Marx is referring. The AMP commune may then be mistaken for the commune under the despotic state, thereby projecting the class content of the one onto the primitive form of the latter.

The AMP or Oriental commune remains primitive regardless of the larger political context in which it sits. It is a primitive commune when it is not under monarchical rule, and it remains a primitive commune when it is under such rule. When the state exists, the commune serves as the foundation of despotic monarchy by surrendering tribute to the despot and suffering exploitation at the hands of the feudal lords. This is equally true of Russia, India, and Java. From the 1850s forward, Marx and Engels constantly make reference to "these idyllic village communities" serving as

"the solid foundation of Oriental despotism," of "the ancient communities" that "have for thousands of years formed the basis of the
cruelest form of state, Oriental despotism."[24] They remain in a
state of "constant immobility" and are untouched by the "unceasing change in the persons and clans that gain control of the political superstructure,"[25] hence the so-called stagnation of the Orient.
We must realize, however, that such references to Asian "society"
speak only of the communal part of society, not society as a whole.
The notion of Oriental "stagnation" otherwise makes no sense.
History and society progressed unceasingly throughout the East. It
is just that the communal part of society by comparison developed
more slowly, thus appearing to be "stagnant."

On the basis of this understanding of the relationship between
the AMP and despotic empires, we can speedily resolve the so-
called problem of the AMP, which has been debated for so many
years. It is only problematic because people did not realize that
AMP communal society under despotic rule remained in the primitive communal stage, instead forcing this preclass society into class
society and making them one. When Marx and Engels speak of
common property in land or of the limited division of labor in
handicrafts, they are referring to the primitive communal period.
To dogmatically misapply such observations to class society and
speak of public ownership in Oriental society as an absence of private property, or of handicraft industry as undeveloped, runs totally counter to historical reality throughout Asia.

The apparent insolubility of the problem has induced some to
argue cavalierly that Oriental class society is distinctive: the
despotic state above, the commune below. Some have called this
"permanent feudalism," others, "the Asiatic formation." Still
others have sought a compromise with the idea of slavery, calling it
"ancient Oriental slavery." The confusion here arises from a failure to understand that although the commune is the foundation of
despotism, the commune and the state belong to two different social epochs and cannot be combined to create a unique (and historically impossible) epoch. The solution is simple. Separate the
two incompatible elements and see them as a combination of two
social formations, not as one.

Engels uses this approach to analyze tsarist Russia during the period of early industrialization. The peasant commune alone of all the elements in Russian society reflects the AMP. To identify the tsar, industrial capital, or the financial oligarchy as belonging to the AMP would reduce capitalism to primitive communalism. In his letter to Vera Zasulich of April 23, 1885, Engels remarks that Russia is a country "where every stage of social development is represented, from the primitive commune to modern large-scale industry and high finance, and where all these contradictions are violently held in check by an unexampled despotism."[26] Similarly, with regard to Java under the Dutch, he says in a letter to Karl Kautsky of February 16, 1884:

> On the basis of the old community communism the Dutch organized production under state control. . . . The result: the people are kept at a stage of primitive stupidity and 70 million marks (now surely more) are annually collected by the Dutch national treasury. . . . Primitive communism furnishes there as well as in India and Russia the finest and broadest basis of exploitation and despotism. . . . In the conditions of modern society it turns out to be a crying anachronism as much as were the independent mark associations of the original [Swiss] cantons.[27]

Engels pictures the simultaneous presence of two social epochs in Java: the primitive communes of the Javanese and the despotic state of the colonial capitalists. In doing so he furnishes us with an excellent example of the AMP under despotic rule, in which, as in Russia and India, we must distinguish two social epochs. Java before the Dutch invasion was without question a society in the stage of AMP primitive communalism: there was no private property, no division of labor between crafts and agriculture, no classes, no state. Under colonialism, Java's basic character remained that of a primitive communist or AMP society, even though it had acquired colonial capitalism, a despotic colonial state, and exploitation.

The problem is thus solved; indeed, it no longer exists. Those who would turn the AMP into a class society and at the same time insist that Oriental society is without private property have forced dogma onto history, thus creating a problem they could not resolve. Our method, on the other hand, is to distinguish two coexisting stages.

The Unity of Rent and Tax, and Commodity
Production under Tribute Relations

One of the questions our formulation solves is how to understand the unity of rent and tax. In places where there is private property, rent is paid by those who use the land to those who own it; tax is paid by landowners to the state. Land is communally owned under the AMP, but in places that have come under the domination of the despotic state, land is under the nominal ownership of the king, though in reality it remains under communal ownership. There is no privately owned land under the AMP, hence no rents are being paid to private landowners. When the state extracts surplus labor from the members of the peasant communities in its guise as the highest landowner, this rent takes the form of tribute, thus uniting rent with tax.

Marx's theory of the unity of rent and tax is an integral component of his theory of the AMP, as he writes in *Capital*:

> Should the direct producers not be confronted by a private landowner, but rather, as in Asia, under direct subordination to a state which stands over them as their landlord and simultaneously as sovereign, then rents and taxes coincide, or rather, there exists no tax which differs from this form of ground-rent. . . . The state is then the supreme lord. Sovereignty here consists in the ownership of land concentrated on a national scale. But, on the other hand, no private ownership of land exists, although there is both private and common possession and use of land.[28]

The unity of rent and tax was found in certain areas under AMP communal ownership, but some have indiscriminately applied it to all periods and places in the East, and even to times after the appearance of landlords and the dynastic state, sowing further confusion.

A second question our formulation resolves is commodity production under the AMP. Commodity production was unknown to the commune, but the state could come in, expropriate the commune's surplus products, and circulate them as commodities. The commune was the producer of the commodities, but the state (the Oriental despot) their possessor. This kind of commodity production based on the primitive community is realized by means of tribute relations with the state. Only when a tributary (i.e., tribute-collecting) state exists is there someone to own and sell the products as commodities.[29] Both components are necessary for commodities to circulate: the primitive community at the one end of the tribute relationship represents the AMP, and the tributary state at the other end is the Oriental despot. What the state is collecting from the primitive communities is tribute; only when this tribute reaches the hands of the state does it become a commodity.

The Role of River-Based Irrigation in the AMP

Another problem with the mismarriage of the AMP to Oriental despotism is its appeal to geographical determinism through artificial irrigation. Many have incorrectly combined the AMP, Oriental despotism, and river-based irrigation to argue that Asia was either a unique socioeconomic formation (the "Oriental despotism" thesis) or a special kind of slave society (the "ancient Orient" thesis).[30]

Both theses accept that the despotic state, state landownership, and slave class relations must be attributed to artificial irrigation. They argue that this is Marx's theory, yet neither Marx nor Engels said anything of the sort. Engels touches on this question in *Anti-Dühring* when he says that irrigation in the East was a type of "common interest" which primitive groups of communities banded together to protect, leading to the formation of the state.[31] Hydraulic projects are simply part of the "common interest" and need not give rise to a despotic political form, although the centralization of power and the unification of a despotic empire could propel the development of artificial irrigation enormously.

The earliest states to appear—the city-states of Sumer, the Indian republics—were not despotic. They did not emerge within river systems; furthermore, the Aegean area of civilization had neither a great river nor a despotic empire. The notion that geographical factors determine the political systems of antiquity certainly does not apply to the Fertile Crescent. What first appeared there were city-state republics, and their hydraulic works did not lead to despotic political rule. In the northern part of this region, where the Assyrian empire arose, there was no need for the sort of irrigation that was found on river plains. Agriculture prospered early on, and the first state was not a despotic empire but an aristocratic republic.

Hydraulic projects, in terms of Marx's theory, are simply one type of variable social function. The great constructions of the Mycenaeans, the Greeks, and the Etruscans are another type of social function. Social functions can only serve political control once classes have differentiated and begun to struggle. The presence of hydraulic projects managed by village communities does not produce class society, the state, or political rule. That can only happen once class differences have emerged and the privileged class seeks to use such functions to serve political goals. Just as these social functions are not restricted to irrigation, so also they are not found only in the East but are universal.

We must accordingly abandon the notion that riverine culture or hydraulic projects caused the appearance of class society or the state in the East. The geographical environment of a society influences its development, but in different ways and at different stages of that development, and never in a way that is decisive. Natural conditions can affect livelihood and the "productiveness of labor," which in turn can play a decisive role depending on the degree to which a society can master and exploit the resources of its environment, and this will vary over time.[32] The danger is to view the role of the geographical environment too mechanistically. It serves simply to provide possible conditions for the creation of surplus value or surplus products: it does not realize them. That depends on society.

During the epoch of the AMP primitive community, agriculture developed. It did so in China not within a large river basin but in the highlands along the edge of the Yellow River. Artificial irrigation thus bore no significant relationship to Oriental communal ownership. Such a relationship developed in China only after the community came under the power of the despotic state. Communal, closed, and isolated, these communities let the responsibility for managing hydraulic resources fall into the hands of the state. As Marx observed of India, the regulation of water supply there became "one of the material bases of the power of the State over the small disconnected producing organisms."[33] But as for the birth of despotic empires and the origin of despotism, river-based irrigation determined nothing.

The AMP in Marx's and Engels' Later Years

To solve the false problem of the AMP, some scholars have faulted the sources that Marx used before the 1870s and argued that Marx and Engels changed their view of the AMP after reading Morgan and Kovalev. This is pure fantasy. Engels may not directly mention the AMP in *The Origin of the Family, Private Property and the State*, but this does not mean that the content of the concept is absent from that work. In fact, it systematizes and deepens the study of the key question of the AMP, primitive communal ownership, by seeking to understand how clan society with public ownership was replaced by class society with private ownership. This concern perfectly complements Marx's discussion of the AMP in the Preface.

In a note to the 1888 English edition of the *Manifesto of the Communist Party*, Engels does say that at the time the *Manifesto* was written in 1847, prehistoric social organization was little understood. As village communities came to be recognized as the universal primitive formation and Morgan discovered the nature of the clan and its relation to the tribe, "the inner organization of this primitive Communistic society was laid bare, in its typical form."[34] All of the work of Marx and Engels in the 1880s and 1890s thus deepened and broadened their earlier research on the AMP and Oriental communal ownership.[35]

When and where did Marx and Engels ever speak of having changed their minds about the AMP? When and where did they say, directly or indirectly, that they no longer found the concept or the term useful? Like many other terms in their writings, such as "tribal ownership," the "AMP" only appears a few times: mostly in the late 1850s, less frequently in the 1860s and 1870s, and hardly at all in the 1880s and 1890s. Yet this is hardly a significant decrease. As we have already pointed out, Marx and Engels tended simply to make use of other terms to signify the primitive period. One term that appears rather late, in Engels' preface to the 1887 American edition of *The Condition of the Working Class in England*, is "Asiatic antiquity." This term, however, bears no relationship to the AMP but refers rather to the ancient [slave] mode of production in the East, for it appears in the phrase "in Asiatic and classical antiquity, the predominant form of class oppression was slavery."[36] The members of the AMP village communities, though they may have seemed like slaves to the despot,[37] did not have their persons appropriated by the despot; so also their land was not appropriated. Thus, the reference to "Asiatic antiquity" in this passage cannot signify AMP communal ownership, nor can the phrase "Asiatic and classical antiquity" be used to prove that the AMP and classical antiquity existed side by side in the ancient world as two kinds of slave society.[38]

The AMP as Problematic

The AMP was something that Marx himself formulated, but it was not a problem for either him or Engels. When Lenin quoted from Marx's works bearing on the AMP, he respected the original formulation of this mode of production and also saw no problem with it.[39] The AMP became problematic only after Lenin's death, beginning late in the 1920s. It was at this time that revolutionary movements in the East, including the Communist-led Chinese revolution then in its bourgeois phase, were flourishing, so questions concerning Oriental history and the character of its society sparked heated debates in the Soviet Union. The first to take part were mostly political theorists and activists, but by the early 1930s historians and sociologists had joined in. A whole series of fundamental questions was posed: What was the AMP? Could the history of the East be divided according the five modes of production and five stages used to analyze Europe? Had there ever been slave society in the East?

In the course of discussion, some argued for fundamental differences between the East and the West. In the East, they said, primitive communalism was followed not by slavery and feudalism but by a special form of AMP society which remained until disturbed by the colonialism of Western capitalism. Others suggested that the East had a prolonged feudal period. Opposing East and

West in this fashion—placing them on different paths of development—amounts to a multiorigin and multilinear view of history.[40]

The earliest advocates of the AMP's peculiarity were political commentators, and in the 1930s this group lost out.[41] Of the later entrants into the debate, the historian Vasilii Struve (1889–1965) was one of the most vocal. Through the 1930s and 1940s he insisted that Oriental history had seen slavery, in accordance with the scheme of five modes of production. Criticized both politically and academically, the AMP was put aside in the Soviet Union.[42] It was also during this period that Josef Stalin's *Dialectical and Historical Materialism* and Marx's *Pre-Capitalist Economic Formations* were published, both of which lent strength to the rejection of AMP peculiarity and the permanent feudalism thesis and helped to confirm the view that there were five modes of production and five historical stages.[43] Multilinearity was rejected in favor of unilinearity. Struve's "ancient Orient" thesis triumphed.[44]

There are many differences within the "ancient Orient" school. All agree that the East had slavery, one of the necessary five modes of production, but thereafter their views divide. A. I. Tiumenev (1880–1957) argued for a total dissimilarity between Eastern and Western culture, picturing Near Eastern and classical Greco-Roman culture as separate types of slavery. Struve saw the ancient Orient as an early slave society that existed before the slavery of the classical world. Still, both share the view that Oriental countries arose out of the need for artificial irrigation and were despotic from the start. Add to this their common acceptance of state ownership of land, the bondage of the peasantry to the state, and general slavery, and the "ancient Orient" approach shows itself to be a descendant of the AMP peculiarity thesis. Both schools base themselves ultimately on environmental determinism.

The first round of controversy over the AMP thus produced no resolution. The victory of the "ancient Orient" thesis proved to be short-lived. A second round began in the late 1950s, and by the early 1970s it had reversed the earlier decision. The controversy intensified in 1964 when Evgenii Varga in the closing chapter of his *Outline of Capitalist Political Economics* attacked Struve on the issue of the AMP. The debate spread among Soviet and foreign scholars, producing a series of books on the topic in the West in the 1970s, including translations of some of Marx's previously un-published manuscripts.[45] On the positive side, this controversy promoted considerable work in historical theory and comparative studies.[46] But the question itself remained unsolved, and Soviet scholars after two decades of debate have basically returned to Struvian orthodoxy.[47]

During the half-century when Marx, Engels, and Lenin were writing, the AMP was not problematic. From the 1920s to the 1970s, the debate went in circles. In the last half-century, anthro-pology and archaeology have made remarkable advances world-wide, yielding rich new findings concerning the history of both primitive and slave society. The Soviet Union is no exception. Why, then, has theoretical work not kept pace with scientific inves-tigation? Is dogmatism the problem? After all, the AMP is Marx's. But the problem is not. It is the product of an erroneous inter-pretation of Marx. Restore the AMP to its original guise, and the problem is rendered unproblematic.

The study of ancient history in the East need not be restricted by concepts like the AMP, since the primitive communal owner-ship it represents is to be found in the early history of all civiliza-tions. Marx and Engels never intended that the theoretical con-struct of the AMP be used to fetter the social reality of Oriental antiquity. The term after all appears only a few times in their writ-ings. In studying such a vast topic we must not allow ourselves to be trapped in empty theorizing about the AMP. There is no need to turn something as simple and straightforward as Marx's AMP into a quandary. The essential thing is to distinguish what Marx said about the AMP from the problem that others have mistakenly fabricated around it.

Notes

1. *CCPE*, p. 21.
2. Ibid., p. 33.
3. Marx, *Capital*, vol. 1 (New York: International Publishers, 1967), pp. 77–78.
4. Ibid., p. 79.
5. Marx, *Grundrisse* (Harmondsworth: Penguin, 1973), p. 106.
6. Marx and Engels, *Manifesto of the Communist Party* (Beijing: Foreign Lan-guages Press, 1965), p. 32.

7. Marx to Engels, March 14, 1868, in *PCEF*, p. 139.

8. G.W.F. Hegel, *The Philosophy of History* (New York: Dover, 1956), pp. 18–19.

9. Cf. Engels, "The Condition of England: The English Constitution," *MECW*, 3:489.

10. K. Marx and F. Engels, *The German Ideology* (New York: International Publishers, 1970), p. 43.

11. Engels in "The Principles of Communism" (*MECW*, 6:343) and Marx in *Wage Labor and Capital* (*MECW*, 9:212), both written in 1847, deal with class oppression and exploitation in history, tracing a development from slave to serf to wage laborer. Change is plotted in terms of property and class relations; history is the history of classes. Similarly, in the *Manifesto of the Communist Party*, written the following winter, historical stages are delineated in relation to the forms of class antagonism and class struggle, thereby laying a scientific basis for the periodization of the history of civilization into ancient, medieval, and modern. Since they discuss only the history of class society or civilization, prehistory or primitive history is not mentioned. Hence "tribal ownership" does not make an appearance in these works.

12. *PCEF*, p. 68.

13. Marx to Engels, March 18, 1852, *MECW*, 39:67.

14. Engels, "On Social Relations in Russia," in Marx and Engels, *Selected Works*, vol. 2 (Moscow: Foreign Languages Publishing House, 1958), p. 55.

15. E.g., Marx, "Elections—Financial Clouds—The Duchess of Sutherland and Slavery" (January 2, 1853), *MECW*, 11:488. Marx to Engels, June 2, 1853; Engels to Marx, June 6, 1853; Marx to Engels, June 14, 1853; Marx, "The British Rule in India"; idem., "The Future Results of the British Rule in India," reprinted in Marx and Engels, *On Colonialism* (New York: International Publishers, 1972), pp. 35–41, 81–87, 313–17.

16. Very occasionally they make reference to primary sources, as Marx does in a letter to Engels, citing the ancient Hindu law code known as Manu (Marx to Engels, June 14, 1853, in *On Colonialism*, p. 317).

17. *CCPE*, p. 33; Marx to Engels, March 14, 1868, in *PCEF*, p. 139.

18. Marx to Kugelmann, February 17, 1870, in *The Letters of Karl Marx*, ed. S. K. Padover (Englewood Cliffs, N.J.: Prentice Hall, 1979), p. 268.

19. Engels, "On Social Relations in Russia," p. 56.

20. Engels' footnote to the English edition of the *Manifesto of the Communist Party*, p. 32.

21. Marx, *Grundrisse*, p. 88.

22. Editor's note: A paragraph on the dissolution of the primitive commune has been omitted.

23. *PCEF*, p. 69.

24. Marx, "The British Rule in India," p. 40; cf. Engels, *Anti-Dühring* (Moscow: Foreign Languages Publishing House, 1962), p. 250.

25. Marx, "Chinese Affairs" (1862), *MECW*, 19:216; see also *Capital*, 1:358.

26. Marx and Engels, *Selected Correspondence* (Moscow: Progress Publishers, 1965), p. 385.

27. Engels to Kautsky, February 16, 1884, in *On Colonialism*, p. 344.

28. Marx, *Capital*, 3:791. Editor's note: The Chinese translation of "supreme lord" as "supreme landlord" (*MEQJ*, 25:891) may have induced the authors to treat the rent/tax couple as unproblematic, whereas some Western scholars have viewed it as incapable of generating a distinct AMP. See, for example, Barry Hindess and Paul Hirst, *Pre-Capitalist Modes of Production* (London: Routledge and Kegan Paul, 1975), pp. 193–200.

29. Marx, *Capital*, 3:325–26, 331.

30. We have criticized the "Oriental despotism" and "ancient Orient" theses in our *Shijie shanggu shigang*, 1:126–27. We have taken the term "ancient Orient" from the title of a paper by the Egyptologist M. A. Korostovtsev, "O poniatii 'Drevnii Vostok'" (The "ancient Orient" concept), *Vestnik drevnei istorii* (Journal of ancient history) 1 (1970): 3–17.

31. Engels, *Anti-Dühring*, p. 205.

32. Marx, *Capital*, 1:512, 514.

33. Ibid., p. 514n.2.

34. Marx and Engels, *Manifesto of the Communist Party*, p. 32.

35. E.g., Marx to Zasulich, March 8, 1881; Engels, "A Contribution to the Early History of the Germans" (1881–82), "The Frankish Period," (1881–82), "The Mark" (1882), "The Afterword to 'Soziales aus Russland' " (1894), in *PCSF*, pp. 274–388, 475–81. See also volumes 2 and 3 of *Capital*, which Engels edited, as well as Engels' letters to Bebel, Kautsky, Danielson, and Lafargue.

36. Engels, *The Condition of the Working Class in England* (Oxford: Basil Blackwell, 1958), p. 355.

37. "Slavery, . . . where the labourer himself appears among the natural conditions of production for a third individual or community, . . . does *not* apply to the general slavery of the Orient, which is so considered *only* from the European point of view" (*PCEF*, p. 95).

38. Editor's note: A further paragraph on Engels' argument in the 1887 preface to *The Condition of the Working Class in England* has been omitted.

39. E.g., Lenin, "What the 'Friends of the People' Are and How They Fight the Social-Democrats" (1894), *LCW*, 1:139; "Karl Marx" (1915), *LCW*, 21:56. In his critique of Plekhanov, Lenin sought to distinguish between the basis for the national ownership of land before Peter the Great (which he refers to as the "Asian mode of production") and the capitalist mode that was established in Russia by the second half of the nineteenth century ("Report on the Stockholm Congress of the Russian Social Democratic Workers' Party," *LCW*, 10:332). Again, Lenin did not view the AMP as problematic.

Editor's note: The authors have misread the Stockholm Report as indicating Lenin's approval of the notion that pre-Petrine Russia was dominated by the AMP, when in fact he is making a rhetorical supposition that he himself rejects. See Stephen Dunn, *The Fall and Rise of the Asiatic Mode of Production* (London: Routledge and Kegan Paul, 1982), pp. 16–17. Among Lenin's references to things "Asiatic" might be added the comment in his first essay on China, published in the inaugural issue of *Iskra* in December 1900, that China is "an Asiatic government that squeezes taxes from the starving peasantry" (*LCW*, 4:377).

40. Lenin, in a lecture delivered in 1919, argued for the unilinearity of historical development ("The State," *LCW*, 29:470–88).

41. Much later, in 1962, Evgenii Varga charged in his *Outline of Capitalist Political Economics*: "The concept of the 'AMP' has been banished from the writings of us Marxists. You do not see it either in political economics texts or in texts on Marxism-Leninism. There is not even a listing for the topic in the fifty-odd volumes of the *Great Soviet Encyclopedia*."

42. One of these was Karl Wittfogel, who by his own account was criticized in 1932 and thereafter could get nothing published in the USSR (*Oriental Despotism: A Comparative Study of Total Power* [New Haven: Yale University Press, 1957], p. 6).

43. Editor's note: The authors' evaluation of *Pre-Capitalist Economic Formations* as discouraging support for the AMP flies in the face of most evaluations of that book's implications.

44. See above, note 30.

45. E.g., Lawrence Krader, *The Ethnological Notebooks of Karl Marx* (Assen: Van Gorcum, 1972).

46. E.g., I. M. D'iakonov, "Slaves, Helots, and Serfs in Early Antiquity," *Soviet Anthropology and Archaeology* 15, 2–3 (1976–77): 50–102.

47. *Istoria drevnego vostoka* (A history of the ancient Orient), published in Russian in 1979, once again divides the ancient world into East and West: the former is plagued with slower development, economic stagnation, and a limited division of labor, its slave relations lacking the depth and breadth of the Greco-Roman. Although the book argues that irrigation stimulated the birth of the despotic state, its argument is more nuanced, noting the existence of primitive monarchy prior to the appearance of despotism, and acknowledging that despotism was not universal in the East. Its shortcoming is its cyclical return—to geographic determinism.

ZHU JIAZHEN

6 | Some Questions Concerning Research on the Theory of the Asiatic Mode of Production

In the sixty years since the Asiatic mode of production (AMP) became an issue of theory within Marxism, a wide-ranging academic debate has gone on both inside and outside China. Although the debate has yielded certain results at the level of theory and has encouraged work on historical evidence, it remains unresolved.

The debate has focused principally on the character of AMP society. Initially, Georgii Plekhanov (1856–1918), Lajos Magyar (1891–1940), and Evgenii Varga held that the AMP was a special mode of production unique to Oriental society and not to be found in the history of Western society. Recently, Umberto Melotti of Italy has advocated that the AMP be considered the sixth mode of production, but this simply continues and extends the notion of Oriental society as special. When the views of Magyar and others came under attack in the Soviet Union, Mikhail Godes proposed the "hypothesis view," which was that the AMP was a "hypothesis" Marx formulated prior to having read Lewis Morgan's *Ancient Society*. Alternatively, Sergei Kovalev (1886–1960) advocated the "variant view," which was that the AMP was a variant of slavery and contributed to the emergence of an Oriental variant of feudalism in the Orient. Lei Hade and Hayakawa Jiro, among others, held that the AMP was a transitional formation between the primi-

From *Jingji yanjiu* (Studies in economics) 6 (1982): 58–64. Translated by Timothy Brook. This article is an abridged version of Zhu Jiazhen (1983).

tive period and slavery. S. M. Dubrovsky opposed the idea of a unique Asiatic mode, arguing that it was simply the feudal mode of production. At roughly the same time, Guo Moruo (1892–1978) and Wang Yanan (1901–1969) in China, M. N. Roy in India, and Moritani Katsumi (1904–1964) in Japan all maintained that the AMP denoted the stage of primitive society directly preceding the period of slavery. Taking a different view, Lü Zhenyu (1900–1980) and Hou Wailu felt that the AMP was a kind of slavery different from that of ancient Greece and Rome.

In the 1950s, Vasilii Struve (1889–1965) and Mikhail Diakonov (1907–1954) among Soviet scholars held that the AMP signified a stage of primitive or domestic slavery prior to the slavery of the classical world. On the other hand, A. I. Tiumenev (1880–1957) argued that the Orient and the classical world had two completely different kinds of slavery that bore no sequential relationship with each other. Among Chinese scholars in this decade, Tong Shuye (1908–1968) and Tian Changwu strengthened the arguments upholding the view that the AMP was a representative form of the primitive mode of production. Concurrently, Wu Ze and Ri Zhi sought to strengthen the view that it represented slave society.

Since the smashing of the "Gang of Four" [1976], the academic world in China, responding to the new creative atmosphere at home and to the global discussion on Third World development, has taken up theoretical study of the question of the AMP. This has produced quite a number of research papers and academic conferences in the past few years. In the course of this discussion, divergent views on certain issues have gradually moved toward a consensus. For instance, many now see the AMP as the early expression by Marx and Engels in theoretical terms of the primitive mode of production. Nonetheless, considerable differences in interpretation remain over a broad range of issues. In this essay I raise a few questions that have come up in the course of theoretical research on the AMP.

The Theory of the AMP and Historical Materialism

For a long time now, many people have consistently understood the AMP as both a concrete social formation and a theory of the character of society that Marx used to evaluate Oriental or ancient Oriental society. I believe that nothing could be further from the truth, and yet many of the theoretical arguments that have been put forward find their bases in these assumptions.

Marx first mentioned the theoretical concept of the AMP in 1859 in his Preface to *A Contribution to the Critique of Political Economy*. In addition to describing the process by which he pursued his own research in political economy, Marx discusses the principles of historical materialism guiding this research and the scientific conclusions that flow from it. After laying out his classic formulations concerning the relationships between the forces and relations of production, and between the economic base and the superstructure, Marx states that "in broad outline, the Asiatic, ancient, feudal and modern bourgeois modes of production may be designated as epochs marking progress in the economic development of society."[1] It is not difficult to see that Marx in this passage is using the principles of historical materialism to examine the rules by which the history of human society has progressed. Since the AMP is here put forward as an economic form of society representing a specific period in the historical development of society, we can see that its logical point of departure is not some specific, concrete Oriental society, but the history of society in general.

In his review of the *Critique*, Engels observed that Marx was writing in the proletarian tradition of German political economy: its essential foundation "is the materialist conception of history whose principle features are briefly outlined in the 'Preface' to the above-named work."[2] Lenin similarly recognized that what Marx was laying out in his Preface was "the fundamental principles of materialism as applied to human society and its history" universally.[3] Some have nonetheless chosen to disregard these evaluations. Zhang Yaqin and Bai Jinfu, for instance, hold that the various periods in the development of the economic forms of society "most certainly do not constitute a high-level generalization concerning the rules of development for all society, but rather provide a scientific summary of the historical process by which the economic rules of capitalism took form." In this view, to regard the Preface as explicating the general rules by which all human society developed would be "to treat the AMP as a social formation or a stage in the development of society and then forcibly insert it into the historical sequence of social development. This conflates the various periods in the development of the economic forms of society, which Marx identified through political-economic analysis, with Marxism's general rules for the development of all society."[4]

This interpretation is very difficult to sustain. It disregards the fact that after Marx proposed in the Preface the various periods for the development of the economic forms of society, he went on to say: "The bourgeois mode of production is the last antagonistic form of the social process of production. . . . The prehistory of human society accordingly closes with this social formation."[5] In this passage, Marx views capitalist relations of production both as a period in the evolution of the economic forms of society and as a social formation in the history of human society. Why should we try to deny that Marx himself "conflated" "two things that belong to different scientific categories," when clearly he saw them as being one and the same thing? The economic forms of society of which Marx spoke in the Preface are set out as modes of production in general that have existed throughout history; their evolution is accordingly also the evolution of the social formations of all societies. Only by using the principles of historical materialism to examine the evolution of the economic forms of society through history can we correctly understand the historical development of all societies.

Although pre-Marxist historians and sociologists provided a wealth of descriptions of the history of societies, they had no way to grasp the rules of social evolution. By basing his explanation in the Preface on the relationships between the forces and relations of production, economic base and superstructure, and social consciousness and social existence, Marx discovered the objective laws governing the economic forms of society and was for the first time able to formulate laws of development applicable to all societies. Marx's thinking here is completely in agreement with what he calls his "standpoint" in the Preface to the first German edition of *Capital*, that "the evolution of the economic formation of society is viewed as a process of natural history." What the Preface lays out is not just "the historical process of the formation of the economic rules of capitalism," but "the materialist principles of human society and the history of human society."[6] This implies that, in theoretical terms, the AMP is both a general historical mode of production and a period in the organic evolution of human society. The AMP is therefore an organic component in the theoretical system of historical materialism.

The AMP and Asian/Oriental Society

Marxists who debated the AMP in the early 1920s all approached it right from the beginning as a theory that Asian/Oriental society was special. Thereafter, though many criticized this view, they still continued to regard the AMP as a theory by which to evaluate the character of Oriental society. Even today, many scholars both in China and abroad study the AMP as a uniquely Asian/Oriental social formation. They fail either to understand or to recognize that in the Preface, Marx proposed the AMP as a mode of production in general; more specifically, that the AMP was Marx's theoretical generalization for the economic form of society in the primitive period. They consistently bring up such issues as despotism, monarchy, slavery, serfdom, and the unity of rent and tax—all of which are characteristic of class society and which Marx mentions in his discussions of the AMP—to deny that the AMP refers to primitive society. I believe that this derives from their failure to understand the methodology behind Marx's references to the AMP.

Just like the slave, feudal, and capitalist modes of production, the AMP presents a theoretical generalization—in this case, of the primitive relations of production that had survived in the societies of Asia, Africa, the Americas, and Europe late into the nineteenth century. To grasp this point correctly, it is essential to draw on the methodology used in *Capital*. The object of analysis in *Capital* is capitalist class society, but it is not any particular capitalist class society. Although England is constantly referred to in the work, this is simply because it serves, as Marx says, "as the chief illustration in the development of my theoretical ideas."[7] *Capital* does not present an analysis of any particular society, not even England's. What it analyzes is the capitalist mode of production in general, which exists in a real sense in all capitalist societies, yet not in a pure form. England is different from France, France from Germany, Germany from the United States, and so forth. It is accordingly inappropriate to maintain that when Marx refers to England, he is analyzing English society in particular. He does this simply to explain the (abstract) theory of the capitalist mode of production in palpable form.

This method of theoretical study in Marx is also the method by which we should study the AMP. Early in the 1850s, when Marx and Engels were researching the relations of production in primitive society, they took their material from the primitive formations surviving among the backward peoples of Asia, Africa, the Americas, and Europe, though from Asia more than the others, and in particular from the village system that still existed in India. Taking this village system as his model, Marx created the theoretical concept of the AMP in the course of generalizing about a social formation based on public property (principally public property in land). What it generalizes, therefore, is only the primitive relations of production as they then existed within particular class societies, not their social formations. It is patently obvious that the concrete social historical conditions of the Indian village, the Russian *mir*, the German *mark*, and the Celtic clan when Marx studied them were all different from each other. The Indian village existed under the feudal system (and also under colonialism after the English had occupied India), the *mir* under capitalist conditions, and so forth. To generalize from these societies, which existed under different historical conditions and at different stages of social development, to create a common, particular mode of social production is not only impossible but would run completely counter to the most basic understanding of Marxist theory. It is not important whether the village or *mark* or clan existed under a despotic or democratic system, or under slave, serf, or capitalist conditions. What is essential is to distinguish between the AMP as a mode of production in general and historical conditions found in particular Asian societies.

From a parenthetical reference by Marx to the "Asiatic communal system" as "primitive communism" in *Theories of Surplus Value*,[8] we can see that he took the AMP to be a mode of production in general. Of this type of commune in India, Marx said: "Within them there is slavery and the caste system"; and again: "We must not forget that these little communities were contaminated by distinctions of caste and by slavery."[9] Here he is saying that because it had passed through slave society, the village community in India unavoidably bore the scars of slavery, not that the village system as it then existed was a form of primitive communism or slavery. In "The Future Results of the British Rule in India," he says: "England has to fulfill a double mission in India: one destructive, the other regenerating—the annihilation of old Asiatic society, and the laying of the material foundation of Western society in Asia."[10] "Asiatic society" here means the feudal society of India within which remnants of the AMP continued to exist; "Western society" means capitalist society. The depiction of social relations in Asia given in volume 3 of *Capital*—of producers "under direct subordination to a state which stands over them as their landlord and simultaneously as sovereign"[11]—similarly describes feudal society.

In the same vein, Marx's concept of "Oriental despotism," which he invoked to characterize particular social systems, is different from the AMP, which is a mode of production, and hence an abstraction.[12] This is a methodological question on which Marx reflected in *Capital*. There he seeks to create the abstraction of the capitalist mode of production on the basis of the concrete capitalist society he observed in England. He says in his Preface to the first German edition that he is concerned with distilling "the natural laws of capitalist production," not with providing a study of England.[13] Marx's methodology therefore requires that we distinguish between particular cases and theoretical abstraction. Failure to do so will create confusion about his theoretical concepts, which are not limited to describing particular societies but must be evaluated as abstractions.

The AMP in Relation to Slavery and Serfdom

Marx and Engels formulated the theory of the AMP to characterize the primitive mode of production as revealed in village systems throughout the world, though mainly in Asia, particularly India. The village community in itself, however, is certainly not an independent socioeconomic formation. It is "the last phase or period of the ancient formation of society," "a transitional phase from common property to private property, from a primary formation to a secondary one."[14] Once they had entered class society, village communities in many areas, and especially in Oriental countries, were preserved over a long period of time, some passing through slave and feudal society, some even surviving all the way down to the capitalist period.

Not only was the village community incomprehensible to Alexander Herzen (1812–1870), Mikhail Bakunin (1814–1876), and Petr Tkachev (1844–1885), but it grew into an utterly remarkable thing in their hands, thereby generating misconceptions among some Marxist historians. Some used historical evidence that these village communities existed in the slave period to equate the village system with slavery, leading them to argue that the AMP is Oriental slavery. Others followed the same logic to equate the village system with feudalism, concluding in turn that the AMP is Oriental feudalism. Guo Moruo maintained that in China's ancient period the internal structure of communities "in slave society was determined by the slave mode of production."[15] To affirm that the village communities in slave society were part of the slave system, he raised the notion of a so-called collective slavery, maintaining that villagers were without exception "collective slaves." On the other hand, Godes and Dubrovsky took the existence of village communities in the feudal period as evidence that the AMP was Oriental feudalism. Some Chinese scholars hold a similar view.

The system of village communities is in essence different from slavery or serfdom. In history, slavery appeared in opposition to the village community: it did not evolve out of relations internal to the village community but negated community relations. The village system protects equality and mutual aid among members and in itself is not a condition for class differentiation. As Engels observed: "In the tribal or village community with common ownership of land . . . a fairly equal distribution of products is a matter of course; where considerable inequality of distribution among the members of the community sets in, this is an indication that the community is already beginning to break up."[16] Equitably distributing land and guaranteeing generally equal conditions of production for members are basic principles of the commune. Hence it cannot produce the conditions for enslaving or exploiting its own members. As we read in *Mencius*, within the village community all are expected to "befriend one another both at home and abroad, help each other to keep watch, and succor each other in illness."[17] Mutual cooperation among village members is a sign of the status and relationship among the direct producers in the process of production. The appearance of class differences within the community is due to improvement in the forces of production, followed in turn by the development of commodity exchange, the widening of the gap between rich and poor, the emergence of a clan aristocracy, and eventually the appearance of relations of exploitation and enslavement. This kind of relation, however, does not appear within a clan but is formed with people outside the clan, tribe, or community. As Engels pointed out, once the forces of production have developed to a sufficiently high level, the product of labor exceeds what is necessary for its basic subsistence, which paves the way for putting this labor to use. The community on its own, however, is unable to furnish surplus labor that it can control in this way; hence, at this point, it is war that furnishes this kind of labor. Whereas in the past hostages were executed or eaten, at this later stage "one let them live and made use of their labor. Thus, . . . slavery had been invented."[18] Hostage-taking in war was the true origin of slavery.

This initial enslavement through warfare took place outside the agricultural community. Within the village, among members of the same clan, mutual equality was still maintained by custom. It was impermissible for the primitive leader to make use of this wealth to exploit other members within his community. On the contrary, those with wealth had a duty to help their comembers. In the rural communities of the Jingpo nationality in Dehong district in Yunnan province, for example, villagers in straitened circumstances can go to the families of fellow villagers, even to the families of clan members living outside their village, "to eat plain rice," as the expression goes. They can also demand assistance from the village headman, who has a certain duty to help households in difficulty. So long as the status of community member exists, slave or serf relations cannot develop between members. Even though free men sank into debt slavery in the classical ancient period, they did not constitute the base of a mode of social production. Theirs was simply a relationship of bondage within a slave society whose foundation was the hostage slave.

Once the origin of slavery is understood in this way, we can identify the unique characteristic of the slave mode of production, which is that slaves can be killed with impunity. Among all the social formations in human history, slavery is the only one under which the slave is reduced to being an object of slaughter. This has nothing to do with the debased character of his status but derives from the fact that he was originally an enemy. On the principle of the fewer the enemy the better, hostages had to be exterminated. It was only as the forces of production developed that the hostage was no longer killed but enslaved, but his identity was still that of an enemy, and hence the slave could still be killed. The study of political economy recognizes this as the essential characteristic of the relations of production under slavery. Within the agricultural community, however, among members of the same clan or the same tribe, even between the nobility and the common people, all were jointly members of the same community (*gongtongti*).

The village system and slavery thus imply two essentially different relations of production. Even though wealthy households in a village might have slaves, the relationship between community members was not thereby transformed into that of master and slave, nor was the village system thereby transformed into slavery. The difference in the nature of these systems meant that the village community existed alongside, rather than within, slavery. It could suffer the exploitation and servitude imposed by the political power of the slave masters, yet the villagers were either free or unfree peasants, not slaves. Their exploitation or servitude did not belong within the category of slavery.

Scholars in China who uphold the theory of "collective slavery," however, confuse the exploited village peasants with slaves, and hence equate the system of agricultural communities with slavery. They maintain that the villages of the Western Zhou dynasty (eleventh to eighth century B.C.) "very much resembled labor concentration camps," and that the villagers had become "collective slaves" in "labor camps under the control of the slave masters."[19] Even though the villagers suffered exploitation and servitude in various forms, their suffering did not make them slaves. The extreme servitude of Russian serfs moved Lenin to observe that their position was no different from that of slaves, yet this is not to say that Russian serfs were slaves, nor that serfdom can be interpreted as slavery. However much an agricultural community in the Western Zhou may have seemed like a labor concentration camp, it in fact was not. The slave master may have "controlled" the village, but the villagers were not his "collective slaves."

In the ancient period, the slave had a clear, specific class status, independent of the degree of his exploitation or servitude. Some, like domestic slaves or personal retainers, could enjoy a better livelihood or treatment than ordinary laboring slaves, but this did not alter their status. As an economic form of society, slavery is a precisely defined category: the master directly and completely owned the person of the slave, and the slave was nothing but his master's living "possession." The degree of exploitation or servitude has nothing to do with it. Accordingly, the notion of "collective slaves" is theoretically incoherent. Proponents of the "collective slave" view nonetheless invoke Marx's comment about "the general slavery of the orient"[20] in their defense. I maintain that this is based on a mistaken understanding. What Marx meant by "generalized slavery" was not slavery in the sense of an economic form of society, but the servitude of the peasants under the rule of despotic lords. It is slavery in a metaphorical sense only.

We can find similar usages elsewhere in Marx's writings. In *The Poverty of Philosophy* and in his letter to Pavel Annenkov, for instance, Marx speaks of "indirect slavery" and "direct slavery." He says: "I do not mean indirect slavery, the slavery of the proletariat; I mean direct slavery, the slavery of the Blacks in Surinam, in Brazil, in the southern regions of North America."[21] "Indirect slavery" he uses to describe capitalist servitude, and "direct slavery" to describe capitalism's enslavement of black slaves. We would never conclude from this comment about indirect slavery that capitalism is a form of slavery. Again, in the *Communist Manifesto* he calls the working class "slaves of the bourgeois class, and of the bourgeois state," and in chapter 13 of *Capital* he refers to the workers under capitalism as "slave-labor."[22] "Slave" and "slavery" are simply being used metaphorically and do not mean slavery in the sense of a socioeconomic formation. Marx's reference to "generalized slavery" falls within the same category of metaphor, and any attempt to use the phrase to create a special form of slavery for China, such as "collective slavery," stems from a failure to recognize this simple fact.

Whereas the village system in slave society may be said to have existed alongside slavery, in feudal society it existed not alongside the feudal economy but within it. Indeed, the village system became an integral component of the feudal economy. The village mode of production did not fit with the slave economy, but it could readily mesh with the feudal economy. This is because the village economy was an economy of independent small producers, and as such it could serve as feudalism's basis of production. What the slave economy demanded was production without individual character or independent management, since the individual laborer was completely possessed by the conditions of his labor. What the feudal economy needed, on the other hand, were laborers with a certain independence who could take initiative in production and were able to manage themselves, which was possible when they were not completely owned but were nonetheless tied to the land. Accordingly, it was only in places where the rulers took over the ownership of land and reduced the villagers to the position of being tied to the land—thereby establishing the basis for feudal ties—that the village community was drawn into the feudal economic system and made the foundation of the feudal economy.

In his description of the emergence of serf relations in Poland and Romania, Marx pointed out how "military and clerical dignitaries usurped, along with the common land, the labor spent upon it. The labor of the free peasants on their common land was transformed into corvée for the thieves of the common land."[23] What Marx reveals here of the process of the feudalization of the village community has important theoretical significance for understanding the character of change in the village system. It argues that within feudal society the village community becomes the basis of the feudal economy and hence comes to be imbued with a distinctly feudal character. The feudalization of the community, however, only explains its character subsequent to its having already changed. We cannot extrapolate backward from its feudal character to understand the character of the AMP.

The AMP is an integral, historically formulated component in the theoretical system of historical materialism. We should therefore treat it historically and distinguish it both from particular Asian/Oriental societies and from slavery and serfdom. Only in this way can we escape from the "Asiatic fantasy" generated by later thinkers who have not understood the concept. When Marx and Engels were investigating the AMP, they came up with many perceptive arguments concerning Asian societies, and these constitute an extremely valuable resource for those of us who study Asia. But it is only after clarifying the basic meaning of the theoretical concept of the AMP [as primitive society] that we can more effectively apply the theoretical resources of Marxism to substantive research.

Notes

1. *CCPE*, p. 21.
2. *CCPE*, p. 220.
3. Lenin, "Karl Marx," *LCW* 21:55. Marx himself, in a passing reference to the *Critique* in the afterword to the second German edition of *Capital*, says that the Preface is "where I discuss the materialistic basis of my method" (*Capital*, vol. 1 [New York: International Publishers, 1967], p. 17).
4. Zhang Yaqin and Bai Jinfu, "Yaxiya shengchan fangshi yanjiu de fangfa wenti," *Xuexi yu tansuo* 1 (1981).
5. *CCPE*, pp. 21–22.
6. Marx, *Capital*, 1:10.
7. Marx, "Preface to the First German Edition," in ibid, p. 8.
8. Marx, *Theories of Surplus Value* (Moscow: Progress Publishers, 1971), pt. 3, p. 423.
9. Marx to Engels, June 14, 1853, in Marx and Engels, *On Colonialism* (New York: International Publishers, 1972), p. 316; "The British Rule in India," in ibid., p. 41.
10. Marx, "The Future Results of the British Rule in India," in ibid., p. 82.
11. Marx, *Capital*, 3:791.
12. Editor's note: A lengthy digression on Marx's methodology in the *Grundrisse* with regard to distinguishing between theoretical abstractions and concrete societies has been omitted.
13. Marx, *Capital*, 1:8.
14. Marx to Zasulich, March 8, 1881, first draft, *MEQJ*, 19:434.
15. Guo Moruo, *Nulizhi shidai* (The slave period) (Beijing: Renmin Chubanshe, 1973), p. 235.
16. Engels, *Anti-Dühring* (Moscow: Foreign Languages Publishing House, 1962), p. 204.

17. D. C. Lau, trans., *Mencius* (Harmondsworth: Penguin, 1970), pp. 99–100 (III.A.3).

18. Engels, *Anti-Dühring*, p. 249.

19. Guo Moruo, *Nulizhi shidai*, pp. 233, 234; Hou Shaozhuang, "Zenyang lijie Guo Moruo tongzhi de gudaishi fenqi xueshuo" (How should we understand Guo Moruo's theory of the periodization of ancient history?), *Lishi yanjiu* 8 (1979): 45.

20. *PCEF*, p. 95.

21. Marx to Annenkov, December 28, 1846, *MECW*, 38:101.

22. *Manifesto of the Communist Party* (Beijing: Foreign Languages Press, 1965), p. 42; *Capital*, 1:332. In the same vein, Marx wrote in a letter to Engels: "Carey, the American economist, has published a new book, *Slavery at Home and Abroad*. Included here under 'slavery' are all forms of servitude, wage slavery, etc." (Marx to Engels, June 14, 1853, in Marx and Engels, *Selected Correspondence* [Moscow: Progress Publishers, 1965], p. 83).

23. Marx, *Capital*, 1:237.

WANG DUNSHU AND YU KE

7 | Further Comments on the "Asiatic Mode of Production"

In the past year or so since we published our first essay on the Asiatic mode of production (AMP),[1] there has been much discussion of this question in academic circles. Some scholars have misunderstood our view, labeling it "a new composite theory" or "a multicausal composite theory,"[2] and arguing that we have applied the AMP to a semicivilized, semiprimitive period.[3] We feel it is necessary for us to make further comments to clarify our position.

The AMP has been a topic of discussion at home and abroad for more than fifty years. No consensus has yet been reached as to its meaning and applicability due to several obscure theoretical points that need to be settled first.

Marx introduced the AMP in the 1850s without offering a clear definition or sustained exposition of the concept. He used the term only once or twice, and in a very restricted fashion, in the Preface to *A Contribution to the Critique of Political Economy* and in *Capital*. What is more, Marx and Engels no longer used this concept after the middle of the 1870s, with the publication of *Anti-Dühring*. That is, as they progressed in their study of primitive society and Oriental society, it seems that they abandoned the term altogether. This makes the problem even more complicated. What was the original idea of Marx and Engels concerning the AMP? And did they still hold to this concept in their later years?

From *Zhongguo shi yanjiu* (Studies in Chinese history) 3 (1981): 103–16. Translated by Li Anshan.

Second, Marx formulated this concept in 1859 while his ideas on the sequence of social development were very much in process. Marx's and Engels' understanding of primitive society and the terms they used to identify the stages of social development were in flux. Hence the position of the AMP in the sequence of developmental stages and its social nature are problematic.

Third, Marx put forward the concept of the AMP on the basis of his knowledge of Oriental history in the 1850s. During the past century and more, research on Oriental nations has been greatly furthered by historians, archaeologists, and ethnologists all over the world. Thus, even if the concept and theory of the AMP were unambiguous, its application would still raise many questions. Since the concept itself is not clear, there are bound to be many different interpretations. For all these reasons we cannot agree with those who insist that this question is "unproblematic."[4]

Since it was Marx who first proposed the concept of the AMP, it is important to understand its original meaning and the subsequent changes it has undergone before applying it to the social history of Oriental nations, as well as the rest of the world. We also think it necessary to examine the concept in relation to what Marx and Engels knew and understood in their own time. What we have since learned from history and ethnography can only serve as indirect verification of Marx's original meaning. This is because Marx's idea of the AMP did not come out of these data but was generated on the basis of the materials available to him.

Marx's Concept of the AMP in 1859

Although Marx did not fully explicate the AMP, he did provide fairly detailed explanations for such related concepts as "Asiatic society," "Oriental society," "Indian society," "the basic Asiatic form," and "Asiatic and Indian communal property." From these one can trace his original idea concerning the AMP. We shall consider these texts in particular: the correspondence between Marx and Engels in June 1853, Marx's "The British Rule in India" and "The Future Results of British Rule in India," which were published about the same time, *A Contribution to the Critique of Political Economy*, *Pre-Capitalist Economic Foundations*, and *Capital*.

We think that the AMP in general outline includes the following six elements:

1. The level of economic development (the productive forces) is dependent on irrigated agriculture. The natural economy is dominant; agriculture is indissolubly linked with domestic handicraft; production is not geared for exchange; and commodity production holds a subordinate position.[5]

2. Within the social organization of the AMP there exist small village communities (rural communes) of a primitive type. Village communities are "the solid foundation of Oriental despotism."[6] They are isolated, dispersed, and closed.

3. The ownership of land is dual: there is the communal ownership by the rural commune, over which has been erected state ownership (or royal ownership) embodied in the person of the despotic monarch. The state is the landlord at the highest level, and there is no private property in land.[7]

4. There exist relationships of power and exploitation between a ruling class headed by the despotic monarch and the broad mass of the peasants in the communes. Within the commune, signs of both caste and slavery have appeared, and officials and superiors have become differentiated from and risen above the other commune members.[8]

5. With regard to exploitation and redistribution, taxes and corvée guarantee that most of the surplus product and falls into the hands of the ruling class headed by the despot. Rent and tax are combined to form a unity.[9]

6. The time frame of the AMP extends from the earliest times to the first decade of the nineteenth century. Indian and Asian society have not undergone change or social revolution since ancient times. Throughout this time they have always been in the AMP stage.[10]

As the above six points indicate, one of the characteristics of the AMP is its primitivity, since within it the rural commune and primitive communal ownership partially continued to exist. But a characteristic even more basic to the AMP is its inescapable class nature, since it contains other elements belonging to class society that are even more important in determining the nature of society, such as the despot, the state, classes, and exploitation. This is certainly quite different from primitive society as we understand it today.

We Should Not Mechanically Divide an Organic Society

In expounding the system of Asiatic rural communal ownership represented by India, Marx often mentioned the domination of the despotic government and the supreme property rights of the despot. The presence of these elements must be explained by those who propose that the AMP represents a type of primitive society. Facing this problem, some scholars have used Engels' comments about tsarist Russia and Dutch Java in letters to Vera Zasulich and Karl Kautsky to distinguish within one society two societies at different stages. According to this theory, Indian or Asiatic society under the despotic state should be divided into two distinct societies. One is the primitive society of the dominated rural communes, which is the part to which the AMP refers. The other is the despotic state, which represents a separate society that does not belong to the AMP system. Otherwise, they say, AMP theorists must combine things that belong to different social stages, dragging elements from primitive society into class society and mixing them to create a strange monster that never existed in history. We think that this method of distinguishing two stages within one society is untenable.

Marxism considers society an organic unity that is structured by the combination of various relations of production and that changes with the development of the forces of production. Within a certain stage of social development, there can exist different systems of ownership and elements belonging to different social stages. A society will have economic elements appropriate to it, but at the same time it may have remnants from the systems of previous societies as well as the seeds of a new society. But it is first of all a society of a specific type at a certain historical stage, the nature of which is determined by the totality of the dominant relations of production (mainly property relations). We cannot deny the existence of this specific social formation and historical stage, nor can we mechanically or artificially carve it up into several different societies or claim it to be an aggregate of several societies, just because elements from different social stages exist simultaneously within it. The remnants of older societies and the seeds of a new society can only exist within a specific society as lingering or emerging elements, governed and restricted by, or organically combined with, the dominant relations of production. But they can never form separate societies on their own, nor replace or represent the society in which they exist.[11]

Marxism also holds that even in a stage of transition from one society to another, one type of ownership and one set of relations of production must determine the social nature of this transitional period. Transition cannot be regarded as a phase in which several societies coexist.[12] Engels said in the letter to Zasulich that tsarist Russia was "where every stage of social development is represented, from the primitive commune to modern large-scale industry and high finance, and where all these contradictions are violently held in check by an unexampled despotism."[13] We should note that Engels was talking about the problem of revolution in Russia and not probing into the social character of tsarist Russia and the relationship between despotism and the rural communes. Neither was he expounding theoretically the general problem of socio-economic formations and stages of development. We should not take one sentence on the situation in Russia and extrapolate from it an abstract and universal theory for distinguishing two social stages where only one exists. In his letter, Engels was only saying that there were elements from different social stages present in tsarist Russia, such as rural communes, modern industry, financial oligarchy, and despotism. He was not denying the capitalist character of Russian society, nor did he intend to divide tsarist Russia into several societies at different stages.

The same is true of Engels' letter to Kautsky, in which he used Dutch rule in Java to criticize the state socialist fallacy. "On the basis of the old community communism the Dutch organized production under state control .... The result: the people are kept at the stage of primitive stupidity and seventy million marks (now surely more) are annually collected by the Dutch national treasury." Engels did not intend to define the Dutch domination of the Javanese in terms of two separate societies. On the contrary, he saw them as a single entity, which he called "state socialism." Although he spoke of the Javanese communes later in the same letter in terms of "primitive communism," he stressed the colonial rule of the capitalist Dutch and regarded the communal system as a sort of remnant. "In the conditions of modern society it turns out to be a crying anachronism . . . as much as were the independent mark associations of the original [Swiss] cantons."[14] It would be historically unrealistic to locate Javanese society before Dutch colonial rule in a primitive communal period that lacked private ownership, a division of labor between agriculture and industry, classes, or the state. When the Dutch invaders arrived in Java, there had already been a history of state formation for over a thousand years. In ancient Chinese and non-Chinese historical records we can find references to such Javanese states as Sjailendra, Mataram, Singasari, Madjapahit, Demak, and Banten. As Marx himself observed, quoting from Raffles' *History of Java*, " 'the sovereign was absolute landlord' of the whole surface of the land, 'where rent to any considerable amount was attainable.' "[15]

In a word, countries like India or Java that retained the rural communal system under a despotic, or even nondespotic, system of government existed as objective, unified entities. Whether we call these societies Asiatic, slave, feudal, or first slave and then feudal, each can be located within a specific sociohistorical stage. No society divides into two coexistent societies or stages.

"Asiatic" or "Indian" Communal Ownership Is Not Equivalent to "Communal Ownership in the Primitive Period"

There are those who maintain that the AMP refers to the period of primitive society. They often quote Marx's footnote on Asiatic and Indian communal property, which appears in both the first chapter of *The Critique* and the second edition of the first volume of *Capital*, as well as a passage in one of Marx's letters to Engels in 1868:

> At present an absurdly biased view is widely held, namely, that *primitive* communal property is a specifically Slavonic, or even exclusively Russian phenomenon. It is an early form which can be

found among Romans, Teutons and Celts, and of which a whole
collection of diverse patterns (though sometimes only remnants
survive) is still in existence in India. A careful study of Asiatic,
particularly Indian, forms of common property would indicate
that the disintegration of different forms of primitive communal
ownership gives rise to diverse forms of property. For instance,
various prototypes of Roman and Germanic private property can
be traced back to certain forms of Indian communal property.[16]

Some have concluded from this footnote that Asiatic communal
ownership is primitive communal ownership. We dispute this conclusion and wish to draw attention to three points: (1) "Asiatic,
particularly Indian, forms of communal property" refers to various
forms of communal ownership in Asia that existed in Marx's time.
"Asiatic" and "Indian" are treated as geographic terms. (2) Communal ownership in Asia and India up to the nineteenth century
had many forms. Most of them were remnants of primitive communal ownership in disintegration, and in that sense not equivalent
to its classic form. (3) In referring to Indian and Asiatic communal
ownership, Marx is not excluding the possibility that other forms of
ownership existed, forms that might even be in a leading or dominant position and could form an important element of the AMP.

From these three points we can see that Asiatic or Indian
ownership here is not equivalent to primitive communal ownership
but refers to the various forms of communal ownership in Asia and
India through the nineteenth century.

In a letter of 1868, Marx wrote to Engels that "the Asiatic or
Indian forms of ownership in various parts of Europe that I have
mentioned are all primitive forms."[17] Although he is associating
"Asiatic" with primitive communal ownership in Europe, this is
not necessarily to say that Asiatic or Indian ownership means
primitive communal ownership. In a letter to Kugelmann in 1870,
however, Marx says: "It is, furthermore, an historic lie that communal property is Mongolian. As I have pointed out in a number
of my writings, it is of Indian origin and is, therefore, to be found
among all nations of European culture at the beginning of their
development."[18] It seems that Marx thought that communal ownership originated in India and for this reason used the terms

Asiatic or Indian to denote primitive communal ownership in early European history. Marx implied nothing more.

The "Ancient AMP" Differs from the AMP

The following passage from the first volume of the English edition of *Capital*, edited by Engels in 1887, is often used as a basis for the interpretation that the AMP is found only in primitive society:

> In the ancient Asiatic and other ancient modes of production, we find that the conversion of products into commodities, and therefore the conversion of men into producers of commodities, holds a subordinate place, which, however, increases in importance as the [primitive] communities approach nearer and nearer to their dissolution. . . . Those ancient social organisms of production are, as compared with bourgeois society, extremely simple and transparent. But they are founded either on the immature development of man individually, who has not yet severed the umbilical cord that unites him with his fellowmen [in a primitive tribal community], or upon direct relations of subjection.[19]

Many commentators, including the authors of *An Outline History of World Antiquity*, think that the phrase "primitive communities" refers specifically to the ancient Asiatic mode of production.[20] From the context, this passage is meant to convey that the commodity economy was underdeveloped and had only a subordinate place in the modes of production of ancient Asia and ancient Greece and Rome in comparison with the bourgeois "social organism of production," and that the more the community declined, the more important the commodity economy became. Regardless of whether "primitive" is added before it, "community" connotes both the ancient Asiatic and the ancient Greek and Roman modes of production.

Similarly, the expression "primitive tribal community," which has been added in the English edition, undoubtedly refers to the above-mentioned ancient Asiatic mode, but this insertion cannot be used to prove that the AMP belongs to the primitive period of the tribal community. This is because the "ancient Asiatic" mode is different from the AMP. In the 1850s, Marx mentioned the AMP,

Oriental society, the Asiatic formation, Asiatic society, and Asiatic communal ownership in the introduction to the *Grundrisse* and the Preface to the *Critique*, but without once adding on the word "ancient." By using the word "ancient" in *Capital*, Marx was singling out the earliest period of the AMP in order to stress its primitive character. The addition of "primitive tribal community" in the English version is in keeping with this emphasis. The difference between the ancient Asiatic mode and other ancient modes of production is that the former reflects the primitive period whereas the latter belong to class society. The AMP thus includes both the early primitive period and the period of class society in the regions of Asia. All this shows that by the time that *Capital* was published, Marx and Engels had developed a deeper understanding of primitive society and had accordingly revised some ideas they had put forward in the 1850s about the sequence, timing, and spatial distribution of the "Asiatic" and "ancient" modes of production. It does not mean that the AMP refers only to primitive society, or that the mode of production of primitive society was prolonged without change.

Marx's Expositions on the Sequence of Social Development

In *The German Ideology*, written in 1845–46, Marx and Engels advanced the idea that there were four forms of ownership in human society: tribal property, ancient communal and state ownership, feudal or estate-property, and modern private property.[21] In *Wage Labor and Capital*, published in 1849, Marx summed up the stages of social development as "ancient society, feudal society, bourgeois society."[22] In 1857–59, in the introduction to the *Grundrisse*, Marx presented the sequence as Oriental, ancient, feudal, and bourgeois economies,[23] and in the Preface to the *Critique*, as "Asiatic, ancient, feudal, and modern bourgeois modes of production."[24]

We can make two observations from these formulations. First, Marx and Engels do not use such terms as primitive society or even primitive communal property. Second, in *The German Ideology*, tribal property is regarded as the first form of ownership. In *Wage Labor and Capital*, ancient society is placed first in the sequence of social development, without any mention of tribal ownership. In the *Grundrisse* and the *Critique*, Oriental society and the AMP respectively are inserted before ancient society and the ancient mode of production.

To reconcile these various formulations, some have claimed that the tribal ownership mentioned in *The German Ideology* refers to the primitive communal period. Marx and Engels then had two formulas to characterize the sequence of social development: when talking about the developmental stages of civilization or class society, as in *Wage Labor and Capital*, they omitted primitive society; but when speaking of the full spectrum of historical development, as in the *Grundrisse* and the *Critique*, they included the primitive period. The concepts of Oriental society and the AMP are thus seen simply as extensions of tribal ownership, all belonging to the period of primitive society.

We think that such an explanation is untenable, for the following reasons. The social structure of tribal ownership is described in *The German Ideology* as "patriarchal family chieftains; below them the members of the tribe; finally slaves."[25] Such elements actually reflect the situation in the period of dissolution of primitive society, not the primitive communal period in the strict sense. No reference is made to Oriental society or communal property. On the contrary, communal property is talked about in relation to the second form of ownership, the combination of communal and state property of the ancient period. This indicates that the Asiatic communal property and the AMP Marx spoke of in the 1850s are quite different from the tribal property in *The German Ideology*.

In the Preface to the *Critique*, Marx lists the AMP as the first of the "epochs marking progress in the economic development of society."[26] But we cannot be sure that this indicates a primitive communal society just because we know now that primitive society is the earliest social formation. Simple analogy cannot solve the problem. The key is whether Marx and Engels had a clear understanding of primitive society.

Engels added this footnote in the 1888 English edition of the *Manifesto of the Communist Party*:

> In 1847, the pre-history of society, the social organization existing

previous to recorded history, was all but unknown. Since then, Haxthausen discovered common ownership of land in Russia, Maurer proved it to be the social foundation from which all Teutonic races started in history, and by and by village communities were found to be, or to have been the primitive form of society everywhere from India to Ireland. The inner organization of this primitive Communistic society was laid bare, in its typical form, by Morgan's crowning discovery of the true nature of the gens and its relation to the tribe. With the dissolution of these primeval communities society begins to be differentiated into separated and finally antagonistic classes.[27]

Engels' observation suggests that in 1847, or even 1859, Marx and Engels had not yet developed a clear idea of primitive society and the primitive community (in which communal ownership is vested in the clan, not the village or the tribe). That is why they did not mention primitive society or the primitive mode of production as specialist terms in the sequence of social development. They thought that the origin of the Roman and Germanic forms of private ownership was deducible from the various forms of village communal ownership in India, hence it was natural for them to put Oriental society and the AMP at the head of the sequence of social development. The AMP and Oriental society may be said generally to comprise the various forms of village communal ownership (with the highest ownership vested in the despot) in Asia, especially in India, from the earliest time to the nineteenth century. But if we wish to determine what society the AMP characterizes, we must do so through a concrete analysis of its characteristics.

The AMP Does Not Belong to the Period of Primitive Society

We now have some approximations concerning the nature of the society that could be characterized by the AMP. First, the AMP—the Asiatic society of which India is typical, or "Asian society" in contrast with "Western society"—did not undergo fundamental changes from earliest antiquity down to the beginning of the nineteenth century. Its geographical scope is mainly Turkey, Iran, and Hindustan. Indian or Asiatic society forms an integral entity, neither exclusively signifying the village community nor separable from it. Marx stated in the first volume of *Capital* that Indian society was based on "the blending of agriculture and handicrafts, and on an unalterable division of labor bought, in Indian society as a whole, by means of the exchange of commodities."[28] So it is clear that Indian society as a whole is not entirely reducible to the Indian commune. The Indian village on its own could not constitute a society. Marx stressed that the commune was the key to explaining the long-term stasis of Asiatic society: the commune and the structure of the basic economic elements of Asiatic society were indivisible.

Second, although the preservation of communal social organization is an important characteristic of Indian and Asiatic society, Marx's Indian rural commune was not the primitive commune: it was at most the remnant of primitive society. It was actually the base-level unit by which the ruling class and the despotic state exploited and oppressed the mass of commune members.

The social community of the primitive commune is based on the common ownership of the means of production in the earliest period of human society. It is characterized by equality among commune members, absence of class exploitation or oppression, and no state system. The clan commune is the typical form of primitive commune; the rural commune (agricultural community) is the form of the primitive commune in its period of dissolution. It is this secondary form that exists as a remnant of the commune in class society and that serves as the basic economic and administrative unit through which the laboring masses are exploited by the ruling class. The Indian rural commune described by Marx is precisely this secondary form of rural commune, as the following three points confirm: (1) Indian rural communes, in Marx's words, were marked "by distinctions of caste and by slavery."[29] (2) Some members of the commune had split off to form an upper stratum. For example, the leader of the commune was the *potail*, "the 'chief inhabitant,' who is judge, police, and tax-gatherer in one."[30] His status had actually become that of a hereditary local-level official of the despotic state. No matter how the organs of political power changed, he always "acts as the petty judge or magistrate, and collector or renter of the village."[31] (3) More important, although the

Indian village community was based on possession in common of the land, such that "the land is tilled in common, and the produce divided among the members,"[32] the community was not the true owner of the land, only its "hereditary possessor."[33]

The main economic function of the community was to pay land tax and tribute to the government of the despot, "into whose hands from time immemorial a certain quantity of these products has found its way in the shape of rent in kind."[34] As Marx pointed out, in ancient Hindu law Indian villages existed as the basic unit of tax payment: "ten villages under a superior collector, then a hundred and then a thousand."[35] We can affirm that the Indian village community had been able to exist for a long time under the storm of constant political struggle, mainly because it had this tax-paying function. Otherwise it would have been wiped out by the ruling classes and conquerors and replaced by other grass-roots administrative units. It is in this fundamental sense that Marx declared that "these idyllic village communities . . . had always been the solid foundation of Oriental despotism."[36]

Third, the Asiatic communal landownership described by Marx was closely tied to, controlled, and dominated by the supreme ownership of the despotic monarch and the state. Marx thought that "the all-embracing unity which stands above all these small common bodies" was personified in the despot, who "appears as the father of all the numerous lesser communities." This greater unity was also the state, "the higher or sole proprietor," while the community was only the "hereditary possessor" whose members were "in fact propertyless." Surplus product thus naturally belonged to the greater unity, and it was "rendered both as tribute and as common labor for the glory of the unity, in part that of the despot, in part that of the imagined tribal entity of the god."[37] Marx also pointed out that in Asia, where the producers were "under direct subordination to a state which stands over them as their landlord and simultaneously as sovereign, then rent and taxes coincide, or rather, there exists no tax which differs from this form of ground-rent. . . . The state is then the supreme lord. Sovereignty here consists in the ownership of land concentrated on a national scale."[38]

The tribute Indian village communities rendered to the despot and the state was a combined form of rent and tax. It was also the embodiment of the supreme ownership of the despot and the state. Subordinated to that supreme ownership, the nature of property under communal ownership was changed. According to Marx, we have no choice but to recognize that the supreme ownership of the despot and the state is an important element of Asiatic society and the AMP.

To summarize, Marx's concepts of Asiatic society and the AMP are characterized by the rural commune, which, however primitive, was in essence a basic organ for the exploitation of the laboring masses by the ruling classes and the despotic state. That is why Marx defined the nature of the Indian village community as "semibarbarian, semicivilized."[39] "Semibarbarian" refers to the considerable legacy of primitive society; "semicivilized" indicates that it had entered class society. Hence Marx spoke of "the peculiar character" of the Indian village system[40] and regarded its form of property as "specifically Oriental,"[41] thereby contrasting it with Greek, Roman, and Germanic forms of private landownership by small producers, as well as with European slavery and serfdom. Offering a broad generalization of the developmental stages of social economy in human history from the earliest times to the nineteenth century, Marx in 1859 called this special form the Asiatic mode of production. This remained Marx's view of Oriental society through the 1850s and 1860s.

Marx and Engels Abandoned the AMP in Their Later Years

Marx's and Engels' knowledge of primitive society, Oriental society, and the sequence of social development changed over time. Although they never stated that they had abandoned the concept of the AMP, from the mid-1870s on they no longer used this term in their published works or manuscripts.[42] We have already dealt with this matter in detail in our earlier essay, "On the Asiatic Mode of Production." Rather than repeat ourselves here, we wish to offer a few additional remarks on this question.

First of all, after further research starting in the mid-1870s, Marx and Engels no longer insisted on their notion of Oriental peculiarity put forward in the 1850s and 1860s but instead emphasized the unitary character of human history. In *Anti-Dühring*, Engels concluded that human history had undergone the modes of production of "slavery, serfdom, wage-labor,"[43] a view with which Marx concurred. In *The Origin of the Family, Private Property and the State*, which Engels finished in 1884, he identified three forms of enslavement in class society: "Slavery is the first form of exploitation, the form peculiar to the ancient world; it is succeeded by serfdom in the middle ages, and wage labor in the more recent period."[44] In his 1887 preface to *The Condition of the Working Class in England*, Engels further pointed out: "In Asiatic and classical antiquity, the predominant form of class oppression was slavery, that is to say, not so much the expropriation of the masses from the land as the appropriation of their persons."[45] These references suggest that according to the historical data available in their later years, Marx and Engels laid more stress on the common character of the Orient and the West, that is, the unitary character of the development of human history. As they formed their theory of social development according to five modes of production, they no longer used the concept of a special Asiatic mode. In the first draft of his letter to Vera Zasulich (March 8, 1881), for instance, Marx spoke of "Semitic, Greek, Roman, . . . and Capitalist societies," but he did not mention the specialized terms "Asiatic society" or "ancient society," which he had used for comparison so frequently in the 1850s and 1860s.

Second, while stressing the commonality of world historical development, Marx and Engels did not neglect the historical particularities of various regions, and they intensified their studies of Oriental countries. For example, in the drafts of his letter to Vera Zasulich and his excerpts from Kovalevsky and Phear, Marx made new progress in his research on the various forms and developmental stages of rural communities, and on landownership and the nature of society in Oriental countries. In their later works they touched on some characteristics of the Orient, but no longer classified them under a special Asiatic mode.

Third, those who do not agree that Marx and Engels abandoned the concept in their later years point to the use of the term "Asiatic" in the third volume of *Capital*, published in 1894. They also take the later manuscripts as evidence of continuing research on the AMP. We think that this argument lacks evidence. It is true that in the third volume of *Capital*, Engels as editor used the phrase "in Asia, in Antiquity, and in the Middle Ages"[46] and several times contrasted "Asiatic" with "Greek and Roman." He also mentioned the concept of "Asiatic land rent and landowner-ship." But Engels states clearly in his preface that the content of the volume was unchanged from Marx's original manuscript of the 1860s.[47] Marx did revise and supplement this volume in his later years, but we do not know whether the parts he changed included these "Asiatic" references. That is why we cannot rely on these references to argue that Marx and Engels continued to support the concept of the AMP.

In conclusion, it is our understanding that the AMP concept was a generalization that Marx used in the 1850s and 1860s for the mode of production in Oriental society in which village communal ownership was preserved. At the time he believed that this forma-tion was unlike both the ancient society of Greece and Rome and either medieval feudal society or the special formation of modern capitalism in Europe. By the mid-1870s, however, as their knowl-edge deepened and developed, Marx and Engels began to abandon in a fundamental sense both the term and the concept of the AMP, and increasingly to stress the unity and common laws governing de-velopment in both East and West. Marxism clearly developed through practice and was not fixed and unchanging. We can nei-ther assert that Marx and Engels from the beginning had formed the idea of a five-stage developmental sequence (and thus equate the AMP with primitive society or Oriental slavery), nor insist that in their later years they continued to advocate a special type of Oriental society or the AMP. Accordingly, contemporary attempts to argue in favor of "Oriental stagnation," "Oriental despotism," or "hydraulic society" by relying on concepts and expositions that Marx held in the 1850s and 1860s but later abandoned are theoretically untenable and politically wrong, even reactionary.

Notes

1. Yu Ke and Wang Dunshu, "Shilun 'Yaxiya shengchan fangshi,' " *Jilin shifan daxue xuebao* 4 (1979).

2. Luo Biyun, "Yaxiya shengchan fangshi de taolun yiji wo dui tade lijie," *Zhongshan daxue xuebao* 2 (1980).

3. "Yaxiya shengchan fangshi taolun qingkuang jianjie," *Tianjin shelian tongxun* 8 (1980).

4. "The Unproblematic AMP," translated in this volume.

5. Karl Marx, "The British Rule in India," in Marx and Engels, *On Colonialism* (New York: International Publishers, 1972), p. 40; Marx, *Capital*, vol. 1 (New York: International Publishers, 1967), p. 337.

6. Marx, "The British Rule in India," p. 40.

7. Marx to Engels, June 2, 1853, and Engels to Marx, June 6, 1853, in *On Colonialism*, pp. 313, 314; Marx, *Capital*, 3:791.

8. Marx. *Capital*, 3:791.

9. Ibid., 1:337; 3:791.

10. Marx, "The British Rule in India," p. 38.

11. For example, feudal society is dominated by relations of production based on the landownership of the feudal lords and landlords. Petty-producer ownership, the remnants of slavery or even the primitive communal system, and elements of incipient capitalism may also exist, but it is still feudal society and can only be called such. We cannot cancel or dismember this society and rename these various elements from different social stages feudal society, petty-producer society, slave society, primitive society, and capitalist society. We cannot regard feudal society as a great hodgepodge of several different societies.

12. For instance, after the founding the the People's Republic, China entered a period of transition from capitalism to socialism. The Constitution of 1953 stipulates that there exist four types of ownership and five economic sectors, but Chinese society at this time was already socialist in character, and state power was in the hands of a proletarian dictatorship. None claimed that there existed several societies within China (excluding Taiwan) or that the Chinese people lived in different societies.

13. Engels to Zasulich, April 23, 1885, in Marx and Engels, *Selected Correspondence* (Moscow: Progress Publishers, 1965), p. 385.

14. Engels to Kautsky, February 16, 1884, in *On Colonialism*, p. 344.

15. Marx to Engels, June 14, 1853, in ibid., p. 317.

16. *CCPE*, p. 33.

17. Marx to Engels, March 14, 1868.

18. Marx to Kugelmann, February 17, 1870, in *The Letters of Karl Marx*, ed. S. K. Padover (Englewood Cliffs, N.J.: Prentice Hall, 1979), p. 268. Marx thought that India was generally the source of European culture. See "The Future Results of the British Rule in India," in *On Colonialism*, p. 86.

19. Marx, *Capital*, 1:79. Words in brackets were added by Engels to the English edition. In the standard Chinese translation, the phrase "other ancient modes of production" is translated more specifically as "such modes of production as the ancient Greek and Roman" (*MEQJ*, 23:96).

20. "The Unproblematic AMP," translated in this volume.

21. Marx and Engels, *The German Ideology* (New York: International Publishers, 1947), pp. 9–11.

22. Marx, *Wage Labor and Capital*, in *MECW*, 9:212.

23. Marx, *Grundrisse* (Harmondsworth: Penguin, 1973), p. 106.

24. *CCPE*, p. 21.

25. Marx and Engels, *The German Ideology*, p. 9.

26. *CCPE*, p. 21.

27. Marx and Engels, *Manifesto of the Communist Party* (Peking: Foreign Languages Press, 1965), p. 32.

28. Marx, *Capital*, 1:337.

29. Marx, "The British Rule in India," p. 41.

30. Marx, *Capital*, 1:337.

31. Marx, "The British Rule in India, " p. 40, quoting from "an old official report of the British House of Commons on Indian affairs."

32. Marx, *Capital*, 1:337.

33. *PCEF*, p. 69.

34. Marx, *Capital*, 1:337.

35. Marx to Engels, June 14, 1853, in *On Colonialism*, p. 317.

36. Marx, "The British Rule in India," p. 40.

37. *PCEF*, pp. 69–70.

38. Marx, *Capital*, 3:791.

39. Marx, "The British Rule in India," p. 40.

40. Ibid.

41. *PCEF*, p. 75.

42. See, e.g., *Anti-Dühring*; the three drafts of Marx's letter to Zasulich; *The Origin of the Family, Private Property and the State*; the preface to the American edition of *The Condition of the Working Class in England*; Lawrence Krader, ed., *The Ethnological Notebooks of Karl Marx* (Assen: Van Gorcum, 1972).

43. Engels, *Anti-Dühring*, *MECW*, 25:267.

44. Engels, *The Origin of the Family, Private Property and the State* (New York: International Publishers, 1942), p. 160.

45. Engels, *The Condition of the Working Class in England* (Oxford: Basil Blackwell, 1971), p. 355.

46. Marx, *Capital*, 3:333.

47. Engels, preface to *Capital*, 3:3.

QI QINGFU

8 | The "Asiatic Mode of Production" Is Not a Marxist Scientific Concept

The question of the "Asiatic mode of production" (AMP) has been debated internationally for a half a century, and great differences of opinion remain unbridged. What is the AMP? Did Marx at some point abandon it? Is it really a Marxist scientific concept? These questions are at the core of the current debate. In this essay I will argue that Marx first proposed the AMP to analyze primitive society, and that later, when knowledge of agricultural communities deepened and a more scientific approach to the history of primitive society was established, he abandoned it as unscientific.

Marx formulated the concept of the AMP while investigating precapitalist property in land, particularly common property. In his Preface to *A Contribution to the Critique of Political Economy*, he arranges the modes of production in a series of successive stages, "epochs marking progress in the economic development of society," beginning with the Asiatic.[1] Given the explicit reference to "progress," it seems undeniable that Marx meant the AMP to indicate primitive society. There are many places, however, where Marx's discussion of the AMP is not compatible with primitive society. Why is this?

In the 1850s Marx was unable to formulate a modern scientific concept regarding the history of primitive society because, at the time, primitive society was still an "unsolved mystery."[2] In a note

From *Zhongyang Minzu Xueyuan xuebao* (Central Minorities Institute journal) 3 (1985): 30–36. Translated by Paul Forage.

to the 1888 English edition of the *Manifesto of the Communist Party,* Engels points out that "in 1847, the pre-history of society, the social organizations existing previous to recorded history, was all but unknown."[3] As late as 1881, Marx said of the different forms of primitive society that "even today we have only rough descriptions."[4] A scientific concept must reflect the nature of the subject described, but when Marx proposed the AMP, the basic laws of primitive society were still not fully known, and as a result he was unable to develop an adequate scientific concept for it.

Marx's main purpose in proposing the AMP was to explain the primitive form of communal property in land. Limited by contemporary knowledge, Marx's research on the AMP was restricted to the ancient agricultural communities of Asia, especially India. He mistook the vestigial forms that could be found within the agricultural communities of Asian feudal society for the primitive social formation.

The primitive community and the agricultural [or village] community must not be confused. Primitive society was the longest age in the history of human society, for it took over a million years for humankind to evolve from the band to the tribal community to the patriarchal community. In contrast, the agricultural community only appeared during the transitional period between the collapse of primitive society and the beginning of class society. Although it may contain vestigial elements of primitive society, including communal property, class society is fundamentally different from primitive society. The "collective ownership/private cultivation" system of landownership in the agricultural community cannot be equated with primitive communal ownership.

Reviewing all of Marx's and Engels' references to the AMP, one cannot help but come to the conclusion that Marx proposed the concept on the basis of materials concerning not the primitive community, but the agricultural community. We must recognize, however, that Marx developed his understanding of the agricultural community gradually. When he first proposed the AMP, his understanding of the agricultural community was cloudy and he could not distinguish its primary [primitive] form from its secondary form. As a result, he considered "despotism" to be characteristic of the agricultural community.

Marx's interest in the AMP was part of his search for the primitive form of human society. The outstanding result of his early research was the discovery that common property is the most primitive form of property. Yet he was unable to discover the objective rules governing the history of primitive society. The AMP was thus a provisional term he used in the course of his research on precapitalist forms of property. As the investigation of the history of primitive society progressed, in the 1870s Marx abandoned the concept in light of newly discovered materials concerning the agricultural community and communal landownership.

The insights that Marx derived from reading Maxim Kovalevsky's *The Communal System of Land Ownership: Its Origins, Development and Conclusion* appear in the three drafts of Marx's letter to Vera Zasulich written in February and March 1881, where for the first time he clearly summarizes the dual nature of the agricultural community. In his third draft he writes: "As the last phase of the primitive formation of society, the agricultural community is at the same time a transitional phase to the secondary formation, i.e., transition from society based on common property to society based on private property. The secondary formation comprises, as you must understand, the series of societies based on slavery and serfdom."[5]

Marx had thus discovered that the agricultural community was nothing more than a transitional passage out of primitive society. He never again stated that the agricultural community was the oldest form, but he saw it instead as "the last phase of the primitive formation of society." What Marx called the "dualism" of this community refers to its property relations, for he discovered that its basic landownership feature was the survival of common property alongside "petty agricultural labor," resulting in a system known as "collective ownership/private cultivation." With his discovery of the dualism of the agricultural community, Marx solved the problem of primitive property and paved the way for a more scientific history of primitive society. This was the reason he abandoned the AMP. Marx's concept of the AMP was nonetheless a big step forward in the development of a scientific history of primitive society.[6]

In the *Critique*, Marx indicated that communal property had originated in India.[7] He repeats this view in 1870 in a letter to Ludwig Kugelmann: "As I have pointed out in a number of my writings, [common property] is of Indian origin and is, therefore, to be found among all nations of European culture at the beginning of their development. Its specific *Slavic* (not Mongolian) form in Russia (which is repeated also among *non-Russian Southern Slavs*) even has most resemblence, *mutatis mutandis*, to the *old-Germanic* modification of Indian type of communal property."[8]

By 1881, however, Marx had changed his mind, as we see in his letter to Zasulich: "The agricultural community in Germany emerged from a relatively ancient type of community. Here it is a product of natural development, not something introduced from its place of origin in Asia. There, eastern India also has this kind of community, which is, moreover, always the last phase or period of the ancient formation."[9]

There are two important changes. First, the Indian community is seen as simply the "last phase or period of the ancient formation." Marx is clearly referring to the agricultural community, not the primitive community. Second, the Indian community is no longer treated as the origin of the community in Europe, nor is it seen as more ancient than the European. Thus it appears that Marx had rejected his view of the 1840s and 1850s that the Indian community was the most ancient of the primitive forms. Since the concept of the AMP was based on the view that the Indian community is the most ancient type, it was necessary to abandon the concept as unscientific. By the 1880s, the AMP no longer appears in the works of Marx or Engels, not even in Engels' *The Origin of the Family, Private Property and the State.*

For more than half a century, people have been studying the published and unpublished writings of Marx and Engels to understand the meaning of the AMP. To this day, however, the discussion has not yielded much. Research limited only to concepts and theories based on chapter-and-verse citations of Marx's and Engels' writings can never solve any problems.

If practice is the sole criterion of truth, the only way to proceed with the AMP is to test it in relation to what is known about the historical development of Asian countries. The AMP was formulated on the basis of research on communal property in India, yet it does not even match the reality of the development of Indian society. The agricultural communities that Marx studied in India were nothing more than remnants within a feudal system. Indian scholars have denied the applicability of the AMP to India, pointing out that (1) private property had emerged in India by the sixth century, and a mature feudal society by the seventh; (2) the village remained the fundamental social unit for irrigation, production, and taxes despite the rise and fall of the four great empires; and (3) changes in the forces of production and even in the caste system demonstrate that Indian society was not stagnant.[10] The Indian scholar R. P. Salaf has further noted that although Marx used the term "Asiatic society" in several articles, neither in these articles nor in his later works did he ever provide a definition or explanation of the term.[11]

Over the years many scholars both in China and abroad have cited evidence from the Western Zhou period (eleventh to eighth century B.C.) as proof for the AMP, finding in the "well-field" system[12] of Western Zhou society many similarities with Marx's and Engels' descriptions of the AMP agricultural community. Yet they have been unable to demonstrate conclusively that the Western Zhou was a classic model of the AMP. First of all, there is no agreement as to whether the well-field system actually represented a form of agricultural community. Second, even if there were agreement on this point, the nature of Western Zhou society is still under debate even today. Some say that it was a slave society, others that it was a feudal society, but no one claims it was a primitive society, much less places it in an "Asiatic" stage.[13]

For years, Indian society and the well-field system of the Western Zhou have been cited as keys for unlocking the AMP. Unfortunately, these keys have rusted and can no longer be used. Is there a shiny new key close at hand that we might use? The Dai ethnic minority of Xishuangbanna prior to democratic reform could be such a key.[14] The Xishuangbanna Autonomous Prefecture is located in Yunnan province on China's southwestern border, and until the early 1950s it had long been under a system of decentralized feudal rule. One of the characteristics of this feudal system was the agricultural community in its classic form.

Prior to democratic reform, each Xishuangbanna village was a separate community, called a *man* in the Dai language. Even today, many Dai place names have prefixes with the word *man*. Much has been published concerning the agricultural communities of Xishuangbanna. Let us compare the villages of Xishuangbanna with the most commonly cited features attributed to the AMP.

Public Landownership

One of the points that Marx repeatedly emphasizes is the absence of private property in land in India:

> In the specifically oriental form, . . . where property exists only as communal property, the individual member as such is only the possessor of a particular part of it, hereditary or not, for any fraction of property belongs to no member for himself, but only as the direct part of the community, consequently as someone in direct unity with the community and not as distinct from it. The individual is therefore only a possessor. What exists is only communal property and private possession.[15]

Marx here is describing collective ownership in the agricultural community, where the individual only "possesses" the land that he cultivates under a system of "collective ownership/private cultivation." In Xishuangbanna, village land was called "public fields of the village," meaning that the fields belonged to everyone within the village. Membership in the village was the precondition for using village land. This communal land was distributed for fixed periods of time. No individual had the right to sell his land, which was in all matters under the management of the village as a whole. But just as the Indian villages discussed by Marx were not the original form of the agricultural community, neither were the Dai villages of Xishuangbanna. Both had undergone substantial changes as class societies.

Marx argued that "in most Asiatic fundamental forms . . . the all-embracing unity which stands above all these small common bodies may appear as the higher or sole proprietor, the real communities only as hereditary possessors."[16] What Marx calls here the "higher or sole proprietor" is the "despotic ruler" to which he so often refers. Within class society, common property in land retains only the external appearance of public ownership. As is clear from Xishuangbanna, behind village communal landownership lay the system of landownership of the feudal lords. The title of the highest ruler in Xishuangbanna, *zhaopianling* (*zao pilin*), means "ruler of the vast land"; that is, he was the owner of all the land of Xishuangbanna. As a result, property had a dual nature: the land belonged both to the village and to the feudal ruler. Under feudal landownership the villagers were bound to the land and had to bear the burden of its cultivation. The "public fields of the village" for this reason were also known as the "fields of burden."

Oriental Despotism

Marx pointed out that "these idyllic village communities, inoffensive though they may appear, had always been the solid foundation of Oriental despotism."[17] More particularly, "the despot . . . appears as the father of all the numerous lesser communities, thus realizing the common unity of all."[18] Engels in *Anti-Dühring* similarly noted that "where the ancient communes have continued to exist, they have for thousands of years formed the basis of the cruelest form of state, Oriental despotism, from India to Russia."[19]

Prior to democratic reform, Xishuangbanna was also subject to despotic rule by feudal lords. The *zhaopianling* was the highest ruler, who administered a full-fledged graded feudal system. Among the ruling class there were different ranks. The chiefs who emerged as leaders from the village had direct control of the serfs. They in turn were subordinate to a *zhaomeng* (*zao meng*), the regional lord enfeoffed by the feudal leader. He had the right to organize soldiers, exact levies and taxes, and adjudicate legal matters within his jurisdiction, but he also had to contribute taxes and soldiers to the highest ruler. The village communal organization facilitated the rule of the greater and lesser feudal lords.

It is important to note, however, that the feudal system in Xishuangbanna was not the type of despotism found in Chinese feudal society. Dai society's most basic cell was the village community, and as a result it also had a strong sense of primitive democracy. The village community on its own has no necessary relationship to the emergence or existence of despotism. Rather, despotism is the product of feudalism.

Irrigation and Public Works

Marx pointed out that in the East, "artificial irrigation is the first prerequisite for agriculture, and this is the responsibility of either the communes, the provinces or the central government."[20] In agrarian societies, irrigation is of the utmost importance, and as a result some writers have taken hydraulics and public works to be the principle feature of the AMP. Some have even gone so far as to posit an "Asiatic hydraulic society."

Irrigation was an important component of public works in Xishuangbanna. At every level, from the *zhaopianling* down to the village, there were people responsible for organizing the maintenance of water channels and distribution of water to the fields. Every year in the fifth and sixth months of the Dai calendar the channels were repaired; following the work, a pig or chicken was offered to the water deity in an "Opening of the Waterways" ceremony. Before the repair work commenced, the head of the public hall would command the *banmen* of each waterway (the villager responsible for the waterworks), the *mengdang banmen* (an official responsible for waterworks at the regional level), and the *nalongda* (the official overseeing cultivation and rents) to supervise their repair. His command reads: "The chief lives in the town, and those who work the fields live in the countryside. When it is time to repair the waterways, the *banmen* calls everyone to work, and no one can refuse. No matter whether he be a chief or a commoner, refusal will be punished according to the ancient rules."[21] Clearly, in Xishuangbanna, irrigation and public works were vital to their economic life. Although this kind of public works was very ancient, it is not the origin of despotism, for irrigation existed prior to the appearance of class society.

Agriculture, Handicrafts, and the Division of Labor

In *Capital*, Marx offers a detailed description of the Indian village:

Those small and extremely ancient Indian communities, some of which have continued down to this day, are based on possession in common of the land, on the blending of agriculture and handicrafts, and on an unalterable division of labour, which serves, whenever a new community is started, as a plan and scheme ready cut and dried. . . . Side by side with the masses . . . occupied with one and the same work, we find the "chief inhabitant," who is judge, police, and tax-gatherer in one; the book-keeper, who keeps the accounts of the tillage and registers everything relating thereto; another official, who prosecutes criminals, protects strangers travelling through and escorts them to the next village; the boundary man, who guards the boundaries against neighbouring communities; the water-overseer, who distributes the water from the common tanks for irrigation; the Brahmin, who conducts the religious services; the schoolmaster, who on the sand teaches the children reading and writing; the calendar-Brahmin, or astrologer, who makes known the lucky or unlucky days for seed-time and harvest, and for every other kind of agricultural work; a smith and a carpenter, who make and repair all the agricultural implements; the potter, who makes all the pottery of the village; the barber, the washerman, who washes clothes, the silversmith, here and there a poet, who in some communities replaces the silversmith, in others the schoolmaster.[22]

We can find a similar scene in Xishuangbanna. There were village members called the "village father" and "village mother," and others whom the feudal lords called the *ba* (*pia*), the *zha*, and the *xian* chiefs. They had authority to manage the movement of residents, represent the village when receiving new members, administer village lands, collect levies and taxes for the ruler, see to religious and marital matters, and resolve disputes. Beneath them were *kunhan*, responsible for militia matters; *taoge* or elders, who passed communications between the villagers and their superiors; *boban* or runners; *kunqian*, responsible for keeping records; *banmen*, who administered the waterworks; *bomo*, responsible for the village deities; and *bozhan*, who looked after Buddhist matters. Some villages had silversmiths, goldsmiths, blacksmiths, carpenters, hunters, butchers, distillers, merchants, doctors, veterinarians, barbers, and so forth. Many also had poet-musicians, the folk singers known as *zanha*. None was divorced from agricultural production.

Isolation, Conservatism, and Stagnation

Whenever Marx discusses the AMP, he frequently mentions the "isolation" and "stagnation" of the agricultural community. He expresses these notions in the passage from *Capital* quoted above:

> The simplicity of the organization for production in these self-sufficing communities that constantly reproduce themselves in the same form, and when accidentally destroyed, spring up again on the spot and with the same name—this simplicity supplies the key to the secret of the unchangeableness of Asiatic societies, an unchangeableness in such striking contrast with the constant dissolution and refounding of Asiatic States, and the never-ceasing changes of dynasty. The structure of the economic elements of society remains untouched by the storm-clouds of the political sky.[23]

The agricultural community as a social structure certainly had a closed and conservative character, and we can easily see this in Xishuangbanna. A glance through the *Le shi* (History of the Xishuangbanna Dai),[24] an annual chronological record, shows that every time the area was leveled in war over the centuries, the villages were always rebuilt immediately in the same places with the same names. Development in a society of agricultural communities like Xishuangbanna was thus very slow. But "slow" does not mean "stagnant." In fact, history tells us that Dai society was continuously developing, and that prior to democratic reform it was in a transition from an economy of feudal lords to an economy of feudal landlords.

From this simple comparison, we cannot deny that there are many similarities between the Dai nationality prior to Liberation and Marx's AMP. But can we therefore conclude that society in Xishuangbanna was "Asiatic"? The answer is no, because the facts of Xishuangbanna would otherwise contradict the position of the AMP in Marx's sequence of modes of production: "Asiatic, ancient, feudal and modern bourgeois."[25] Before Liberation, according to Marxist analysis, the Dai people lived under a system of feudal lords and serfdom. This conclusion has been verified by the experience of democratic reform in Xishuangbanna. Can we say that the AMP means the system of feudal lords? No, because to place the AMP at the head of the sequence of modes of production means having to place the feudal lords of Xishuangbanna in that position. There is no way that Marx could conceive of preceding "ancient, feudal and bourgeois" with a mode of production consisting of feudal lords.

Why do we see so many similarities between the decentralized feudalism of the Dai nationality and the AMP? The crux of the matter is that they are merely similarities of form. The material available to Marx on the remnant agricultural communities of feudal India is almost identical to what we know of Dai village communities. But however much Dai society seems to fit the AMP, it runs counter to the order of social development Marx proposed. The factual content of the AMP does not match Marx's intention when he first raised the concept. No matter whether we consider ancient historical records or modern ethnological materials, Xishuangbanna presents the best case for the AMP in China, and yet the Dai system of feudal lords cannot be interpreted as "Asiatic." We can only conclude that the concept of the AMP itself is confused, and that it was nothing more than a provisional term of inquiry that Marx used in the course of his research. It is not a scientific concept.

Notes

1. *CCPE*, p. 21.
2. Engels, *The Origin of the Family, Private Property, and the State* (New York: International Publishers, 1947).
3. Marx and Engels, *Manifesto of the Communist Party* (Beijing: Foreign Languages Press, 1965), p. 32.
4. Marx to Zasulich, March 8, 1881, first draft.
5. Marx to Zasulich, March 8, 1881, in *PCEF*, p. 145.
6. Marx to Engels, January 13, 1859, *MECW*, 40:368. Marx and Engels are no exception to the general rule that the process of investigation may require modification of earlier ideas. As Marx said in a letter to Ferdinand Lassalle, "no sooner does one set about finally disposing of subjects to which one has devoted years of study than they start revealing new aspects and demand to be thought out further" (Marx to Lassalle, February 22, 1858, *MECW*, 40:270). Continual "disposal" is the sign of a serious and fact-based attitude to scientific research. In keeping with this attitude, Marx "disposed" of the AMP in the course of his research.

Translator's note: The Chinese translation (*MEQJ*, 29:530) suggests that Marx had disposed of certain "subjects" more thoroughly than does the English translation. The author's point that Marx "disposed" of the AMP is based on this reading.

7. *CCPE*, p. 33.

8. Marx to Kugelmann, February 17, 1870, in *The Letters of Karl Marx*, ed. S. K. Papover (Englewood Cliffs, N.J.: Prentice Hall, 1979), p. 268.

9. Marx to Zasulich, *MEQJ*, 19:433–34.

10. " 'Yaxiya shengchan fangshi' xueshu taolunhui jiyao," *Zhongguo shi yanjiu* 3 (1981): 12–13, especially concerning the views of Chen Hongjin and Liu Chuangyuan.

11. R. P. Saraf, *The Indian Society: A Process of People's Revolutionary Struggle Through the Ages* (Kashmir: Progressive Studies, 1974), pp. 477–81.

12. Editor's note: The well-field system describes an arrangement by which land for eight households was divided into nine plots, the produce of the central plot going to the lord and that of each of the other eight plots to its respective household. For more information see Zhao Lisheng's essay in this volume.

13. Cf. Wang Zhenxing, "Xi Zhou shi ruogan wenti yanjiu zongshu" (Summary of research on several questions concerning the history of the Western Zhou), *Renwen zazhi* (Humanities magazine) 4 (1983).

14. Material for the following discussion has been drawn from Liao Luanhe, *Xishuangbanna Daizu zizhizhou de guoqu he xianzai* (Past and present in the Xishuangbanna Dai Nationality Autonomous Prefecture) (Kunming: Yunnan Renmin Chubanshe, 1957); Yun Lan, "Xishuangbanna diqu minzhu gaige yiqian de fengjian lingzhu jingji" (The economy of decentralized feudalism in the Xishuangbanna region prior to democratic reform), *Minzu yanjiu* (Nationalities research) 4 (1959); Song Shuhua, "Jiefang qian Daizu de fengjian lingzhu tudi suoyouzhi ji qi he nongcun gongshe de guanxi" (The relationship between decentralized feudal landownership among the preliberation Dai nationality and the agricultural community), *Minzu tuanjie* (Ethnic unity) 4 (1963).

Editor's note: For a fuller study of Dai society, see Chen Han-seng, *Frontier Land Systems in Southernmost China* (New York: Institute of Pacific Relations, 1949). Chen characterizes Xishuangbanna as a "protofeudal" society. Feudal relations there took form not in the wake of slavery, "but as a result of the dissolution of the structure of primitive society." He contrasts this with the emergence of feudal relations in the Western Zhou from the "interaction between slaveowning elements and patriarchal elements" (p. 34). The partial Chinese edition (Chen Hansheng, *Jiefang qian Xishuangbanna tudi zhidu* [The land system in Xishuangbanna before Liberation] [Beijing: Zhongguo Shehui Kexue Chubanshe, 1984]) carries an introduction by Qi Qingfu, in which Qi claims that Chen's "protofeudalism" is simply "baronial feudalism" (*lingzhu fengjianzhuyi*), thereby implicitly equating the structure of Dai society with that of the Zhou dynasty (p. 10). I am grateful to Professor Qi for supplying me with a copy of the Chinese edition.

15. *PCEF*, p. 75.

16. *PCEF*, p. 69.

17. Marx, "The British Rule in India," in Marx and Engels, *On Colonialism*

(New York: International Publishers, 1972), p. 40.

18. *PCEF*, p. 69.

19. Engels, *Anti-Dühring* (Moscow: Foreign Languages Publishing House, 1962), p. 250.

20. Marx to Engels, June 6, 1853, *MECW*, 39:339.

21. See "Xishuangbanna Mengjinghong de guangai xitong ji qi guanli he guantian fenbu" (The irrigation system, its management, and the distribution of public land in Mengjinghong, Xishuangbanna), *Daizu shehui lishi diaocha* (Investigation into the history of Dai society) (Kunming: Yunnan Minzu Chubanshe, 1983).

22. Marx, *Capital* (New York: International Publishers, 1967), 1:357–58.

Editor's note: Marx in this passage is paraphrasing Hegel's description of the organization of the Indian village; see *The Philosophy of History* (New York: Dover, 1956), p. 154. The notion that Indian villages were integrated communities has been challenged by Jean Baechler, who argues that the existence of castes means that a village is not a community but a juxtaposition of elements centered on realities external to the village, unlike village communities elsewhere in the world, including China (*La solution Indienne: Essai sur les origines du régime des castes* [Paris: Presses Universitaires de France, 1988], pp. 20, 171).

23. Marx, *Capital*, 1:358.

24. Li Fuyi, trans., *Le shi* (Kunming: Guoli Yunnan Daxue Xinan Wenhua Yanjiushi, 1946). Editor's note: "Le" is another name for the Dai minority of Xishuangbanna.

25. *CCPE*, p. 21.

SONG MIN

9 | The Scientific Validity of the Concept of the Asiatic Mode of Production

It has been argued that the Asiatic mode of production (AMP) formulated by Marx and Engels in 1859 is not a Marxist scientific concept.[1] The AMP appears at the head of the sequence of socioeconomic formations listed in the Preface to *A Contribution to the Critique of Political Economy*—"Asiatic, ancient, feudal and modern bourgeois modes of production." Many have seized on its location to deduce that Marx must have understood Asiatic to mean primitive communal society based on a clan system. According to this view, because the key component of the AMP is in fact the [postprimitive] village commune rather than the [primitive] clan commune, accompanied by the despotic state, the AMP cannot be regarded as a scientific concept.

We should not base our understanding of the AMP on the subsequent theory of the five modes of production. Nor should we rely solely on one sentence from the Preface. It is certainly true that Marx and Engels in the 1850s did take the AMP to be society's most primitive form. It was primitive communalism, the starting point of all civilizations. As Marx observes in a footnote in the *Critique*, certain "Asiatic, particularly Indian, forms" of "primitive communal property" were the origins of "various prototypes of

From *Shehui kexue zhanxian* (Social science frontline) 4 (1986): 128–34. Translated by Timothy Brook.

Roman and Germanic private property."[2] The AMP, as the ownership of land in common by village communities, existed at "the
threshold of the history of all civilized races."[3] For Marx in the
1850s, the AMP was primitive communalism, the starting point of
all civilizations.

Thirty years later, in a footnote to the 1888 English edition of
the *Manifesto of the Communist Party*, Engels outlines the process
by which he and Marx further developed their understanding of
primitive society. He notes the extensive discoveries that had been
made since the *Manifesto* was written, and he credits Lewis
Morgan with discovering that the "gens" or primitive clan community was not the same as the tribal village community, the latter
emerging at the point at which "society begins to be differentiated
into separate and finally antagonistic classes."[4] Engels thus makes
very clear that in the 1880s he and Marx no longer regarded the
village community, which in the 1850s they had taken to be representative of the AMP, as the primitive form of society. Only after
Morgan's "crowning discovery" did they grasp primitive communal
society in its pure form.

Can we take this revision as justification for claiming that "the
AMP is not a Marxist scientific concept"? Absolutely not. The
proper way to determine the scientific validity of the AMP is to as-
sess it in terms of Marx's "guiding principle" of historical
materialism, which he lays out in the same Preface to the *Critique*:
"It is not the consciousness of men that determines their existence,
but their social existence that determines their consciousness."[5]
We cannot take the shift in Marx's view of the AMP between the
late 1850s and the 1880s, which reflects the influence of social existence on their consciousness, as proof that the concept is inherent-
ly unscientific. We must look instead at the content of the AMP
and determine whether it can be said to have had an objective existence. The existence of the [postprimitive] village community is
certainly not contradicted by Morgan's discovery of the [primitive]
clan community; rather, its place in the development of society is
simply made more precise.[6] The concept cannot be dismissed as
unscientific.

It has also been argued that what Marx was examining within
the rubric of the AMP was simply the village community as it ex-

isted in Asia, particularly India. In fact, however, Marx's research touched on the early history of all civilizations, not just India. Returning again to Engels' footnote to the *Manifesto*, we find him stressing the impact that the research by Haxthausen and Maurer had on Marx's understanding of the village community. Indeed, there he makes no reference to Marx's interest in India. This goes to show that Marx and Engels studied the village community and formulated the AMP in relation to the general laws of social development, not Asia alone.

The Soviet historian V. N. Nikiforov has charged that Marx's AMP carried on the "erroneous perceptions of the socioeconomic systems of Oriental countries of the previous two centuries" in Europe.[7] He lists "the lingering impact of Aristotle," travelers' accounts, Montesquieu, Hegel, Adam Smith, John Stuart Mill, and James Mill among the influences on this concept. Marx revolutionized social science by absorbing as well as criticizing previous philosophical, economic, and socialist doctrines. According to Nikiforov, Marx abandoned the AMP in the 1880s, once he had thoroughly overcome these two centuries of influence. There is no basis for this opinion in the writings of Marx and Engels. At the same time, however, Nikiforov follows Georgii Plekhanov (1856-1918) in his suggestion that Marx by 1880 or 1881 understood the Asiatic system and ancient society to be "two coexisting types of economic development."[8] Thus Nikiforov admits, rather curiously, that the AMP, whose influences Marx was supposed to have "thoroughly overcome," did have an objective existence.[9]

The notion that the AMP could exist contemporaneously with the ancient mode of production contradicts one of Marx's basic principles. In the preface to the first volume of *Capital*, Marx states that his "standpoint" is to view "the evolution of the economic formation of society . . . as a process of natural history." This process is strict: "Even when a society has got upon the right track for the discovery of the natural laws of its movement—and it is the ultimate aim of this work, to lay bare the economic law of motion of modern society—it can neither clear by bold leaps, nor remove by legal enactments, the obstacles offered by the successive phases of its normal development."[10] When Marx points out in the *Economic Manuscripts* of 1861–63 that "the natural laws of the Asiatic, ancient and feudal modes of production are in reality different laws,"[11] he is once again stressing that socioeconomic formations and the rules by which they develop are natural, inescapable, and inviolable. The Preface to the *Critique* says that the AMP existed prior to ancient society and in fact "produced" ancient society. To place it in parallel with ancient society thus contradicts this basic principle of the natural historical process.

Marx's reading of Morgan's *Ancient Society* did not cause him to abandon the AMP or to place it alongside ancient society. In his letter to Vera Zasulich, written in 1881 after he had read Morgan, he clearly states that the stage of the village community exists in the "transition from society based on common property to society based on private property," and he cites slavery as one of the series of societies that follow historically after this transition.[12] The society of village communities—the AMP— thus preceded the ancient mode of production but was no longer the starting point of all civilized peoples, being preceded in turn, as Marx and Engels came to realize after reading Morgan, by true primitive society.[13]

Marx and Engels Never Abandoned the Concept of the AMP

After the publication of Morgan's *Ancient Society*, Marx did not have time to revise thoroughly his old formulations concerning archaic society. Engels, on the other hand, was able to make some revisions in their work. For example, in the first (1867) and second (1873) editions of volume 1 of *Capital*, Marx held that the household preceded the clan. In the third edition of 1883, however, Engels added this footnote:

> Subsequent very searching study of the primitive condition of man, led the author to the conclusion, that it was not the family that originally developed into the tribe, but that, on the contrary, the tribe was the primitive and spontaneously developed form of human association, on the basis of blood relationship, and that out of the first incipient loosening of the tribal bonds, the many and various forms of the family were afterwards developed.[14]

This observation is in complete agreement with Marx's own reading note to Morgan's *Ancient Society*:

> Mode: *patriarchal family*—in *Latin or Hebrew form*—zur typical family of primitive society zu machen. The *gens* [clan], as it appeared in the later period of barbarism, was understood, but erroneously supposed to be *subsequent in point of time to the monogamian family*. The gens was treated as an aggregation of families.[15]

The note in *Capital* thus shows that Engels made considerable effort to have that work reflect Marx's revised views of the 1880s. Indeed, he says as much in his preface to the fourth edition of 1890, where he explains that he has "added a few more explanatory notes, especially where changed historical conditions seemed to demand this."[16] The final edition of volume 1 thus reflects Engels' thinking in 1890.

By the time the third volume of *Capital* appeared in 1894, Engels added many footnotes to Marx's text on the basis of subsequent new knowledge. His doing so brought Marx's original text into line with his and Marx's new ideas of the 1880s, making it truly a work of the 1890s.[17] In this regard, we should pay close attention to his footnote to Marx's statement: "Unlike the English, Russian commerce, on the other hand, leaves the economic groundwork of Asiatic production untouched."[18] The note reads: "Since Russia has been making frantic exertions to develop its own capitalist production, which is extensively dependent upon its domestic and neighboring Asiatic market, this is also beginning to change." The note is significant in that it in no way denies the existence of "the economic groundwork of Asiatic production" but suggests only that in Russia by the 1890s it had been weakened by the advent of capitalist production. This shows that Marx and Engels had not abandoned the concept of the AMP in their later years.

The essential content of the AMP—common property in land—is dealt with in many places in Marx's writings, especially in the descriptions of "Asiatic forms of property" in *Pre-Capitalist Economic Formations*, and in the discussion of primitive communal ownership in *Theories of Surplus Value*. In a letter to Engels in

1868, he includes the system of common property Maurer discovered in Germany among the "Asiatic or Indian forms of ownership in various parts of Europe."[19] In other words, Marx thought that the AMP had once existed in Europe. Similar comments by Marx in a letter to Danielson of March 13, 1873, and by Engels in his *Anti-Dühring* of 1878 repeat the point that "the primitive common ownership of the land," that is, the AMP, is a necessary stage to be found "among all civilized peoples of Europe and Asia."[20]

Even in the 1880s, after they had read Morgan's *Ancient Society*, Marx and Engels still maintained that the AMP was a necessary stage in the development of society. We see this in the third draft of Marx's letter to Vera Zasulich, in which he remarks that, while common ownership of land can be found in the early history of all areas of Europe, "primitive communities are not all cut to a single pattern."

> On the contrary, taken together they form a series of social groupings, differing both in type and in age, and marking successive phases of development. One of these types, now by general agreement called "the agricultural community," is the type of the *Russian community*. Its counterpart in the West is the *Germanic community*, which is of very recent date.[21]

Marx does not use the term AMP here, yet he has certainly not given up the idea that common property in land—the core content of the AMP—is a necessary social stage. Engels makes the same point in 1888 in his footnote to the new English edition of the *Manifesto*, and again in 1894:

> Common ownership of land flourished in the primitive period among the Germanic, Celtic and India peoples; in short, was the form of possession that flourished among all Indo-European peoples. This form of possession still exists in India today, only recently was forcibly dissolved in Ireland and Scotland, and in Germany even now can still be seen in various places. It is a form of possession in decline. *As a specific stage of development it was in fact a phenomenon common to all peoples.*[22]

Marx and Engels thus continued over several decades to view the

AMP, which Marx originally formulated in the 1850s as a concept based on common property in land, as the first of a series of epochs in the evolution of the economic forms of society. At no point did they discard the AMP.

We have reviewed Marx's and Engels' writings on common property in land, which is the core content of the AMP, to verify its existence for them as a stage in the development of society. Contrary to Nikiforov, this was no "guess" on their part, no "hypothetical concept." Although Morgan proved that there existed prior to the village community an even more primitive social formation based on clans, his discovery in no way brought into question the scientific validity of the AMP as a distinct epoch in the history of socieconomic formations.[23]

Notes

1. Qi Qingfu, "The AMP Is Not a Marxist Scientific Concept," in this volume.

2. *CCPE*, p. 33.

3. Marx, *Capital*, vol. 1 (New York: International Publishers, 1967), p. 77. Editor's note: Marx appends the foregoing quote from the *Critique* to this phrase in *Capital*.

4. Marx and Engels, *Manifesto of the Communist Party* (Beijing: Foreign Languages Press, 1965), p. 32.

5. *CCPE*, p. 21.

6. Marx makes the same point in the third draft of his letter to Vera Zasulich of March 8, 1881: "As the last phase of the primitive formation of society, the agricultural community is at the same time a transitional phase to the secondary formation, i.e. transition from society based on common property to society based on private property. The secondary formation comprises, as you must understand, the series of societies based on slavery and serfdom" (*PCEF*, p. 145).

7. Cited in *Waiguo xuezhe lun Yaxiya shengchan fangshi*, 1:259. Editor's note: Nikiforov's views are summarized in Gilbert Rozman, ed., *Soviet Studies of Premodern China: Assessments of Recent Scholarship* (Ann Arbor: Center for Chinese Studies, University of Michigan, 1984), pp. 150–52.

8. Georgii Plekhanov, *Fundamental Problems of Marxism* (New York: International Publishers, 1969), p. 63.

9. Editor's note: The author's further comments on Nikiforov and Plekhanov have been ommitted from the translation.

10. Marx, *Capital*, 1:10.

11. Marx, *Economic Manuscripts*, *MEQJ*, 48:163–64.

12. See above, note 6.

13. Editor's note: Three paragraphs of the original text have been omitted here.

14. Marx, *Capital*, 1:351n.2.

15. Lawrence Krader, *The Ethnological Notebooks of Karl Marx* (Assen, The Netherlands: Van Gorcum, 1972), p. 119.

16. Engels, "Preface to the Fourth German Edition," in Marx, *Capital*, 1:26.

17. See, e.g., the new data and revisions Engels has appended in *Capital*, 3:542n.12, and 605n.24.

18. Ibid., p. 334.

19. Marx to Engels, March 14, 1868, in *PCEF*, p. 139.

20. Engels, *Anti-Dühring* (Moscow: Foreign Languages Publishing House, 1962), p. 243.

21. *PCEF*, p. 144. Italics in original.

22. Engels, "The Afterword to 'Soziales aus Russland,' " *MEQJ*, 22:494. Emphasis added.

23. Editor's note: A closing paragraph discussing Marx's assessment of his *Critique* as a scientific work has been omitted.

SU KAIHUA

10 | The Meaning of the "Asiatic Mode of Production" and the Origin of the Term

From Marx's comment that "the Asiatic, ancient, feudal and modern bourgeois modes of production may be designated as epochs marking progress in the economic development of society"[1] has arisen the great unresolved debate over the question of an "Asiatic" mode of production (AMP). He Ziquan in his 1985 essay "The Meaning of the 'Asiatic Mode of Production' "[2] is perceptive in seeing the AMP as the period or stage prior to ancient society and insisting on the need to distinguish the AMP from "Oriental despotism." But I think he has not correctly understood the basic meaning of the AMP, for he concludes on the basis of *Theories of Surplus Value* and *Capital* that it denotes primitive society, or the primitive communal period.

Let us begin by considering the passage He Ziquan cites from *Theories of Surplus Value*:

> The original unity between the worker and the conditions of production (abstracting from slavery, where the labourer himself belongs to the objective conditions of production) has two main forms: the Asiatic communal system (primitive communism) and small-scale agriculture based on the family (and linked with domestic industry) in one form or another.[3]

From *Zhengming* (Contending) 4 (1986): 62–65. Translated by Timothy Brook.

This passage in no way implies that slavery (that is, of "ancient" society) necessarily follows chronologically "the two main forms" of "the original unity between the worker and the conditions of production." In fact, as Marx himself recognized, slavery is not exclusive to "antiquity" but can be found to exist to varying degrees both within the period of tribal ownership predating "ancient ownership" and in the subsequent medieval and modern periods.

Second, and even more crucially, we cannot state conclusively that the "Asiatic communal system" of which Marx speaks in this passage is the "village community" of the AMP period. Village communities can exist in different periods and accordingly may have different characters, as Marx himself later discovered: "To mix together all primitive communities is mistaken. Just like geological formations, there are primary and secondary forms in the formation of history."[4] The existence of communes or village communities in a later period cannot be used to determine the mode of production of a previous period.

According to the various drafts of Marx's letter to Vera Zasulich in 1881, "the very youngest type" of the village community, which he called "the last word of the archaic formation of societies," has three characteristics: (1) It is "based on blood relationships between the members of the community. These communities have only blood relatives or adopted relatives. Their structure is the structure of a genealogical tree." (2) The "economic foundation" of this community is "common housing and collective residence." (3) "Production is carried out cooperatively; apart from what is set aside for the reproduction of the laborers, the product is distributed on the basis of consumption needs."[5] This "community" is what we speak of today as the clan community.[6]

What follows the clan community chronologically is the "primitive tribal community." Communities of this sort are founded "on the immature development of man individually, who has not yet severed the umbilical cord that unites him with his fellowmen."[7] Marx's "primitive tribal community" is nomadic, for he observes that the tribe does "not settle in a fixed place but uses up what it finds locally and then passes on."[8] Given that Marx understood tribal ownership to be "the first form of ownership,"[9] we may conclude that by "primitive tribal community" he means the community of the pastoral (nomadic) period.[10]

As settled agricultural livelihood came to replace nomadic livelihood, and as locality relations replaced blood relations, the patriarchal community dissolved in favor of the "village community" (which Marx also called the "agricultural" or "peasant community"[11]). The village community is a broad concept susceptible to differentiation into many types. From a temporal perspective, remnants or variants can be found to exist from antiquity down to the medieval period and even into the modern period. In geographical terms, one can find both Oriental and Western village communities.

What kind of village communities, then, is Marx speaking of in the following passage from *Capital*, which He Ziquan quotes:

> The obstacles presented by the internal solidarity and organisation of pre-capitalistic, national modes of production to the corrosive influence of commerce are strikingly illustrated in the intercourse of the English with India and China. The broad basis of the mode of production here is formed by the unity of small-scale agriculture and home industry, to which in India we should add the form of village communities built upon the common ownership of land, which, incidentally, was the original form in China as well.[12]

From the context, the references are clearly to communities that have survived as remnants in modern Oriental society. These are what Marx in many places refers to as the foundation for "Oriental despotism." Although Marx did parenthetically insert "primitive communism" in the passage from *Theories of Surplus Value*, he did so to indicate that this kind of community still bore a "primitive communal" character. He was not saying that these communities were those of the primitive communal period. Hence, this kind of nonprimitive Oriental community cannot be invoked to prove that the AMP refers to primitive society.

If the Oriental "village community" and the AMP are not indissolubly linked, then at what period did the AMP exist? I maintain that the concept describes the mode of production of pastoral society, immediately prior to the time when people settled down to an agricultural way of life; in other words, the patriarchal tribal community. It to be found in both Oriental and Western history [between primitive society and the emergence of agricultural society].

There can be no doubt that, according to the Preface to the *Critique*, Marx regarded the AMP as the earliest mode of production in human history, the first "socioeconomic formation." On the opening page of the *Grundrisse* Marx rules out "the individual and isolated hunter and fisherman" from the sequence of modes of production, as they are not "individuals producing in society."[13] For Marx, the starting point of social production (and property) is nomadism or pastoralism. He says in *Pre-Capitalist Economic Formations*: "We may take it for granted that pastoralism, or more generally a migratory life, is the first form of maintaining existence."[14] Clearly, Marx's approach to modes of production and the progress of society in general is to treat the pastoral age as "the beginning point of true development." On this basis we can see that Marx regarded the AMP as the mode of production of the pastoral age.

This conclusion also provides an answer to the question of why Marx, even after his later discovery of the existence of the clan community, which predated both pastoral and agricultural livelihood, did not abandon the idea that the AMP was the earliest mode of production in human history, for the AMP, the first socioeconomic formation, could now be identified with pastoralism, "the first form of maintaining existence" after the clan stage. The sequence of historical forms of ownership in *The German Ideology* (tribal, ancient communal and state ownership, and feudal or estate-property[15]) thus matches perfectly the sequence of "modes of production" given in the Preface. In other words, tribal ownership and the AMP both belong to the age prior to "ancient" society and are both products of the same period, pastoralism.

Why did Marx choose the term "Asiatic" for this mode of production? Is it, as He Ziquan says, a reflection of the limitations of the age in which Marx lived, when the history of Europe prior to ancient society was little researched? He Ziquan rests his argument on Engels' note to the first sentence in the 1888 English edition of the *Manifesto of the Communist Party*:

In 1847, the pre-history of society, the social organization existing previous to recorded history, was all but unknown. Since then, Haxthausen discovered common ownership of land in Russia, Maurer proved it to be the social foundation from which all Teutonic races started in history, and by and by, village communities were found to be, or to have been, the primitive form of society everywhere from India to Ireland. The inner organization of this primitive Communistic society was laid bare, in its typical form, by Morgan's crowning discovery of the true nature of the *gens* [clan] and its relation to the *tribe*. With the dissolution of these primeval communities, society begins to be differentiated into separate and finally antagonistic classes.[16]

Maurer was the first person to prove that the "common ownership of land" found in the Orient had also existed in Western history, but Marx came to his own awareness of this fact independently. Marx suggests as much in a letter to Engels in which he says that, although Maurer "knew nothing of the view I have put forward, namely that the Asian or Indian forms of property constitute the initial ones everywhere in Europe, he provides further proof of it."[17] He Ziquan's argument that Marx's reason for using "Asiatic" was that European prehistory was insufficiently studied at the time thus lacks substance.

In fact, the type of "property" and "community" that Maurer verified for Marx was not, as He Ziquan tells us, the product of "a stage prior to ancient society." Rather, the property and community Maurer studied came *after* the ancient period. This view is corroborated in the first draft of Marx's letter to Vera Zasulich:

When the Germanic tribes occupied Italy, Spain, and Gaul, the ancient form of the community no longer existed. . . . Most importantly, the stamp of the old community is manifested with great clarity in the community that replaced it, for in the new community, the cultivable soil belongs to the peasants as private property, whereas woodlands, pastures, and waste still remain common land. Thus Maurer, who investigated the community in its secondary form, was able to reconstruct it in its archaic primary form.[18]

We can see that the Germanic community Maurer studied was a "secondary" community, preceded by the "archaic" type. If the

"Asiatic mode" is recognized as having preceded ancient society, then the "Germanic" form cannot be located within the same period in the development of society. Hence the kind of community Maurer studied cannot be associated with the AMP, nor can the source for the term "Asiatic" be explained in this way.[19]

What, then, was Marx's basis for calling the earliest form of property in human history "Asiatic"? The reason is rooted in Marx's great "hypothesis" concerning the origin of civilization. Let us return to his discussion of "the form of Asiatic property" in *Pre-Capitalist Economic Formations*, which we have already quoted in part and now present in full:

> The first prerequisite of this earliest form of landed property appears as a human community, such as emerges from spontaneous evolution: the family, the family expanded into a tribe, or the tribe created by the inter-marriage of families or combination of tribes. We may take it for granted that pastoralism, or more generally a migratory life, is the first form of maintaining existence, the tribe not settling in a fixed place but using up what it finds locally and then passing on. Men are not settled by nature (unless perhaps in such fertile environments that they could subsist on a single tree like the monkeys; otherwise they would roam, like the wild animals). Hence the tribal community, the natural common body, appears not as the consequence, but as the precondition for the joint (temporary) appropriation and use of the soil.[20]

Marx thus located the "true origin" of human society in the pastoral period. But Marx "hypothesized" further that the earliest pastoral society originated in Asia, and for this reason he called the earliest mode of production in history "Asiatic."

To attribute the origin of pastoral society to Asia was initially a bold hypothesis, and subsequent research during Marx's lifetime by Morgan and others was to prove him right. According to Morgan, pastoralism began among Aryan and Semitic peoples in West or South Asia.[21] As they moved westward and northward during the pastoral period,[22] they carried the form of property of the tribal period (i.e., what we have come to call the "Asiatic" form) with them throughout the Eurasian continent. Thus, we can see that the AMP came to exist historically in the West as well as the

Orient, but that it first appeared in Asia. It was for this reason that Marx used the term "Asiatic mode of production."

Notes

1. Marx, *CCPE*, p. 21.
2. He Ziquan, " 'Yaxiya shengchan fangshi' de benyi," *Shehui kexue jikan* 1 (1985): 103–106.
3. Marx, *Theories of Surplus Value* (Moscow: Progress Publishers, 1971), pt. 3, pp. 422–23.
4. Marx to Zasulich, March 8, 1881, first draft.
5. Marx to Zasulich, third draft, in *PCEF*, p. 145.
6. Editor's note: Marx characterized primitive society in terms of the clan community on the basis of Morgan's *Ancient Society*. In the argument to follow, Su Kaihua differentiates the clan community (primitive society) from the tribal community (the Asiatic mode), later followed by the agricultural community (the ancient mode).
7. Marx, *Capital*, vol. 1 (New York: International Publishers, 1967), p. 79.
8. *PCEF*, p. 68.
9. Marx and Engels, *The German Ideology* (New York: International Publishers, 1970), p. 43.
10. Engels called it "the patriarchal household community." See *The Origin of the Family, Private Property, and the State* (New York: International Publishers, 1942), p. 53.
11. *PCEF*, p. 68.
12. Marx, *Capital*, 3:333.
13. Marx, *Grundrisse* (Harmondsworth: Penguin, 1973), p. 83.
14. *PCEF*, p. 68.
15. Marx and Engels, *The German Ideology*, pp. 43–45.
16. Marx and Engels, *Manifesto of the Communist Party* (Beijing: Foreign Languages Press, 1965), p. 32.
17. Marx to Engels, March 14, 1868, in *PCEF*, p. 139.
18. Marx to Zasulich, first draft.
19. Note also that the form of property Maurer was verifying was landed property. When Marx wrote to Engels that Maurer had verified for him the existence of "the Asian or Indian forms of property . . . everywhere in Europe," he was clearly talking about property in its landed form. Although the "Asiatic form of property" was the first form of landed property (*PCEF*, p. 68), landed property is not property's first form. If we understand the Asiatic form of property to be the tribal ownership of the pastoral period, Asiatic property is seen to be not solely landed. Hence, the earliest form of landed property noted by Maurer for Europe cannot be used to explain the earliest form of property in human history, nor be offered as the reason why Marx used the term "Asiatic" to indicate it.
20. *PCEF*, p. 68.
21. Lewis H. Morgan, *Ancient Society* (New York: Henry Holt, 1877), p. 25.
22. Ibid., p. 23; cf. Engels, *The Origin of the Family*, p. 21.

HU ZHONGDA

11 | The Asiatic Mode of Production and the Theory of Five Modes of Production

Marx's earliest reference to the Asiatic mode of production (AMP) in his 1859 Preface to *A Contribution to the Critique of Political Economy*[1] has led to disagreement over how this concept should be understood, and exactly what type of socioeconomic formation it represents. The debate over the AMP involves not only questions of theoretical significance, but also matters of practical value. After all, the definition of a nation's social character is for all developing countries a necessary ideological prerequisite to determining that nation's path toward revolution. The first debate in the 1920s and 1930s on the AMP and its relation to China centered on the practical issue of the Chinese revolution. Unfortunately, the debate became a victim of factional struggles within the Comintern and the Soviet Communist Party. Once Stalin affirmed that there were exactly five stages in the development of every society, the AMP debate disappeared from academic discussion. An even larger debate was launched in the late 1950s and 1960s in response to national liberation movements. Now, once again, the issue of the AMP has reemerged, and there is as yet no consensus.

The AMP must be understood in relation to the slave and feudal modes of production. This forces us to confront the broader questions of whether human history unfolds along a unilinear as

From *Zhongguo shi yanjiu* (Studies in Chinese history) 3 (1981): 30–43. Translated by André Schmid.

opposed to multilinear path, and whether there are four, five, or even six modes of production.

Returning to the Original Meaning of the AMP

What was Karl Marx's original understanding of the AMP? In his comments on the subject, Marx portrayed the AMP as having several characteristics. First, in the AMP, two types of landownership existed. One type was public ownership by village communities; the other, more common than the former, was state landownership, usually under a despotic ruler. In the latter the state is the "higher or sole proprieter," whereas the former are "hereditary possessors."[2] Marx summarizes this situation: "The state is then the supreme lord. Sovereignty here consists in the ownership of land concentrated on a national scale. But, on the other hand, no private ownership of land exists, although there is both private and common possession of land."[3] Marx and Engels concluded that "the absence of private landed property is the real key, even to the eastern heaven."[4]

The second characteristic identified by Marx was that the village community, the fundamental unit of Oriental society, formed the basic structure of the AMP. He took Indian communities to be representative of the rest of the Orient. In India, "a village, geographically considered, is a tract of country comprising some 100 or 1,000 acres of arable and wastelands.. . . In some of these communities the lands of the village [are] cultivated in common, in most of them each occupant tills his own field. . . . Wastelands [are used] for common pasture."[5]

The major distinguishing feature of Indian communities was a "blending of agriculture and handicrafts and an unalterable division of labour." Each village community "forms a compact whole, producing all it requires. The chief part of the products is destined for direct use by the community itself, and does not take the form of a commodity." In addition, "spinning and weaving are carried on in each family as subsidiary industries."[6] Indian villages also manifested certain social divisions. They had leaders, accountants, guards, and a range of other hereditary positions forming an administrative structure. This structure had a dual function: on the one hand, it was an organization for self-governance at the local level; on the other, it served as the grass-roots unit for the exploitation and rule of the villages by the despotic state. The class divisions within the villages were already "contaminated by distinctions of caste and slavery."[7]

The economic function of this type of village was not merely its own reproduction. It also served as a source of revenue and corvée labor for the despotic state. In *Pre-Capitalist Economic Formations*, Marx pointed out: "Part of its surplus labour belongs to the higher community, which ultimately appears as a *person*. This surplus labour is rendered both as tribute and as common labour for the glory of the unity, in part that of the imagined tribal entity of the god."[8] In *Capital* Marx further stated: "Should the direct producers not be confronted by a private landowner, but rather, as in Asia, under direct subordination to a state which stands over them as their landlord and simultaneously as sovereign, then rent and taxes coincide, or rather, there exists no tax which differs from this form of ground rent."[9]

The third characteristic of the AMP, stasis, also concerns the village communities. In an article in the *New York Daily Tribune*, Marx reminds his readers: "We must not forget that these idyllic village-communities, inoffensive though they may appear, had always been the solid foundation of Oriental despotism, that they restrained the human mind within the smallest possible compass, making it the unresisting tool of superstition, enslaving it beneath traditional rules, depriving it of all grandeur and historical energies."[10] Because of their self-sufficient nature, communities of this type could "constantly reproduce themselves in the same form, and when accidentally destroyed, spring up again on the spot and with the same name." As Marx observes in *Capital*, their simplicity was "the key to the unchangeableness of Asiatic societies, an unchangeableness in such striking contrast with the constant dissolution and refounding of Asiatic states, and the never ceasing changes of dynasty. The structure of the economic elements of society remains untouched by the storm clouds of the political sky."[11]

Marx was adamant in stressing that "however changing the political aspect of India's past must appear, its social condition has remained unaltered since its remotest antiquity, until the first decennium of the nineteenth century." At this point, the "semi-barbarian, semi-civilized communities" were destroyed by the invading forces of capitalist Britain. This "produced the greatest, and to speak the truth the only *social* revolution ever heard of in Asia."[12]

The fourth characteristic of the AMP is its geographic extent. Within "Oriental society" or the "Asiatic mode," Marx included such countries as India, Indonesia, Persia, Turkey, Arabia, Egypt, and, of course, the Chinese empire.

Finally, Marx repeatedly pointed out that in China the small peasant economy was closely integrated with household handicraft production. As in India, in China "the broad basis of the mode of production . . . is formed by the unity of small-scale agriculture and home industry" within the village.[13] In this ancient empire, as in all Oriental nations, there existed "unceasing change in the persons and clans that gain control of the political superstructure" while the "social substructure" remained constantly immobile. For this reason, Marx dubbed China the "living fossil."[14]

To summarize, the AMP was a mode of production based on a village communal system of ownership. Having only the right to occupy and utilize the land, these communities and their members were subordinate to the despotic state. Agriculture and handicraft production were closely linked, creating a high degree of self-sufficiency. The bulk of their production was geared toward satisfying their own immediate needs and ensuring their reproduction, though surplus production and surplus labor were transferred in the form of tax and corvée to the despotic state and the exploiting classes. In this way, these villages served as the basic unit for the exploitation and domination of the working masses by the ruling class. In Oriental societies, changes of dynasty and regime were of little importance since the basic unit of society, the village community, remained unchanged. Throughout the long history of the Orient, these villages created a firm foundation for the rule of despotic regimes. It was not until Western capitalism encroached upon the Orient that this traditional order was upset. This, in short, is how Marx conceived of the AMP.

Having reviewed Marx's vision of the AMP, we are now in a

position to deal with the question of whether primitive village communities can be classified as being under the AMP. As Marx wrote in a letter to Vera Zasulich, "primitive communities are not all cut to a single pattern. On the contrary, taken together they form a series of social groupings, differing both in type and age, and marking successive phases of development."[15] The AMP-type village communities preserved many vestiges of their original, pre-AMP forms. However, the AMP-type village had already advanced to the point of producing surplus value, the hallmark differentiating the AMP-type village community from the primitive community. Since only the former has the surplus product and labor to transfer to the despotic state, it cannot represent the initial stage in the historical development of the community; rather, it forms a derivative or secondary stage. One must be careful to distinguish between these two types of communities and not group them into one stage of development.

The next issue to address is whether the AMP, or an early stage of the AMP, accurately describes the mode of production of Oriental slavery. Marx acknowledged the existence of slavery within Indian village communities, but he believed that during the AMP stage "slavery neither puts an end to the conditions of labour, nor does it modify the essential relationship."[16] Since slavery could not become the leading mode of production during the AMP stage, Marx never considered ancient India or any other ancient Oriental country to be a slave society.[17]

If we accept that it does not represent the slave mode of production, can the AMP, or a late stage of the AMP, be applied to the mode of production of Oriental feudalism? According to Marx, it cannot. Early definitions of the term feudalism equated it with the fief system. In such a system, the distribution of land—including, of course, the peasants who tilled the land—determined the personal status, powers, and obligations of the rulers, lords, and vassals. It is essentially the concept of this system that is embodied in both the Western term "feudalism" and its Chinese counterpart *fengjian* [enfeoffment]. Thus the fief system in political terms was the converse of a centralized state; and in economic terms, it acted as a system for the ruling classes to divide rent profits by rank. To develop a complete understanding of feudalism, however, we must move beyond the fief system and discuss serfdom as well. It is the combination of these two systems, enfeoffment and serfdom, that constituted the typical feudal system as found in Europe during the Middle Ages as well as in China during the Western Zhou and Spring and Autumn periods (eleventh to sixth century B.C.).

Marx did not believe that the ancient Orient, with the exception of Japan, was a feudal society; nor did Engels.[18] Throughout his works, Marx referred to China as "the Heavenly Kingdom," "the Chinese Empire," even "a living fossil," but none of these names signifies feudalism. His analysis of the integration of agriculture and handicraft clearly shows that "feudal" is not an appropriate adjective for China. In the eyes of Marx, feudalism never existed there.

Is it possible that in his later years Marx abandoned his concept of the AMP? During the 1870s and 1880s, as he obtained more information on Oriental societies, Marx did revise his views on certain issues, but his basic conviction that Oriental society consisted of village communities dominated by despotic powerholders remained unchanged.[19] In short, Marx considered the AMP to be a unique form of production, different from both the primitive communal mode of production and the ancient slavery and medieval feudalism characteristic of the West. It was a unique precapitalist economic formation in Oriental history.

Asiatic, Ancient, and Feudal Modes of Production as the Same Stage of Development

In 1859 Marx proposed in his Preface a schema for delineating the different stages of social development: "the Asiatic, ancient, feudal and modern bourgeois modes of production." Subsequent attempts to ascertain the relationships among these socioeconomic stages have divided scholars in China and abroad into two camps. Their divergent positions can perhaps best be portrayed by figures 1 and 2. Figure 1 represents a modified version of the five-stages theory, the only difference being the inclusion of the AMP. Figure 2 amounts to a rejection of the five-stages theory insofar as it contends that feudal society did not evolve from ancient slave society but developed directly out of primitive society. Proponents of this

Figure 1. Modified Five-Stages Theory

Primitive Communal MP (mode of production)

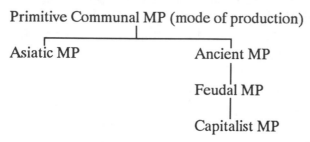

Asiatic MP   Ancient MP

Feudal MP

Capitalist MP

Figure 2. Multilinear Theory

Primitive Communal MP

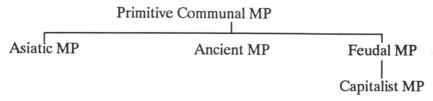

Asiatic MP   Ancient MP   Feudal MP

Capitalist MP

second view, including myself, argue that the Asiatic, ancient, and feudal modes of production are all representative of a single stage of development. They are simply three different forms of class society found in the same precapitalist stage.

This arrangement raises many question, including the chronological relationship between slavery and serfdom. It has generally been maintained that serfdom could exist only in the latter period of slave society, facilitating the emergence of the following stage, feudalism. Yet we find Marx pointing out in *Pre-Capitalist Economic Formations* that slavery and serfdom could appear simultaneously in the transition from primitive society to class society:

> The fundamental condition of property based on tribalism (which is originally formed out of the community) is to be a member of the tribe. Consequently, a tribe conquered and subjugated by another becomes *propertyless* and part of the *inorganic conditions* of the conquering tribe's reproduction, which that community regards as its own. Slavery and serfdom are therefore simply further developments of property based on tribalism. They necessarily modify all its forms. This they are least able to do in the Asiatic form.[20]

Hence, in late primitive society, conquest could lead to enslavement or serfdom.[21] Marx did not view serfdom merely as a "sprout of feudalism" rooted in late slave society.

The model of feudalism used by Marx and Engels in their studies was Western European feudalism. Established by the Germanic people, feudal society there evolved directly from the primitive stage. According to the pattern of historical development espoused by the five-stages theory, the Germanic barbarians should have first passed through a slave stage before entering feudalism. But, as we have seen, this was not the case: the Germanic people were able to bypass slavery and enter feudalism directly. This seemingly anomalous sequence of development was made possible, it is argued, because of the influence of the more advanced production forces of the Romans—an external factor without which the primitive Germans could not have skipped the slave stage.

Marx believed that conquest could lead to three possible outcomes when different modes of production came into conflict. The conquerors might impose their own mode of production on their defeated foes; they might allow the mode of production of their enemies to continue, satisfying themselves with the extraction of taxes and tribute from that system; or the two modes of production might mutually influence one another, synthesizing a new mode of production. The Germanic conquest of the western Roman empire, in particular the Frankish subjugation of Gaul, is an example of the third case. Feudalism emerged in Western Europe from a combination of Germanic and Roman elements: on the Germanic side, military organization and a long history of agricultural serfdom; on the Roman side, a high level of productive forces and the manorial land system.[22]

Serfdom and the parcelization of sovereignty through fiefs were combined in feudalism. In terms of their role in the mode of production, however, the two were by no means equal. Serfdom was the central component, whereas enfeoffment played an essential but subordinate role. The Germanic military system, consisting of "armed bodies of retainers" loyal to their military commanders, provided the foundation for the development of serfdom. By means of this system, rewards and honors were dispensed to create a "hierarchical structure of land ownership."[23] It was precisely this pattern of stratified landholding that provided the economic basis for the fief system.[24]

During the Merovingian period, the Frankish military nobility were granted large tracts of land, which, as "sprouts of feudalism," became a major element of the economy. It is not immediately apparent, however, whether these sprouts blossomed into the feudal mode of production that entrapped the majority of the peasantry, or whether, as Engels said, the Germans were "able to develop and universally introduce the milder forms of servitude they had been practicing at home."[25] To clarify this issue we must investigate the condition of the Germanic communal peasantry after their move to Roman territory.

Prior to the movement of Germanic peasants into newly conquered Roman territory, agricultural and pasture land had been periodically reallocated by household. Once these peasants moved to Roman territory and formed *mark* communities, however, the status of this program of land redistribution becomes difficult to ascertain. Although it may have been implemented at first—and even this is not certain—it could not have lasted long, for soon afterward there is evidence that shares in communal land had already become the private property of individual peasants. By synthesizing both Germanic and Roman elements, the Franks effected the transition from primitive to feudal society, bypassing the slave stage altogether.

It has been suggested that this pattern of development was made possible only because the Franks encountered in the Roman empire a system whose productive forces were already more advanced than slavery. In fact, the situation was exactly the opposite: what the Franks encountered was not a mode of production more advanced than a slave-based system, but rather a system where the productive forces were insufficiently developed to create the requisite conditions for a slave system. It was the decline of the forces of production and the general economic deterioration in the later years of the Roman empire that led to the rise of "big ruling landowners and dependent small peasants," producing the relations of production of serfdom, the foundation of feudalism.[26] The mode of production in the Merovingian and Carolingian periods was not

sufficiently developed, nor their commodity and monetary economies sufficiently strong, to support a large-scale slave economy.
(This is confirmed by Charlemagne's abortive experiments with imperial estates.) Serfdom was their adaptation to the lower level of
productive forces.[27]

Conclusion

We have identified two common misconceptions: that feudal
societies can emerge only from slave societies, and that a primitive
society, lacking advanced forces of production, can only develop
into a slave, not a feudal, society. We can now return to Marx's
statement in the Preface. I have argued that in terms of their social
development, the Asiatic, ancient, and feudal modes of production
may be found at the same stage of development, as shown in figure
2. All three are class societies that took form in the wake of the
disintegration of primitive society and preceded the advent of capitalism.

In the course of history, Oriental societies were the first to
evolve into what we refer to today as civilization. Following close
behind were Greece and Rome. Western European feudalism was
established in turn on the ruins of the Roman empire by the
Germanic peoples. From a chronological perspective, then, the
Asiatic, ancient, and feudal modes of production appeared in succession. Since Western historiography well before Marx's time periodized history into ancient, medieval, and modern, Marx was led
to assume that the Asiatic, ancient, and feudal modes of production were progressive epochs. In fact, in terms of their socioeconomic formations, these three modes of production should be
seen as three variants within a single stage of development.

Being at the same stage of socioeconomic development, these
forms manifest several similarities. (1) All three had at some point
entered the iron age, though, with the exception of a few sectors
that employed simple mechanization, technology remained at the
level of manual production. (2) Agriculture was the main production sector. Households in this sector often integrated handicraft
production with cultivation. The urban handicraft industry and
commodity/money economy expanded, but on the whole, the natu-

ral economy was still dominant. (3) Land rent was the major form of exploitation. It was extracted through the use of extra-economic coercion exerted on the direct producers, who were placed under varying degrees of personal bondage.

These three socioeconomic forms, whether in their level of productive forces, the extent of their division of labor, or the degree to which labor was exploited and bound, are dissimilar only in degree. In terms of their basic nature, there is no substantial difference.[28]

According to Marxist theory, society originates in the primitive communal stage, then enters class society, culminating ultimately in communist society. Socialism is the route through which humanity must pass for the classes that history has created to be destroyed. This is the basic view of Marxism. Where questions have arisen is in determining the forms of class society that existed prior to the advent of capitalism. Did Asiatic, ancient, and feudal socioeconomic formations coexist? Were slavery and feudalism the only two types of precapitalist socioeconomic formation? Was there only one form of feudalism? If two or more socioeconomic formations existed concurrently, what was their relationship? We should not dismiss these questions by maintaining that the only legitimate view on these issues is embodied in the five-stages theory. Differing ideas should not be considered heterodox. Only through public debate and painstaking research can these issues concerning the nature of precapitalist socioeconomic formations be resolved.

Notes

1. *CCPE*, p. 21.
2. *PCEF*, p. 69.
3. Marx, *Capital*, vol. 3 (New York: International Publishers, 1967), p. 791.
4. Marx to Engels, June 2, 1853, in Marx and Engels, *Selected Correspondence* (New York: Progress Publishers, 1942), p. 66.
5. Marx to Engels, June 14, 1853, *MECW*, 39:347.
6. Marx, *Capital*, 1:337.
7. Marx, "The British Rule in India," *MECW*, 12:132.
8. *PCEF*, p. 70.
9. *Capital*, 3:791.
10. Marx, "British Rule in India," *MECW*, 12:131.
11. Marx, *Capital*, 1:358.

12. Marx, "The British Rule in India," *MECW*, 12:132.

13. Marx, *Capital*, 3:393.

14. Marx, "Chinese Affairs," *MECW*, 19:216.

15. *PCEF*, p. 144.

16. *PCEF*, p. 92.

17. Engels is the author of some puzzling comments on slavery in the ancient Orient. In 1884 he wrote in *The Origin of the Family, Private Property and the State* that Oriental domestic slavery was quite developed (Marx and Engels, *Selected Works* [Moscow: Foreign Language Publishing House, 1958], p. 307). Three years later, Engels continued this line of thought, asserting that "in Asiatic . . . antiquity the predominant form of class oppression was slavery" (*The Condition of the Working Class in England* [Oxford: Basil Blackwell, 1958], p. 355). We do not understand the basis for Engels' change of heart, nor did he ever expand on these comments. In themselves, however, these two statements are insufficient reason for us to reject Marx's theory.

18. Engels to Marx, June 6, 1853, in *Selected Correspondence*, p. 67.

19. E.g., Marx to Zasulich, March 8, 1881, in *PCEF*, p. 143.

20. *PCEF*, p. 91.

21. See also the third draft of his letter to Vera Zasulich, and *Capital*, 1:227–28.

22. Marx and Engels, *The German Ideology, MECW*, 5:85; Marx, *Grundrisse* (Harmondsworth: Penguin, 1973), pp. 97–98.

23. Marx and Engels, *The German Ideology, MECW*, 5:34.

24. Editor's note: A paragraph on the term "slave" in Tacitus's *Germania* has been omitted here.

25. Engels, *The Origin of the Family*, p. 307.

26. Ibid., p. 305.

27. Editor's note: A discussion of the rise and decline of slavery in the Roman empire has been omitted here.

28. Editor's note: The final section of the original essay concerning the issues of feudalism and slavery in China has been omitted.

MA XIN

12 | The Theory of Marx's "Four Modes of Production"

It has become conventional to interpret Marx's statement in the Preface to *A Contribution to the Critique of Political Economy*—that "in broad outline, the Asiatic, ancient, feudal and modern bourgeois modes of production may be designated as epochs marking progress in the economic development of society"[1]—in accordance with the unilinear "five-stages" theory of social development proposed by Soviet scholars in the 1920s and 1930s. This five-stage theory has been so consistently applied to the "four modes of production" in the Preface that the theory has come to be regarded as Marx's own, and therefore unassailable. Who would now dare to suggest anything other than that the five-stages theory guides the history of every country and every people? To describe history in any other way would be to commit the sin of heresy. And yet a whole host of questions has cropped up because of this theory. Our inability to reach conclusions concerning many major questions of Chinese and world history, despite years of debate, is not unrelated to this assumption. In my opinion, this is the reason why we are still disputing the periodization of ancient Chinese history even after all these years.

How we understand the Preface directly influences our grasp of the laws of historical development. It is well known that Marx based his views in the Preface on his work in the *Grundrisse*, which was written during 1857 and 1858 and anticipates his work in *Capi-*

From *Xinhua wenzhai* (New China digest) 8 (1987): 54–57. Translated by Timothy Brook.

tal. Marx's writings on political economy differ from most works of historical analysis of the time in his use of a consistent, logical system of categories and concepts. It is similarly well known that the object of analysis in Marx's work is the capitalist mode of production. Unlike the bourgeois theorists of his time, Marx saw capitalism not as an eternal category found equally in the past and the present, but as a historical category. Like all previous modes of production, capitalism is a certain stage in the development of property relations corresponding to a stage in the development of the forces of production. It is both the culmination of all past history and the historical precondition for the creation of a higher stage of development. To investigate the historical process of capitalism's emergence, Marx had to study the various modes of production that generated capitalism. His investigation of these earlier modes of production was consistently done in order to understand the later appearance of capitalism.

Marx describes and sequences these modes of production in relation to their distance from pure capitalism in its ideal form, rather than limiting his study of them to the concrete forms or actual chronological sequence in which they appeared in history. Although the ideal and the actual are largely unified in their analysis, they do diverge in certain ways. By going from the abstract to the concrete, Marx and Engels sought to generalize theoretically beyond concrete historical forms to a purer, more representative abstraction, thereby enabling them to grasp the basic characteristics and developmental laws of the material world. They were nonetheless also aware that this logical process could not start from pure thought, as idealism did, but had to begin from tangible facts. This is the methodology that we find Marx using in *A Contribution to the Critique of Political Economy*: searching for the abstract form of the historical currents leading to the emergence of the capitalist mode of production, but doing so on the basis of historical reality.

To reveal the laws governing the developmental process of precapitalist production and the social formations appropriate to it, Marx in the *Grundrisse* focused on the formation of modern private property. From the various modes of production that have existed in history he selected the Asiatic, ancient, and Germanic forms of property in particular for study. Each of these forms of communal property, based on landed property and the management of agriculture, matured in the course of history into a distinct social formation, and each can be examined through both written records and historical relics. Even so, in his search for the classic forms of landownership in each historical period, Marx did not restrict himself to the actualities of a particular period or place.

The Asiatic form is direct ownership in common, the most primitive form of property, and for this reason it appears first in Marx's sequence. Germanic ownership is primarily collective private property, augmented by a limited degree of ownership in common; being closest to the pure private property of modern times, it is placed last. Ancient ownership is also a type of mixed public and private property; having become partly privatized, it is in the second place. These several types of community represent several stages in the evolution of property, and these stages structure the step-by-step process in the history of property. Logically coherent and at the same time globally based, this formulation of the sequence of property forms escapes the restrictions of historical particularity. In purely historical terms, the Asiatic form of ownership may have been the earliest of the three, but it was preserved in some ancient Oriental countries all the way down to the modern period, whereas the later Germanic form disappeared in Europe at an earlier period. What Marx's logically constructed sequence reflects is thus the gradual process of the general evolution of socioeconomic formations rather than their particular histories.

While it is true that Marx in the *Grundrisse* examines the history of earlier socioeconomic formations in order to understand what led to the emergence of capitalist private property, his sequencing of forms of property is also intended to describe historical stages. The first form of ownership (Asiatic), both logically and historically, is the point of origin of capitalist private property; the others are links between the two. This sense of the historical evolution of all precapitalist forms of private property, which Marx once referred to as "capital not yet fully developed,"[2] in the direction of capitalist property runs throughout Marx's writings, from his *Economic and Philosophic Manuscripts* of 1844 and *The German Ideology*, written with Engels in 1845–46,[3] to the *Grundrisse* (specifically, the section published as *Pre-Capitalist Economic Formations*) of 1857–58. For instance, the "common property" that Marx speaks of in relation to the Asiatic form of property in the *Grundrisse* is the earliest form of incipient private property.[4] There is no justification to suppose that this is equivalent to the "common property" of the primitive period, when "all under heaven was held in common." Rather, it stands in relation to the forms of "common property" under the capitalist system of ownership by "private individuals," that is, public or collective ownership. Were it otherwise, it would be difficult to understand why Marx would speak of the exploitation of these communities through slavery and tribute, and the emergence of trade in cities that "arise by the side of these villages."[5] When he speaks of the Asiatic form of property as "primitive," he means it not in the sense of "primitive society," but as a primitive form of private ownership. The "four modes of production" listed in the Preface must therefore not be interpreted in terms of the "five stages" formula.

Compared to the Asiatic form, the forms of property Marx outlines in the *Grundrisse* are somewhat more developed and therefore less primitive. The Asiatic commune derives directly out of tribal (or clan) pastoralism in which fixed land property had not yet been devised, for it is a form of property involving settled residence. Although Marx acknowledged that this settled agricultural existence was historically a great step forward, he did not completely separate it from the pastoral tribalism that preceded it, for two reasons: the gap between them is very small, and their internal structures are basically similar. Hence Marx included them both in his exposition of the AMP. In this sense, the concept of the AMP in general refers to Asiatic communal ownership, but it can also be understood in much larger terms as embracing the developmental process from pastoralism through primitive agriculture to the Asiatic commune.

From this perspective, the pastoral tribe or clan community should be seen as the embryonic form of Asiatic property, and the commune as its developed form. The ancient and Germanic forms of property also derive from the primitive form, of which they are later metamorphoses, serving as the foundations for the separate emergence of classical slavery and medieval feudalism. The original structures of slavery and feudalism are thus based on the ancient and Germanic forms of property, just as the despotic society of the ancient Orient derived from the Asiatic form.

The Preface is a polemic, but it is entirely consistent with the *Grundrisse* (along with Marx's other earlier writings). Where the expositions differ is in their emphases. The *Grundrisse* concentrates on the forms and historical remnants of precapitalist property, whereas the Preface, which seeks to generalize at a theoretical level, presents only a few abstract concepts and logical sequences. To resolve the differences between "modes of production" in the one and "forms of property" in the other, let us consider the "ancient form of property." Its original structure is the ancient urban commune, its developed form is Greek and Roman slavery, and its remnant form in the modern age is plantation slavery in the southern United States. Marx combined these particular historical expressions to conceptualize the "ancient mode of production." Similarly, the original structure of the "Germanic form of property" is the dispersed rural commune, its developed form the feudal serfdom of the Middle Ages, and its remnants the various forms of personal bondage that have been preserved in modern society. Marx has abstracted from these historical data the "feudal mode of production." The AMP is a somewhat more complicated concept, but we can approach it in the same way by proceeding from the "Asiatic form of property" to the AMP, which is how the latter concept took shape. We shall do so by first examining the three ways in which the "Asiatic form of property" is used in the *Grundrisse*, for all three will of course be found within the category of the AMP.

First, the basic structure of the "Asiatic form of property" according to Marx is the agricultural commune in its representative Asiatic form. It is based on common property, tied to the enlarged organization of the patrilineal patriarchal household, and characterized by a productive system in which agriculture and handicraft industry are firmly united. Although a primitive form of ownership, its organization has been advanced by pastoralism; for this reason, this society cannot be called primitive.

Second, the "Asiatic form of property," broadly interpreted, applies to the period from the emergence of pastoralism to the agricultural commune. In the *Grundrisse* it is viewed as the original structure of all forms of precapitalist property, the mother of history; hence, in the Preface, it is placed first. When Marx much later, in the first volume of *Capital*, speaks of the "ancient Asiatic" mode of production,[6] he means it in this sense. This use of the concept by Marx was not simply a logical induction on his part but was related to the knowledge then available to him. For quite a long time, Marx thought that the ancient Orient (principally India) was the origin of human civilization, and that not just European civilization but even the earliest tribes and communes of the Western world had come across from the Orient. As these nomadic peoples encountered different environments and historical conditions, they altered their way of life in ways that led the Asiatic-style tribes and communes to become transformed and thence evolve separately into the ancient and Germanic forms of property. Marx revised this view somewhat in his later years.

Third, the "Asiatic form of property" is used to signify the village communes preserved throughout the ancient Oriental world from the time of earliest antiquity. Marx believed that the peoples that remained in the ancient Orient, unlike those that migrated west, continued to organize their societies on the basis of communes. They did so because of the natural environment and particular historical conditions in the Orient. The internal property relations of the commune, no matter what its age, continued to be primitive, though gradually over several thousand years it was absorbed into the despotic systems of certain ancient Oriental states, serving as the foundation on which rested state ownership of land vested in the despot. This development worked inevitable changes in the internal property relations of the commune and in the status of its members, though the degree and rate of these changes were limited and slow. Ancient Oriental society thus embraced at one extreme the village commune, and at the other the monarchical state, which systematically oppressed and exploited the commune members. This unique combination, the social formation of the ancient Orient, structured something very different from classical [Greco-Roman] slave society and the feudal social formation of the Middle Ages. For this social formation, slow and cyclical in its development, Marx used such expressions as "oriental" society, "the Oriental heaven," "Oriental despotism," and "semi-barbarian, semi-civilized" society.[7] For good reason, he never spoke of it as either slave or feudal society.

What the foregoing demonstrates is that Marx himself did not subscribe to a unilinear view of historical development but saw human societies emanating from a single origin along several different lines. The "AMP" is the mother of world history, whereas the slave and feudal modes of production are the fraternal twins to which she gave birth. The passage from the first to the fourth mode of production in the Preface thus presents a logical sequence of one type of property relations. It conforms in a general way to the course of development of world history, but we should not read it as a strict lineage passing necessarily from one to the other. The first three— Asiatic, slave, and feudal—all shared the same origin but followed different courses as they encountered different conditions. Furthermore, in comparison with capitalism, their mutual differences appear even less striking. For this reason, Marx, from the *Grundrisse* to *Capital*, often spoke generically of pre-capitalist society as a whole, using terms such as "primitive community," "primitive forms of property," and "the prehistory of human society."[8]

Thus I conclude that the period from the emergence of the AMP to the demise of feudalism should be considered a single, unified epoch in human history. Close contact with the natural world, the existence of the community (*gongtongti*), direct relations of personal dominance and servitude, production and exchange that are underdeveloped and restricted, forms of property that are primitive and rough: all these aspects are possessed in common by the three modes of production of this epoch. The feudal mode of production diverges most significantly, for it was able to increase the productive capacity of society more than slavery, and it gave birth to the capitalist mode of production in medieval Europe.

If I am not mistaken in my interpretation of Marx's exposition of the development of socioeconomic formations, then we are now freed from the notion of having to combine his "four modes of production" with the "five stages" into a single, unilinear theory of history. This explains the significance of the opening phrase of the sentence in the Preface, "in broad outline." In my view, "broad outline" comprises two levels of meaning: it means that Marx is abbreviating a far more complicated historical process into a few words, but it also indicates a certain unwillingness on Marx's part to be definitive here. Marx is speaking colloquially. This reading is in keeping with my impression that Marx maintained great flexibility when writing about the course of human history and never stuck precisely to any one periodization. On no account must we read Marx in a rigid fashion, nor should we commit him, or ourselves, to a unilinear view of history.

Notes

1. *CCPE*, pp. 21–22.

2. Marx, *Economic and Philosophic Manuscripts of 1844* (New York: International Publishers, 1964), p. 126.

3. Marx and Engels, *The German Ideology* (New York: International Publishers, 1970), pp. 43–47.

4. *PCEF*, p. 70.

5. Ibid., p. 71.

6. Marx, *Capital*, vol. 1 (New York: International Publishers, 1967), p. 79.

7. Marx, *Grundrisse* (Harmondsworth: Penguin, 1973), p. 106; Marx to Engels, June 2, 1853, in Marx and Engels, *On Colonialism* (New York: International Publishers, 1972), p. 313; Marx, "The British Rule in India," in *On Colonialism*, p. 40.

8. *PCEF*, pp. 81, 101; *CCPE*, p. 22. Editor's note: To this list might be added "ancient social organisms," which Marx contrasts with "bourgeois society" in *Capital*, p. 79.

BIBLIOGRAPHY
CHINESE PUBLICATIONS ON THE ASIATIC
MODE OF PRODUCTION, 1978–1988

The bibliography does not include roughly twenty foreign essays on the AMP translated and published in Chinese journals during this decade.

Abbreviations

BZX   *Baokan ziliao xuanhui* (Selected materials from periodicals), after 1985
FBZ   *Fuyin baokan ziliao* (Reprinted materials from periodicals), to 1985

"Beijing daxue, Jilin shida lianhe zhaokai 'Yaxiya shengchan fangshi' wenti taolunhui" (A conference on the question of the "AMP" jointly sponsored by Beijing University and Jilin Normal University). *Jilin Shida xuebao* (Jilin Normal University journal) 4 (1978).
Cao Gecheng. " 'Yaxiya shengchan fangshi' de benyi jiujing shi shemma" (What is the basic meaning of the "AMP"?). *Beifang luncong* (Northern essays) 6 (1986): 80–86. Reprinted in *BZX* 1 (1987): 11–17.
———. "Yaxiya shengchan fangshi de cunshe tezheng ji yu erzhongxing de guanxi" (Characteristics of the village under the AMP and its dual nature). *Daqing Shizhuan xuebao* (Daqing Normal School journal) 1 (1987).
Chen Gaohua. "Makesi Engesi guanyu yuanshi gongshe fazhan shi de lunshu" (Marx's and Engels' discussions of the history of the development of the primitive community). *Yanjiu jikan* (Research papers), ed. Yunnan Sheng Lishi Yanjiusuo (Yunnan Provincial History Research Institute) 3 (1979).
Chen Hongjin. "Lun Yaxiya shengchan fangshi" (On the AMP). *Shijie lishi* (World history) 5 (1981): 3–11.
Cui Lianzhong. "Guanyu gudai Yindu tudi suoyouzhi wenti" (On the

question of landownership in ancient India). *Lishixue* (The study of history) 1 (1979).

Dong Zhi. " 'Yaxiya shengchan fangshi' yu shijieshi yanjiu: 'Yaxiya shengchan fangshi' xueshu taolunhui ceji" (The "AMP" and the study of world history: Some observations on the academic conference on the "AMP"). *Shijie lishi* 4 (1981): 75–78.

Du Zhangzhi, trans. "Weitefugeer tan Yaxiya shengchan fangshi" (Wittfogel on the AMP). *Guowai shehui kexue dongtai* (Trends in the social sciences outside China) 2 (1981).

Gao Xian. "Lunshu 'Yaxiya shengchan fangshi' de *Makesi yu disan shijie* yishu neirong zhaibian" (Summary of *Marx and the Third World* on the "AMP"). *Makesizhuyi yanjiu cankao ziliao* (Reference materials on research on Marxism) 17 (1980).

Guo Yuanhang. "Xifang xueshujie taolun Yaxiya shengchan fangshi de qingkuang zongshu" (The discussion of the AMP in Western academic circles). *Xueshu dongtai* (Academic trends) 3 (1982).

Hao Zhenhua. "Guowai dui Yaxiya shengchan fangshi wenti de taolun" (Discussion of the question of the AMP outside China). *Guowai shehui kexue dongtai* 2 (1981).

———. "Guowai guanyu Yaxiya shengchan fangshi wenti de taolun" (Discussion of the question of the AMP outside China). *Makesizhuyi yanjiu cankao ziliao* 38 (1981): 57–68.

He Shaoying. "Cong he chu tupo? 'Yaxiya shengchan fangshi' wenti yanjiu de huigu yu zhaowang" (Where can we break through? A retrospective on and prospects for research on the question of the "AMP"). *Yunnan Minzu Xueyuan xuebao* (Yunnan Nationalities Institute journal) 4 (1986): 68–73. Reprinted in *BZX* 1 (1987): 5–10.

He Xin. "Lun Makesi de lishi guandian yu shehui fazhan de wujieduan gongshi" (Marx's view of history and the five-stages formula of social development). *Jinyang xuekan* (Jinyang journal) 6 (1981).

He Xinfu. "Shilun Makesizhuyi 'wuzhong shehui xingtai' xueshuo de jige wenti" (Several questions concerning the Marxist doctrine of "five social formations"). *Qiusuo* (Explorations) 2 (1983).

He Ziquan. " 'Yaxiya shengchan fangshi' de benyi" (The meaning of the "AMP"). *Shehui kexue jikan* (Social sciences journal) 1 (1985): 103–106. Reprinted in *BZX* 1 (1987): 18–21.

He Zuorong. "Ye tan 'Yaxiya shengchan fangshi' " (Further comments on the "AMP"). *Lishi yanjiu* (Studies in history) 5 (1980).

Hu Deping. "Makesi dui Yaxiya shengchan fangshi de tichu, yanjiu he jielun" (Marx's formulation, research, and conclusions on the AMP). *Shehui kexue* (Social sciences) 5 (1980): 118–23. Reprinted in *FBZ* 12 (1980): 3–8.

Hu Zhongda. "Shilun Yaxiya shengchan fangshi jian ping wuzhong fang-shi shuo" (The AMP and the theory of five modes of production). *Zhongguo shi yanjiu* (Studies in Chinese history) 3 (1981): 30–43. Translated in this volume.

———. "Shilun Yaxiya shengchan fangshi jian ping wuzhong shengchan fangshi shuo" (On the AMP, with a critique of the theory of five modes of production). *Nei Menggu Daxue xuebao* (Inner Mongolia University journal) 2 (1982).

———. "Zai ping wuzhong shengchan fangshi shuo" (Further criticism of the theory of five modes of production). *Lishi yanjiu* 1 (1986): 33–51.

Huang Songying. "Yaxiya shengchan fangshi shi dongfang zhuguo de nuli zhanyouzhi xingtai—jian yu *Shijie shanggu shigang* bianxiezu de tongzhi shangque" (The AMP is the form of slavery in Oriental countries: A critique of the authors of *An Outline History of World Antiquity*). *Zhongguo shi yanjiu* 3 (1981): 59–71.

Huang Weicheng. "Yaxiya shengchan fangshi bushi nulizhi de shengchan fangshi" (The AMP is not the slave mode of production). *Guangxi Minzu Xueyuan xuebao* (Guangxi Nationalities College journal) 4 (1986).

———. "Yaxiya shengchan fangshi ke guishu yu fengjian shengchan fangshi" (The AMP belongs within the feudal mode of production). *Guangxi Minzu Xueyuan xuebao* 1 (1987).

Huang Yingxian. "Lun gudai dongfang shehui de xingzhi" (The character of ancient Oriental society). *Huanan Shiyuan xuebao* (Huanan Normal College journal) 4 (1980).

Jiang Hong and Jiang Jie. "Makesi zai wannian fangqi le 'Yaxiya' zheyi gainian ma?" (Did Marx abandon the concept of 'Asiatic' in his later years?). *Wen shi zhe* (Literature, history, philosophy) 5 (1981): 19–27.

Ke Changji. "Cong Yaxiya shengchan fangshi kan Zhongguo de gudai shehui" (Ancient Chinese society and the AMP). *Lanzhou Daxue xuebao* (Lanzhou University journal) 3 (1983): 16–25. Translated in this volume.

———. "Xian-Qin de Yaxiya shehui" (Pre-Qin Asiatic society). *Shehui kexue (Gansu)* (Social sciences [Gansu]) 1 (1988).

Li Tianyou. "Ye tan Yaxiya shengchan fangshi wenti" (Further comments on the question of the AMP). *Lanzhou Daxue xuebao* 2 (1981).

Li Xihou. "Makesi shi zai 'Zhengzhi jingjixue pipan, xuyan' zhong shouci tichu 'Yaxiya shengchan fangshi' wenti de ma?" (Did Marx first raise the question of the "AMP" in the preface to *A Contribution to the Critique of Political Economy*?). *Guoji Zhengzhi Xueyuan xuebao* (International Politics Institute journal) 1 (1983).

Li Yongcai and Wei Maoheng. "Guanyu Yaxiya shengchan fangshi yan-jiu fangfa de jige wenti" (Some questions concerning the methodology of research on the AMP). *Wen shi zhe* 1 (1986): 13–16.

Li Zutang. "Guanyu Makesizhuyi yu Yaxiya shengchan fangshi de wenti" (Marxism and the question of the AMP). *Guizhou Shida xuebao* (Guizhou Normal University journal) 4 (1987).

Liang Youyao and Xie Baogeng. *Zhongguo shi wenti taolun ji qi guandian* (Discussions and viewpoints on questions in Chinese history), pp. 30–41. Taiyuan: Shanxi Renmin Chubanshe, 1984.

Liao Xuesheng. "Guanyu 'dongfangzhizhuyi'" (On "Orientalism"). *Shijie lishi* 1 (1980).

Lin Ganquan. "Yaxiya shengchan fangshi yu Zhongguo gudai she-hui—jian ping Wengbeituo Meiluodi de *Makesi yu disan shijie* dui Zhongguo lishi de waiqu" (The AMP and China's ancient society: A criticism of Umberto Melotti's distortion of Chinese history in his *Marx and the Third World*). *Zhongguo shi yanjiu* 3 (1981): 133–46.

Lin Ganquan, Tian Renlong, and Li Zude. "Guanyu 'Yaxiya shengchan fangshi' de zhenglun" (The debate over the "AMP"); " 'Yaxiya sheng-chan fangshi' de xin jieda" (New interpretations of the "AMP"); "'Yaxiya shengchan fangshi' de zai tantao" (The reexamination of the "AMP"). In their *Zhongguo gudaishi fenqi taolun wushinian (1929–1979)* (Fifty years of discussions of the periodization of ancient Chinese history) (Shanghai: Shanghai Renmin Chubanshe, 1982), pp. 21–35, 86–90, 147–60.

Lin Hong. " 'Yaxiya shengchan fangshi' shijie" (A tentative interpretation of the "AMP"). *Sichuan Daxue xuebao* (Sichuan University journal) 3 (1982).

[Lin] Zhichun and [Liao] Xuesheng. "Zenyang lijie Makesi shuode Yaxiya shengchan fangshi?" (How should we understand Marx's AMP?). *Shijie lishi* 2 (1979): 13–19.

Liu Jiahe. "Gongyuan qian liu zhi si shiji bei Yindu shehui xingzhi he fazhan quxiang lice" (An analysis of the character and direction of development of north Indian society from the sixth to the fourth century B.C.). *Nanya yanjiu* (South Asian studies) 1 (1983).

Liu Fangjun. "Zhongguo shi fou zai Yaxiya shengchan fangshi? 1925-1931 nian zai Sulian de bianlun" (Is China in the AMP? The debate in the USSR, 1925–1931). *Guowai shehui kexue xueshu qingbao* (The social sciences abroad) 6 (1981).

Liu Xiaming and Xu Haoming. "Guanyu Yaxiya shengchan fangshi ji qi youguan gainian de tantao" (An inquiry into the AMP and related concepts). *Anhui Daxue xuebao* (Anhui University journal) 3 (1980): 20–24.

Lu Kaiwan. "Jianxi 'Yaxiya shengchan fangshi' diyici dalunzhan" (A brief analysis of the first controversy over the "AMP"). *Wuhan Daxue xuebao* (Wuhan University journal) 2 (1984): 45–48.

Luo Biyun. "Yaxiya shengchan fangshi de taolun yiji wo dui tade lijie" (My understanding of the discussion of the AMP). *Zhongshan Daxue xuebao* (Sun Yatsen University journal) 2 (1980).

Ma Keyao. "Xuexi Makesi, Engesi lun dongfang gudai shehui de jidian tihui" (Some thoughts on studying Marx's and Engels' discussions of ancient Oriental society). *Beijing Daxue xuebao* (Beijing University journal) 4 (1978).

Ma Xin. "Lun Makesi de 'sizhong shengchan fangshi' shuo yu gushi fenqi" (On the Marx's theory of "four modes of production" and the periodization of ancient history). *Zhongguo Renmin Daxue xuebao* (China People's University journal) 2 (1987): 104–11.

———. "Lun Makesi de 'sizhong shengchan fangshi' shuo" (The theory of Marx's "four modes of production"). *Xinhua wenzhai* (New China digest) 8 (1987): 54–57. Condensed version of the previous entry. Translated in this volume.

"Nankai Daxue lishixi taolun 'Yaxiya shengchan fangshi wenti' " (The history department of Nankai University discusses the "AMP question"). *Guangming ribao* (Guangming daily), December 4, 1979.

Pan Jiansheng. "Yaxiya shengchan fangshi yu Zhongguo gudaishi de yanjiu" (The AMP and research on China's ancient history). *Lishi jiaoxue wenti* (Questions in historical pedagogy) 1 (1983).

Pang Zhuoheng and Gao Zhongjun. "Youguan Yaxiya shengchan fangshi jige wenti de shangque" (A discussion of several questions concerning the AMP). *Zhongguo shi yanjiu* 3 (1981): 72–85.

Pang Zhuoheng, Huang Sijun, Tian Shusheng, and Yu Ke. " 'Yaxiya shengchan fangshi' xueshu taolunhui jiyao" (Report on the conference on the "AMP"). *Zhongguo shi yanjiu* 3 (1981): 3–17.

Qi Qingfu. " 'Yaxiya shengchan fangshi' zhide shi yuanshi shehui ma? Yu Zhichun, Xuesheng tongzhi shangque" (Does the "AMP" denote primitive society? A critique of [Lin] Zhichun and [Liao] Xuesheng). *Shijie lishi* 1 (1980): 55–64.

———. " 'Yaxiya shengchan fangshi' bushi Makesizhuyi de kexue gainian" (The "AMP" is not a Marxist scientific concept). *Zhongyang Minzu Xueyuan xuebao* (Central Minorities Institute journal) 3 (1985): 30–36. Reprinted in *FBZ* 9 (1985): 23–29. Translated in this volume.

She Shusheng. "Guanyu Yaxiya shengchan fangshi wenti—yu Wu Dakun tongzhi shangque" (On the question of the AMP: A critique of Wu Dakun). *Lishi yanjiu* 5 (1980).

————. "Lun Yaxiya shengchan fangshi" (On the AMP). 2 parts. *Lilun yanjiu* (Theoretical studies) 1 and 2 (1981).

————. "Makesi yu dongfangxue ji qita" (Marx and the study of the Orient). *Shehui kexue zhanxian* (Social sciences frontline) 3 (1983): 109–22.

Shijie shanggu shigang bianxiezu (Authors of *An Outline History of World Antiquity*). "Yaxiya shengchan fangshi—bu cheng qi wei wenti de wenti" (The unproblematic AMP). *Lishi yanjiu* 2 (1980): 3–24. Translated in this volume.

————. "Duoxianshuo haishi danxianshuo?" (Multilinear or unilinear?) *Shijie lishi* 5 (1981).

————. "Yaxiya shengchan fangshi yu guojia" (The AMP and the state). *Lishi yanjiu* 3 (1982): 39–52.

Song Min. "Cong Makesi zhuyi de fazhan kan 'Yaxiya shengchan fangshi'—yu Zhichun, Xuesheng tongzhi shangque" (The "AMP" from the perspective of the development of Marxism: A critique of [Lin] Zhichun and [Liao] Xuesheng). *Jilin Shida xuebao* 4 (1979).

————. " 'Yaxiya shengchan fangshi—bu cheng qi wei wenti de wenti' yiwen zhiyi" (In criticism of "The unproblematic AMP"). *Lishi yanjiu* 5 (1980).

————. " 'Yaxiya shengchan fangshi wenti de zhengjiedian zai nali?' yiwen zhiyi" (In criticism of "Where lies the weakness in the question of the AMP?"). *Shijie lishi* 1 (1982).

————. " 'Makesi yu dongfangxue ji qita' yiwen shangque" (A critique of "Marx and the study of the Orient"). *Shehui kexue zhanxian* 1 (1984): 138–43.

————. "Tan Yaxiya shengchan fangshi wenti de liangzhong shengchan fangshi shuo" (Two theories of modes of production in the question of the AMP). *Dongbei Shida xuebao* (Northeast Normal University journal) 4 (1984): 79–87.

————. "Lun Makesizhuyi wuzhong shehui xingtai lilun de queli—Makesi zai *Ziben zhuyi shengchan yiqian de gezhong xingtai* zhong queli 'wuzhong shehui xingtai lilun' shuo zhiyi" (On the definition of the Marxist theory of five social formations: In criticism of the view that Marx defined a "theory of five social formations" in *Precapitalist Economic Formations*). *Jilin Daxue xuebao* 3 (1985).

————. "Guanyu Yaxiya shengchan fangshi gainian de kexuexing wenti—'Yaxiya shengchan fangshi bu shi Makesizhuyi de kexue gainian' shuo shangque" (The scientific validity of the concept of the AMP: A critique of "The AMP is not a Marxist scientific concept"). *Shehui kexue zhanxian* 4 (1986): 128–34. Translated in this volume.

————. "Yaxiya shengchan fangshi ji yuanshi shizu gongshezhi" (The

AMP is the primitive patriarchal commune system). *Xueshu yanjiu congkan* (Academic studies) 1 (1987).

———. "Lun Yaxiya shengchan fangshi yu guojia—'Yaxiya shengchan fangshi buzhi guojia wei hewu' shuo zhiyi" (The AMP and the state: In criticism of the view that "the AMP does not know what the state is"). *Shehui kexue zhanxian* 4 (1987).

Su Fengjie. "Guanyu shehui xingtai wenti de zhiyi he tansuo" (A critical inquiry into the problem of social formations). *Zhongguo shi yanjiu* 3 (1981): 117–32.

———. "Makesi de shehui xingtai xueshuo yu Yaxiya shengchan fangshi wenti—yu He Xin tongzhi shangque" (Marx's theory of social formations and the question of the AMP: A critique of He Xin). *Fuyang Shifan Xueyuan xuebao* (Fuyang Normal College journal) 2 (1983).

———. "Qianzibenzhuyi shehui xingtai de tantao" (An inquiry into precapitalist social formations). *Shehui kexue pinglun* (Essays in the social sciences) 12 (1985).

Su Kaihua. "Guanyu 'Yaxiya shengchan fangshi' de benyi ji qi mingcheng youlai—jian yu He Ziquan xiansheng shangque" (The meaning of the "AMP" and the origin of the term: A critique of He Ziquan). *Zhengming* (Contending) 4 (1986): 62–65. Reprinted in *BZX* 1 (1987): 22–25. Translated in this volume.

Sun Jian. "Yaxiya shengchan fangshi shi gudai dongfang nulizhi" (The AMP is ancient Oriental slavery). *Jingji lilun yu jingji guanli* (Economic theory and economic management) 3 (1981).

Sun Wenfan. "Yaxiya shengchan fangshi yu lishi renwu pingjia" (The AMP and the evaluation of historical figures). *Shixue yuekan* (History monthly) 1 (1982).

Tian Changwu. "Yaxiya shengchan fangshi wenti de wenti" (The question of "the question of the AMP"). *Zhongguo shi yanjiu* 3 (1981): 86–102.

———. "Ping jinnian lai Yaxiya shengchan fangshi wenti de taolun" (An evaluation of the discussion in recent years of the question of the AMP). *Renwen zazhi* (Humanities magazine) 6 (1981).

———. "Tan Yaxiya shengchan fangshi wenti" (Comments on the question of the AMP). *Guangming ribao* (Guangming daily), April 26, 1982. Reprinted in *Lishi lilun yanjiu* (Studies in historical theory), ed. Guangming Ribaoshe (*Guangming Daily*) (Chongqing: Chongqing Chubanshe, 1984), pp. 104–12.

Tian Renlong. "Jianguo yilai Yaxiya shengchan fangshi wenti taolun zongshu" (A survey of the discussion of the question of the AMP since 1949). *Zhongguo shi yanjiu* 3 (1981): 147–59. Includes a bibliography of articles on the AMP, 1951–1981.

————. "Yaxiya shengchan fangshi taolun de huigu" (A retrospective on the discussion of the AMP). In his *Jianguo yilai shixue lilun wenti taolun juyao* (Discussions on questions of historical theory since 1949) (Jinan: Qi Lu Shushe, 1983), pp. 1–31.

Wang Dunshu and Yu Ke. See Yu Ke and Wang Dunshu.

Wang Gesen. "Woguo shixuejie dui shijie gudaishi shang ruogan zhongyao wenti de tantao" (The inquiry within Chinese historical circles into certain important questions relating to world antiquity). *Qi Lu xuekan* (Shandong study journal) 1 (1980).

Wang Guoqing. "Yaxiya shengchan fangshi shi Ma-En lilun tantao zhong de yige jiashe" (The AMP was a hypothesis in the theoretical explorations of Marx and Engels). *Ningxia shehui kexue* (Ningxia social science) 5 (1987).

Wang Miandan. "Dui Makesi de 'Yaxiya shengchan fangshi' gainian de tantao—jian ping yizhong lilun guandian" (An inquiry into Marx's concept of the "AMP": Critical comments on a theoretical standpoint). *Makesizhuyi yanjiu* (Studies in Marxism) 3 (1985): 74–86.

Wang Sijin. "Lun Yaxiya shengchan fangshi yu Kong xue de guanxi" (The relationship between the AMP and Confucianism). *Jiang–Han Daxue xuebao* (Jiang–Han University journal) 1 (1986).

Wu Dakun. "Guanyu Yaxiya shengchan fangshi yanjiu de jige wenti" (Some questions concerning research on the AMP). *Xueshu yanjiu* (Academic research) 1 (1980): 11–18. Translated in this volume.

————. "Guanyu Yaxiya shengchan fangshi de yanjiu" (Research on the AMP). *Makesizhuyi yanjiu cankao ziliao* 17 (1980). Reprinted as the introduction to Umberto Melotti, *Makesi yu disan shijie* (Marx and the Third World) (Beijing: Shangwu Yinshuguan, 1981), Chinese translation of *Marx e il terzo mundo*.

————. "Cong guangyi zhengzhi jingjixue kan lishi shang de Yaxiya shengchan fangshi" (The AMP in history as viewed by political economy in its broad sense). *Zhongguo shi yanjiu* 3 (1981): 18–29. Translated in *Selected Writings on Studies in Marxism* (Beijing: Institute of Marxism–Leninism–Mao Zedong Thought, Chinese Academy of Social Sciences, 1981). Reprinted in Su Shaozhi et al., *Marxism in China* (London: Spokesman, 1983), pp. 53–77.

————. "Guanyu Zhongguo lishi shang de Yaxiya shengchan fangshi ji qi shehui jingji jiegou" (The AMP and its socioeconomic formation in Chinese history). *Ma–Lie zhuzuo yanjiu tongxin* (Newsletter for research on the works of Marx and Lenin) 12 (1981).

————. "Bo Kaer Weitefu de *Dongfang zhuanzhizhuyi*" (Repudiating Karl Wittfogel's *Oriental Despotism*). *Lishi yanjiu* 4 (1982): 27–36.

"Wu Dakun jiaoshou tan Yaxiya shengchan fangshi" (Professor Wu

Dakun on the AMP). *Zhejiang xuekan* (Zhejiang journal) 3 (1981).

Wu Xinfu. "Shilun Makesizhuyi 'wuzhong shehui xingtai' xueshuo de jige wenti" (Several questions concerning the Marxist theory of "five social formations"). *Qiusuo* (Explorations) 2 (1983).

Wu Ze. "Makesi lun gudai tudi suoyouzhi zhu xingtai" (Marx on ancient forms of landed property). *Huadong Shifan Daxue xuebao* (East China Normal University journal) 1 (1983).

―――. *"Zibenzhuyi shengchan yiqian de gezhong xingshi* yu gudai dongfang shehuishi yanjiu" (*Pre-Capitalist Economic Formations* and the study of the history of ancient Oriental society). *Shanghai Shehui Kexueyuan xueshu jikan* (Shanghai Academy of Social Sciences quarterly) 3 (1987).

―――. "Yaxiya shengchan fangshi wenti de zhenglun yu Zhongguo Makesizhuyi shixue de fazhan" (The controversy over the AMP and the development of Marxist historiography in China). *Hebei xuekan* (Hebei journal) 5 (1987).

―――. "Yaxiya shengchan fangshi lilun yu gudai dongfang shehui tedian yanjiu" (The theory of the AMP and research into the characteristics of ancient Oriental society). *Shehui kexue jikan* 1 (1988).

Wu Ze and Ding Jihua. "Guanyu Yaxiya shengchan fangshi de jige wenti" (Several questions concerning the AMP). *Lishi jiaoxue wenti* 2 (1981).

Xia Yang. *"Waiguo xuezhe lun Yaxiya shengchan fangshi* jianjie" (Introducing *Foreign Scholars on the AMP*). *Zhongguo shi yanjiu dongtai* (Trends in research on Chinese history) 11 (1981).

Xiang Guanqi. "Lun Makesi xinmu zhong de Yaxiya shengchan fangshi" (Marx's view of the AMP). *Wen shi zhe* 1 (1986).

―――. "Lun wuzhong shengchan fangshi lilun de xingshi" (On the form of the theory of five modes of production). *Lishi yanjiu* 6 (1987): 3–17.

Xu Hongxiu. "Nongcun gongshe yu 'Yaxiya shengchan fangshi'—dui Makesi, Engesi youguan nongcun gongshe lunshu de lishi kaocha" (The village community and the "AMP": A historical investigation of Marx's and Engels' discussions of the village community). *Wen shi zhe* 4 (1982): 48–57. Reprinted in *FBZ* 8 (1982): 3–12.

Xu Houshan. "Guanyu gudai dongfang shehui de shehui xingzhi wenti" (The question of the social character of ancient Oriental society). *Huazhong Shiyuan xuebao* (Huazhong Normal College journal) 1 (1979).

Xu Qiji. "Guanyu Yaxiya shengchan fangshi gainian de tantao" (An inquiry into the concept of the AMP). *Xueshu yuekan* (Academic monthly) 11 (1979).

Yang Shanqun. " 'Yaxiya shengchan fangshi' bian" (Critique of the "AMP"). *Jiang–Han luntan* (Jiang–Han forum) 9 (1982).

Yao Nianci. "Shilun 'Yaxiya shengchan fangshi' zai lishi weiwulun fazhan zhong de diwei" (On the place of the "AMP" in the development of historical materialism). *Wuhan Shifan Xueyuan xuebao* (Wuhan Normal College journal) 3 (1983).

"Yaxiya shengchan fangshi taolun qingkuang jianjie" (Brief report on the conference on the AMP). *Tianjin shelian tongxun* 8 (1980).

Yu Ke and Wang Dunshu. "Shilun 'Yaxiya shengchan fangshi' " (A tentative discussion of the "AMP"). *Jilin Shida xuebao* 4 (1979).

———. "Zai tan 'Yaxiya shengchan fangshi' wenti—jian yu chi yuanshi shehui shuo de tongzhi shangque" (Further comments on the "AMP": A critique of those who interpret it as primitive society). *Zhongguo shi yanjiu* 3 (1981): 103–16. Translated in this volume.

Yu Qinghe. "Guanyu Yaxiya shengchan fangshi wenti" (On the question of the AMP). *Jilin Shida xuebao* 1 (1980).

Zhan Yikang. "Cong lishi fazhan jieduan de sanzhong tifa kan Yaxiya shengchan fangshi" (The AMP in relation to three ways of referring to the stages of historical development). *Zhengming* 1 (1981).

Zhan Yikang and Chen Chun'e. "Cong Zhongguo geming de shijian kan Yaxiya shengchan fangshi wenti de zhenglun" (The debate over the question of the AMP from the viewpoint of the Chinese revolution). *Jiangxi Shifan Xueyuan xuebao* (Jiangxi Normal College journal) 3 (1983).

Zhang Shudong. "Makesi 'Yaxiya shengchan fangshi' gainian de lishi kaocha" (An historical investigation into Marx's concept of the "AMP"). *Nanjing Daxue xuebao* (Nanjing University journal), special issue (1983).

———. "Jianshu Makesizhuyi guanyu renlei lishi fazhan de 'wuduanlun' sixiang" (Marx's thinking concerning the "five- stages model" of human historical development). *Nanjing Daxue xuebao* 4 (1984).

Zhang Shusheng. "Sulian shixuejie guanyu 'Yaxiya shengchan fangshi' he Zhongguo gudaishi fenqi wenti de lunzhu xuanyi" (Translated selections from Soviet historians on the "AMP" and the periodization of ancient Chinese history). *Zhongguo shi yanjiu dongtai* 2 (1979).

Zhang Yaqin and Bai Jinfu. "Yaxiya shengchan fangshi yanjiu fangfa wenti" (Methodological questions concerning research on the AMP). *Xuexi yu tansuo* (Study and exploration) 1 (1981).

———. "Yaxiya shengchan fangshi wenti de zhengjiedian zai nar?" (Where is the flaw in the question of the AMP?) *Shijie lishi* 4 (1981): 29–35.

Zhang Zhongmin. "Makesi, Engesi zhuzuo zhong de 'Yaxiya shengchan fangshih' yu 'Yaxiya de suoyouzhi xingtai' " (The "AMP" and "Asiatic forms of property" in the works of Marx and Engels). *Xuzhou Shifan Xueyuan xuebao* (Xuzhou Normal College journal) 2 (1982).

Zhang Zuoyao. "Yaxiya shengchan fangshi" (The AMP). *Zhongguo lishixue nianjian* (Chinese historical studies annual) (Beijing: Xinhua Shudian, 1981), pp. 190–98.

Zhao Jiaxiang. " 'Yaxiya shengchan fangshi' yu Makesi de wuzhong shehui xingtai lilun" (The "AMP" and the theory of Marx's five social formations). *Shanxi Shiyuan xuebao* (Shanxi Normal College journal), special edition (1983).

Zhao Lisheng. "Yaxiya shengchan fangshi ji qi zai Zhongguo lishi shang de yicun" (The AMP and its remnants in Chinese history). *Wen shi zhe* 5 (1981): 13–18. Reprinted in *FBZ* 11 (1981): 25–30.

———. "Cong Yaxiya shengchan fangshi kan Zhongguo gushi shang de jingtian zhidu" (The well-field system in relation to the AMP). *Shehui kexue zhanxian* 3 (1982): 109–15. Reprinted in *FBZ* 19 (1982): 2–7. Reprinted in the author's *Zhongguo tudi zhidu shi* (History of China's land systems) (Jinan: Qi Lu Shushe, 1984), pp. 22–35. Translated in this volume.

———. "Yaxiya shengchan fangshi lilun shi xian-Qin shi yanjiu de tuidongli" (The theory of the AMP is a force for promoting research on pre-Qin history). *Xueshu yuekan* 8 (1982).

Zheng Deliang. "Yaxiya shengchan fangshi he Xianggang de lishi fazhan yu 'yiguo erzhi' " (The AMP and the historical development of Hong Kong in relation to the "one country, two systems" formula). *Zhongshan Daxue xuebao* 2 (1988).

Zhou Ziqiang. "Shi liuzhong shengchan fangshi, haishi wuzhong shengchan fangshi?" (Are there six modes of production or five?) *Zhongguo shi yanjiu* 3 (1981): 44–58.

Zhu Jiazhen. "Guanyu Yaxiya shengchan fangshi lilun yanjiu zhong de jige wenti" (Some questions concerning research on the theory of the AMP). *Jingji yanjiu* (Studies in economics) 6 (1982): 58–64. Translated in this volume.

———. "Yaxiya shengchan fangshi lilun yu woguo cunshe zhidu de tantao" (An inquiry into the theory of the AMP and China's village system). *Minzu xuebao* (Minorities journal) 3 (1983): 339-74.

Zhu Xiaoyuan. "Gudai Zhongguo sanzhong xingshi" (Ancient China's three formations). *Shanghai Shifan Xueyuan xuebao* (Shanghai Normal College journal) 1 (1984).

Zhu Zhongxi. "Shilun xiangsui zhidu yu Yaxiya shengchan fangshi" (The ancient rural administrative system and the AMP). *Lishi jiaoxue yu yanjiu* (The teaching and study of history) 1 (1984).

Zuo Wenhua. "Guanyu nuli shehui shi de jige wenti—jian *Shijie shanggu shigang* bianxie xiaozu shangque" (Several questions concerning the history of slave society: A critique of the authors of *An Outline History of World Antiquity*). *Jilin Shida xuebao* 2 (1980): 98–103.

———. "Ye tan Yaxiya shengchan fangshi wenti" (Further comments on the question of the AMP). *Sixiang zhanxian* (Ideological frontline) 3 (1981).

INDEX

agricultural community. *See* village community

Analects, 73

"ancient Asiatic" mode of production, 86, 125-26

ancient mode of production, 7, 180. *See also* forms of property; slavery

"ancient Orient," 99, 102n.30, 181

"ancient Oriental slavery," 92

ancient society, 23, 49

Anderson, Perry, 28

Annenkov, Pavel, 114

Anti-Dühring, 95, 118, 132, 142, 154

archaeology, 16

Aristotle, 4, 151

Asia, as origin of civilization, 173, 181

"Asiatic": Marx's use of the term, 7, 25, 48-49, 62n.4, 88-90, 124-25, 160-63, 167; negative connotation of, 7-8, 30n.11

"Asiatic antiquity," 98, 132

Asiatic mode of production (AMP): alleged abandonment of, 15, 23, 26-27, 131-33, 138-39, 151; associated with Trotskyism, 13, 15, 36; characteristics of, 67, 119-20, 165-67; class nature of, 120; contemporaneous with ancient mode, 151; as critique of capitalism, 12-13; debates in China over, 13, 14-17, 105; debates in Europe over, 44, 99-100; debates in Japan over, 13, 104-5; debates in USSR over, 13-14, 36, 98-100, 104-5, 164; and development of historical materialism, 105-8; and development of new historiography, 15; as earliest mode, 160; as an economic formation, 34, 106-7; as equivalent to ancient and feudal modes, 26, 169-70, 173-74; historiographical function of, 20-21; in Marx's later years, 97-98; opposition to, 21-23; political significance of, 43-45, 133, 164; as primitive society, 15, 22-23, 37, 90-96, 108-10, 137-38; as provisional concept, 138; in relation to Asian society, 108-10; in relation to slavery, 105; rhetorical function of, 15-16, 20-21; as sixth mode of production, 24-25; as slave society,